Kurosaki Killed the Cat

John Jarvis

Kurosaki Killed the Cat

Gulliver Press

The opinions expressed in this manuscript are solely the opinions of the author and do not represent the opinions or thoughts of the publisher. The author has represented and warranted full ownership and/or legal right to publish all the materials in this book.

Kurosaki Killed The Cat
All Rights Reserved.
Copyright © 2010 John Jarvis
v1.0

Cover Photo by John Jarvis

This book may not be reproduced, transmitted, or stored in whole or in part by any means, including graphic, electronic, or mechanical without the express written consent of the publisher except in the case of brief quotations embodied in critical articles and reviews.

Gulliver Press

ISBN: 978-0-9582728-0-3

PRINTED IN THE UNITED STATES OF AMERICA

Table of Contents

Chapter One 1
Chapter Two 23
Chapter Three 47
Chapter Four 61
Chapter Five 91
Chapter Six 123
Chapter Seven 161
Chapter Eight 195
Chapter Nine 221
Chapter Ten 245
Chapter Eleven 267
Chapter Twelve 293
Postscript 301
Acknowledgements 305

BY THE SAME AUTHOR

The Handy Self Defence Book
Weight Training For Self Defence
Okinawa Goju Ryu Karate Training Manual

Dedication

To everyone who gave me a laugh along the way, and to those who made a serious attempt at improving me as a person. A few of the stories came to me indirectly, but in all cases I can vouch for the sources. I make no excuses if these have been changed somewhat and fall back on George Bernard Shaw's words, "Embellishing a good story never did any harm."

I have avoided using names except in obvious situations, old comrades I interviewed asked for 'no names no pack drill', and a few of my contemporary martial art teachers are still practicing. I wish them all well.

John Jarvis
Silverstream N.Z. 2005

Chapter One

My first exposure to the martial arts was having to drop my trousers at the Army Recruiting Centre in Buckle Street, Wellington.

I had arrived by tram, a Victorian left-over with four doors each side, once gleaming brass handles now thick with verdigris where continuous hands had worn them to a dull gleam and an imperial bell at each end. Trams would still have five years to run in the Capital, but I doubted this one would have made it as it travelled up the road to Mt Cook, power pole fizzing and wheels shrieking.

I approached a modern looking building with an impressive crest, George VI, above the doorway and two muzzle loading cannons with shot impeccably stacked flanking the steps. A bored sergeant directed me across the road and went back to reading his Sports Digest.

The building on the southern side was an old concrete affair with an add-on wooden drill hall; the gates to the car park were hung onto two muzzle loading cannons, probably the first to use rounds shaped as a projectile instead of shot. I noticed that the ammunition welded on top was the wrong size for the bore, not an inspiring sight for someone wanting to join the Ordnance Corps.

After showing my papers that had arrived only that morning, giving me just two hours to report, I was passed from one corporal clerk to another and was given my first lesson in how to "hurry up and wait".

I sat down on a long well-worn bench filled with other hopefuls and waited my turn. Finally I was called to a harassed looking doctor with the rank of major who looked at my papers, looked annoyed and asked,

"Why didn't you say you were Regular?" I was about to reply in innocence that nobody had asked me about my bowel habits when fortunately he hurried on,

"You shouldn't have been waiting with the Territorials." He glanced disdainfully towards the others.

"We always process regular soldiers first". He then gave me a very rudimentary medical check: pulse, tongue and embarrassing questions about whether I had ever had leprosy or ingrown toe nails. Then the pants had to come down for the customary check of the privates.

"Turn your head sideways and cough," he said, giving a couple of Latin types who were waiting a scornful look, obviously suspecting they had garlic on their breath.

Finally it was over; I had passed and had a stamp on my file to prove it. Five days later I was presented to a staff officer, sworn in with my hand on a Bible and signed to the Official Secrets Act that forbade me to say anything I shouldn't for seventy-five years or death, whichever came soonest. I was 718258 Private J JARVIS Royal NZ Army Ordnance Corp.

I was handed a rail travel voucher to Trentham Camp in the Hutt Valley and was met on arrival by a large Women's Army Corps corporal. She delivered me to the Quartermaster's Issue Centre to sign for a bewildering array of clothes and equipment and then to a private room in barracks that were built temporarily for World War One. She left me alone and wondering what would happen next.

'Next' was Corporal Jim Price: a red faced, mustached rotund Welshman, ex-armourer, Royal Canadian Air Force and held back from higher rank and responsibilities in the Army's opinion only because of his love of and addiction to beer. We hit it off immediately after discovering that we were both "Goon" fans which divided all senses of humour in the 1950's. He was to become a great friend, mentor and to have a bearing on my future. He gave advice on how to settle in, what to wear, and why, before I was trained north to Waiouru Camp for Basic Military Training. I arrived there with thirty other new entrants, fortunately in spring. I was about to be, for the first time in my life, 'subjected to discipline'. The basic training I found hard but fair. I struggled at times with the physical side, having done nothing sports wise since leaving school but I enjoyed the structured system and found out the difference between a 'friend' and a 'comrade'. I soon realised that the armed services served to attract both the best and the worst type of person.

I surprised myself by winning the first trophy in my life: 'Champion at Arms' for Squad 33 - a highly polished, of course, 40mm inscribed shell case. Although not the best shot in the squad I managed to perform better under pressure than the target shooters.

On graduating our commanding officer said something that surprised me, "Good to see better soldiers joining the service corps." Did this mean that the 'better types' joined the fighting units and the service corps took what was left over? Many years later, watching my own son graduate on the same parade ground, I noticed that the change had almost been full circle. Then the lads who were winning all the awards were going into the service corps, attracted by technology and longer term qualifications.

On returning to Trentham I was put to work in the Ammunitions' Depot Laboratory where we wore felt overshoes to avoid sparks and constantly had to earth ourselves by touching pipes to avoid build up of static energy, especially when handling gunpowder. The work was interesting at first but soon became repetitive with the sheer volume of work to process.

A directive then came to destroy all stockpiled obsolete World War I ammunition, some of which was stacked rusting outside at New Zealand's largest ammunition area in Belmont on the Western Hills of the Hutt Valley. Belmont was reached by a narrow winding road and consisted of over one hundred thick concrete ammunition storehouses (never call them magazines) scattered around the crests of the hills, protected from each other by hillsides or man-made hillocks to prevent sympathetic detonation in the event of an accidental explosion.

The demolition area resembled the surface of the moon but, like most of the demolition areas in New Zealand, it was too close to a residential area to allow large quantities to be detonated. This meant much smaller detonations that were both time consuming and work intensive. The labour was hard and dangerous. The ammunition stacked in rusty boxes on the sides of hills was either six pounder ten hundredweight - cwt coastal defence, or six pound sevencwt anti-tank. The Army, for some reason best known to itself, measured the weight of the projectile six lbs and the weight of the breach block ten cwt.

The ammunition had no fuses and therefore should have been safe but because of age and deterioration was considered 'unstable'.

The boxes were stacked carefully at the back of the 'Red Terror': a 4x4 gun-towing vehicle adapted for this specialised use. It had two inch armour plate protecting the driver, and danger signs, skulls and crossbones to terrify everyone else. The vehicle was then driven by a driver, whose I.Q. roughly matched the low speed, to the demolition site where the rounds were removed from their boxes and gently laid out in rows on prepared level areas at the bottom of the craters.

Even the explosive being used to destroy them was obsolescent, being slabs of 'Gun Cotton' rather than T.N.T. A primer resembling a cotton reel was placed in a hole in the middle of the slab and a detonator in turn placed inside the hole of the primer. The detonators were all linked by 'Cordtex' explosive fuse; these white cords snaked all round the area linking up the many different nests of shells. Finally they were all taped together to a master electric detonator with wires leading back to the underground bunker a hundred metres away. At the last moment, when all personnel were accounted for in the bunker and a hand siren had cranked out a warning wail, the wires were connected to the terminals of a hand cranked generator. We placed our fingers in our ears (no ear protectors in those days) and opened our mouths. The tit was pressed. A concussion shook the bunker, covering us and filling our mouths with dust. We then started all over again.

After months of this routine it all came a bit too familiar, and, while safety procedures were still strictly observed, one corporal paid the price of perhaps working a little too quickly. After each explosion the high explosive shells were completely destroyed with only hot shrapnel scattered around the site or hissing in puddles of water. The brass shell cases were also scattered about in jagged forms looking like modern art work where some sculptor had had a hangover. The contents of these cases, the propellant, was in most cases also destroyed along with the primer at the base of the shell case but in many cases the tiny cap at the centre of the primer (the part that starts the ignition when struck by the firing pin) was left intact. These had to be fired before the Ammunition Technical Officer could declare the site F.F.E. - Free From Explosive.

One corporal had the not too arduous job of wandering around with a little sharpened mallet and a tap hammer firing any intact caps by hitting them; his little 'cracks' all over the site signaling the final demise of the rounds. He overlooked one of the cases that was not completely destroyed. Worse perhaps, the end of the shattered shell case had bent over, sealing in some remaining propellant. This time there was no 'crack' but a dull bang. When we discovered the corporal, he had lost three fingers and suffered a piece of shrapnel through his chest. After the inevitable court of inquiry, work resumed with a noticeable increase in care and attention.

During the break, while waiting for the court of inquiry to convene, we were given various fill-in jobs around Trentham Camp. Those that could be were sent on various courses and I found myself with several others on a clean up duty of Camp HQ. Our job was to empty out old 'Orders of the Day Part Two', now deemed to be of no strategic value. Some of them dated back to before World War One. One caught my eye as we were loading the dusty cardboard boxes onto a Landrover and I have always regretted not keeping it. It was dated just prior to hostilities in 1914 and ordered officers to hand in their swords to the camp blacksmith for sharpening! That would have struck fear into the hearts of Kaiser Bill and his Imperial General Staff if word of it had ever been leaked.

The ammunition that had been stored outside had now been destroyed and attention was turned towards the ammunition stored inside. These were old but in very good condition and were mostly World War One four and a half inch howitzer high explosive shells. Cases were selected at random to be inspected to ensure they were in good condition. Some of these had been manufactured in South Africa and almost ten percent were found to be filled with sand, giving some idea of the extent of sabotage that existed in that country during the First World War.

Destroying them by detonation was not practical so it was decided correctly that it would be faster, easier and safer to dump them at sea. Enter the Royal New Zealand Navy in the form of HMNZS 'Endeavour'. The original Endeavour was wooden and had been used largely to supply the Antarctic. There was much speculation after boarding as to which bunk had been used by Sir Edmund Hillary.

The ammunition boxes had been offloaded from trucks and stacked into the forward hold. We cast off from the wharf at Shelly Bay, all of us looking forward to the sea voyage onto Christchurch and catching the ferry back to Wellington. The novelty soon wore off. One of the characteristics of the Endeavour was not only did she roll at sea but she pitched as well - a feature that would have been helpful in breaking sheet ice but did nothing for the stomachs of soldiers and crew alike. Everyone seemed to be seasick as the Endeavour hit rough water off Cape Palliser - chosen by the Navy (which was in complete charge once we had cast off) for deeper waters.

Dumping in rough waters was a nightmare. Four others and I were given the worst job for no other reason than we seemed to be not as sick as everyone else. We had to load the boxes into the hoist at the bottom of a hold that was moving in all directions at once. When the hoist got up to the top of the hold gravity, chutes and the sea's trampoline effect did the rest. Good timing was essential. The boxes had to be dumped before a wave hit to avoid them returned with interest. By the time the hold was empty everyone was absolutely exhausted and lay in their bunks unable to sleep yet being sneered at by passing naval ranks.

One of our corporals plotted revenge. He had acquired two hand grenades sometime previously by simply 'writing them off' and suggested that we go fishing with these weapons that did not actually exist, to cheer ourselves up. He had already been in strife over hand grenades in the past. After inspecting a box he had written a note: "These are thirty-six grenades - hand for the use of - mark one and it will explode in the hand". The recruits on the range had been suitably terrified and were reluctant to throw them. Their Sergeant had been suitably furious and had made an official complaint. Making their way to Endeavour's port side, they pulled the pin on the first grenade and lobbed it in true grenadier fashion over the side. After four seconds nothing happened. Undeterred, the second one went over the side. Everything seemed to happen! Bells clanged and the ship's tannoy made sounds only understood by sailors who disappeared below, possibly to battle stations if there was anything to battle with.

Endeavour drifted, engines shutdown. The only noise was the seagulls that were screaming over the dead fish floating to the surface astern. The perpetrators stood ashen faced, what had they done? Was there still a yard-arm they could be hung from? After what seemed a very long time, Endeavour's engines restarted at an idle, then were progressively brought up to speed; we were under way again.

A petty officer passing, concerned enough to speak to soldiers, asked,

"Did you lads see logs or anything hit the side? The chief engineer heard a God almighty bang and thought we had broken a driveshaft".

"No"

"No" and

"No" said the others.

The wooden Endeavour was duly replaced by a more modern

vessel built of steel, its bridge and main superstructure situated aft and much more suitable for loading and unloading. The new Endeavour berthed and loaded at Shelly Bay in Wellington and for some reason half the ship's crew were given shore leave. The Ammunition Technical Officer was summoned to the Captain, who was in fact a commander, and was told that the Army would assist in certain duties, the first being to come aboard and help secure the 'deck cargo' which meant the ammo boxes.

The army captain went ashore and told the assembled soldiers consisting of Army service corps drivers, ordnance corps store men and ammunition technicians, most of them from Auckland and the most part of them Maoris, what was required of them. They all surged up the gangway, hobnails clattering on metal plates, and looked around the deck looking for ropes to tie granny knots with.

The ships tannoy shrieked something completely unintelligible ending in "----iately". The army captain, guessing it could be for him, weaved his way around the deck cargo, pounded up several sets of companionways and presented himself panting to the captain on the bridge. The captain was annoyed,

"Your men came directly aboard without saluting the quarterdeck." He pointed to the area concerned to make sure there was no confusion.

"Have your larrikins disembark and re-embark doing it properly, respecting our traditions".

The army officer ordered his men back ashore and had them fall in. They were used to this sort of thing.

"Now men," he said patiently, "When you get to the top of the gangway you face aft and salute".

"Where's aft sir?" Inevitably from one of the privates.

"It's the thick end there".

"Why do we have to salute some stacks of wood and piles of rope?" asked another.

"It's tradition," said the officer a little less patiently, "It's the quarterdeck where Nelson fell."

"Who's Nelson?"

"Quiet," snorted the officer, completely out of patience, "Just follow orders".

The quarterdeck duly received some twenty or so army style salutes and the ship prepared to cast off. The lines were dropped into the sea, the naval ratings handling the bow and the soldiers the stern. As the ship was making way the tannoy shrieked again "Ble___ ah___ oh____ em__ ar_____iately". The army officer, correctly deducing that it was for him again, ran the gauntlet of deck cargo, swayed his way up the passageways and reported to the bridge, out of breath, once again.

The captain was furious.

"May I direct your attention to that," he said, indicating forward.

"What's that sir?" said the army officer confused.

"The coil of rope." The captain pointed to a perfect spiral of rope neatly on the bow.

"And also to that," he said acidly, waving his arm towards the stern but not daring to look.

There on the stern was the army's effort: a tangled mass of rope, seaweed, Coke cans and other unmentionables, the end tied to

CHAPTER ONE | 11

the mast with a bow so that it would not all fall overboard again. The army officer didn't wait and, retracing his steps, had his men put the offending rope in some sort of order. The ship's tannoy stayed mercifully silent.

At the area designated for dumping, the sea was rough. The captain, annoyed at the delay caused entirely by the army, was anxious to dump both the ammunition and the soldiers as soon as possible. He waited for the forecasted better weather to arrive but it didn't.

"We can't dump this load in sea like this," advised an experienced petty officer to the soldiers on the deck.

"We will get it straight back in our faces".

The captain felt that he had delayed enough. "Commence dumping" was passed to the deck by various intermediaries. The soldiers heaved the first load overboard. Lightened, the deck immediately cantered to one side then, aided by the sea, over-corrected in perfect time to receive most of the ammunition boxes back on board. The deck looked as if it had been attacked; half the soldiers ended up in sick bay. The petty officer had been right.

No sooner had the last ammunition box been consigned to the deep than the tannoy squeaked again, "ou____ i____ ar____ iately". The army officer, a dab hand by now, approached the bridge.

"Because of the delays," informed the captain, leaving no doubt as to who was to blame for that, "we will not be returning to Wellington but will instead sail directly to Auckland". The captain seemed disappointed that the army officer was not about to argue but he knew who had all the authority and, besides, seeing that most of the soldiers came from Auckland in the first place, the Navy would be saving the Army money. Smiling internally, he left the captain wondering.

The Endeavour had an uneventful passage to Auckland and, arriving outside of Devonport Naval Base, the ship's tannoy came back to life, "wr___ it___... immediately." Caught by surprise, the army officer raced down the cleared decks, along the companionways and back yet again to the bridge. The captain was back to his agitated old self again.

"Your chaps will have to help our hands paint one side of the ship. We were in the Antarctic previously and ice has scarred the sides."

"One side of the ship, sir?" the captain was ready for that.

"Yes, dammit, we have been ordered to take part in a review tomorrow and one side is all the brass will see; we will have to make do."

Navy ratings and soldiers went over the side together to paint half of the ship regulation grey. By this time (unlike the officers) they had begun to get on well with each other, working out who was a good 'hand' or 'mate' and sharing a common distrust of all commanding officers. When the job was finished to the petty officer's satisfaction, everyone celebrated with a rum (rum ration was still in force in New Zealand naval ships). The feeling of accomplishment, however, was not to last.

"Scr___ bai___ __uy ___tely." The army officer reacted like a Pavlovian dog; he knew the way backwards by now but the captain was almost apologetic this time.

"Well, you see...tides changed... tricky currents around here... fact is, we'll have to paint the port side as well, we will have to anchor the other way about." The army officer was at last relishing his small advantage.

"What about my men's gear, they are all filthy and can't go ashore like that?" The captain was by now eager to please.

CHAPTER ONE | 13

"The ship's laundry will wash and press all your men's kits; my men will collect all items at eight Bells," the captain still couldn't help himself.

The port side was duly painted regulation grey and HMNZS Endeavour took part in the naval review with the band playing and everyone saluting with their hands the wrong way down. The Navy had the last laugh however; the soldiers' gear came back from the laundry to many curses and loud complaints - the Navy had ironed their trouser creases horizontally, all seven of them, one for each sea in the world.

The Ammunition Depots' Tours of Duty were a way of avoiding posting people permanently to unpleasant areas, and could last up to two years. I found myself on tour of duty to Waiouru Camp in the middle of the North Island while still officially being stationed at Trentham. I even retained my room there until someone tired of the farce and packed up my gear and stored it.

I enjoyed Waiouru - the isolation and the extreme in the weather - the dry colds. I never tired of Mt Ruapehu on a clear day. The ammunition depot there was smaller but busy and we rarely had time on our hands. On the few occasions that we did, we had to run courses for infantrymen to qualify for a 'Blind Disposal Ticket'. Rounds of ammunition that failed to explode were called blinds, never duds. The course was designed to allow infantry N.C.O's, staff sergeants and above to deal with their own unexploded ammunition and not be calling upon Ordnance at awkward times.

This was an ideal vehicle for revenge: these N.C.O's were often as not the very unforgiving types that had made our life a misery through Basic Training. Instruction for them was fairly simple: all they had to do was first find the blind, identify it and then destroy it by placing a charge to it but not touching it. All ammunition have safety devices to prevent them from exploding prematurely by using centrifugal force, springs and the 'set back' principle (similar to the feeling you get when in a lift and press the 'UP' button). These devices would all have been triggered during the projectile's flight, leaving it potentially very dangerous.

Our job was to place real, but safe, mortar bombs or hand grenades around the range for the trainees to find and destroy. A sergeant major was first. He had in his career once told a recruit to water a garden and when the recruit replied

"But, sir, it's raining," was told,

"Well, you have a raincoat don't you?" We had prepared something special for him.

The craters at the demolition site had been overlooked by the army's long term strategic planning staff and therefore lacked any sort of drainage system. Many were filled with thick, still water, undisturbed from previous demolitions several months ago and home to approximately 100 divisions of starved mosquitoes.

The sergeant major in question had made an exhaustive search of the area and with a stroke of genius came to the conclusion that the offending 'blind' was submerged.

"Do I have to search each crater? Can't you tell me which one it's in?" We all looked blank as if such common sense was beyond us.

"You did this on purpose, didn't you?" His voice was rising to parade ground strength and our officer decided we needed support.

"You can't expect every round to land on a billiard table, all nice and easy for you to deal with, can you?"

The sergeant major, realising he had been set up, attempted to march down the crater's slope. After several steps the march

CHAPTER ONE | 15

changed into a desperately quick jogging on the spot to avoid falling headlong into the slime. We kept regulation blank looks on our faces.

He began to slurp around in the slime using his S.M.'s baton, with a highly polished 50 calibre shell case attached to its end, as a prodder. It wasn't long before he was covered in mud and losing the last controls over his temper.

Our officer had decided enough was enough.

"Show him where it is, chaps, will you?"

One of us, with great alacrity, shallied down the bank and stood ankle deep in the mud to mark the blind with a red flag. We had previously dug a shell into the side of the bank, just below water level. The sergeant major clambered back out, gathered his gear together and proceeded to lay his charges and destroy the offending water bomb with a satisfying 'crump'. He was, by this time, completely covered in mud but, to his credit, began to take it all in good humour. Our respect for him increased markedly.

The next sergeant found his hand grenade imbedded in a pile of four cow pats; he too joined in the festive occasion.

"Christ, the cows around here must be as big as elephants," he muttered as he exploded more manure about that any politician could ever hope to achieve.

We got very technical on the last one. Found imbedded in the fork of a skeletal tree too flimsy to climb was a three inch mortar bomb resplendent in various colours and codes announcing that it was filled with phosphorous - a compound that was devised for smoke but had a nasty habit of sticking to and burning anything . But we had met our match: the staff sergeant calmly cut a pole from an adjacent scrub, measured the distance to the offending bomb, tied the explosive charge and fuses to the pole and gently pushed it next to but not touching the mortar round. Lighting the fuse, he whistled as he retired behind a hill. The bomb, fuse and stake all disappeared in the blast. Impressed, we called it a day, glad to be up two - one.

To break routine, a visit to the camp cinema was worthwhile; the comments from the audience often being more entertaining than the film itself. It was here, on a Pathe Pictorial slot that I saw karate for the first time. The slot showed only breaking techniques: squat, expressionless Orientals displaying callused hands and feet, calmly smashing their way through stacks of roof tiles. I was left with the question: was this a circus style act, or were the Japanese so seemingly indestructible they justified having two atomic bombs dropped on them?

This was the time that the army decided to replace its ageing WW2 Valentine tanks with US M41 tanks which in fact were not tanks but armoured reconnaissance vehicles. I suspected the difference was in how quickly they could be destroyed. The M41's would augment the aging armoured corps Centurion Mk1's which couldn't drive anywhere outside of Waiouru anyway because of bridge weight restrictions. The M41's 76mm gun looked far more business-like than the Valentine's puny little two inch pounders. I suspect that the United States gave the dozen or so M41's to the NZ Army, intending to fleece them later when charging for ammunition and spare parts.

The ammunition duly arrived and had to be 'duly inspected'. This proved somewhat of a problem. The casings, unlike British ammunition, were made of steel not brass, obviously meant for throwing away after use and not re-using like good conservationists or the poor relations which we were. There was also no separate 'gauge' available to test that the rounds actually fitted the breech so that a tank had to be parked outside our workshop, the rounds passed down through the hatch into the turret and loaded into the gun's breech itself.

CHAPTER ONE | 17

After half an hour's work someone noticed that the gun was pointed back in the direction of Waiouru Camp. It was hurriedly unloaded and cranked around to face a large hill covered with unsuspecting sheep.

Worse was to come. When the fuses were removed, the high explosive fillings broke up, making the rounds unserviceable. Complaints flew across the Pacific and an expert was dispatched from Washington. I picked him up from the railway station at 0100 hours. He was a small man, impeccably dressed in a dark suit and Ivy League tie. He seemed none the worse for his trip down from Auckland, 1st class but no sleeper. Surprisingly he was a civilian working under contract for the US Defence Department which showed how far apart our two military systems were. It also enabled him to not be intimidated by senior ranks.

We were driving through camp trying to make polite conversation, when he remarked,

"That's a mighty fine tank museum you guys have got there ". I mumbled something like "thank you". I was too embarrassed to tell him that that was in fact our tank parking area.

There was much discussion over the next week about the different standards of British versus U.S. ammunition. Finally the American said it all.

"The goddamn things are meant to be fired, not pulled apart to be looked at."

We never did get to hear what decisions were finally arrived at, but most inspections stopped.

The NZ Army announced one of its few amnesties for war souvenirs after the Police complained they were spending too much time dealing with items handed into them in the first instance. Wide publicity was given to the amnesty, encouraging people to come forward with new items. Some could be checked to see if they were free from explosives and returned. In some cases they could pay for the items to be rendered harmless, and in a few cases told to leave it on the table and walk away tiptoe. Rarest of all but by far the most dangerous were items dug up in the garden or found underneath houses. We all dreamed selfishly of finding such a menace under a building far too dangerous to move, and therefore destroying it along with the building as well.

We were told that we would only be dealing with 'the tip of the iceberg'. If that were the case, New Zealand soldiers returning from abroad must have staggered ashore with tons of contraband. Shells, mortar bombs, grenades, rockets, small arms, ammunition of every nationality were gathered for destruction.

One farmer, in a fit of patriotism, called to check his tractor counterweight, which was a huge rusty blob resembling a projectile. To humour him, and justify the expense of travelling out there and staying overnight in a hotel, the seemingly inert mass was lugged to a hollow, a charge placed beside it, and detonated. The resulting explosion left a huge crater, stunned technicians, and an absolutely terrified farmer who stammered he had been carting it around for about 20 years.

McKay's crossing, north of Wellington, was a thorn in our side. It had been a base camp for an American marine division during the Second World War, and the visitors, true to their 'throwaway economy' ideals, bulldozed tons of unwanted trivia, including condoms and high explosives, underground. Unfortunately the ammunition had a nasty habit of working its way to the surface, resulting in continuous visits to destroy it. Today it is Queen Elizabeth the Second Park, and as I drive past on Highway One and see young people playing sport on the fields, I can't help wondering what still lies underneath.

Back at Waiouru the ammunition technical officer was retiring and returning to the United Kingdom. We still had hundreds of amnesty items to be individually destroyed by the book and officially 'written off'. Our officer was far too busy organizing his future to worry about such trivialities, and left Corporal Price and me alone to finish the work. His trust was at first justified as we laboriously destroyed each round. We soon tired with this, though, and Corporal Price came up with the great idea of throwing all the remainders into a box and blowing up everything at once. I proudly came up with an even better idea: why don't we throw all the remainders into one box, throw it into the river, and blow it up and some fish as well!

We packed the rounds into an old wooden ammo box. These were lightly skinned items, concussion grenades, rocket heads, and various flares labelled as pyrotechnics. We carefully measured the fuse for thirty seconds, placed the charge firmly in the centre of the box, secured the lid, and carried it by its rope handles to the river. Lighting the fuse, we swung the box one, two, and tossed it into the centre of the river. Feeling very pleased with ourselves, we ran along the bank down river, and around a bend to await results.

With approximately ten seconds remaining, the box floated around the bend, fizzing blue grey smoke from its fuse. Corporal Price weighed in at two hundred and thirty pounds, and he passed me fleeing in the direction away from the river, his short stout legs pounding up and down like pistons.

We were both well clear when the box exploded, sending a column of water ten metres into the air. Putting on a brave face to cover our fright, we nonchalantly walked back to the river to collect our fish. Not a fish was to be found. Later, someone told us there had never been fish in the river as its sulphur content, washed down from the mountains, was too high.

When we returned to report, a message awaited us from the Camp Commandant complaining that the explosion had shaken his office windows. We blamed 'atmospheric conditions'.

From time to time the Army would be asked to assist in pageants or put on some form of 'tattoo' for a community or an organization. This entailed hauling out ancient pieces of ordnance and dressing up in uniforms from the 1820's - red coats and all. Fitting was a problem as the soldiers in the last century were a lot smaller than their modern counterparts.

To commemorate one particular anniversary the old signal cannon on top of Wellington's Mt Victoria was to be prepared for firing after being silent for many decades, and suffering the ignominy of having its barrel slowly filled up with Coke bottles and other unmentionable things. It was a sizeable old piece, and to clear its barrel a large crane had to be used to lift the rear clear of the ground, pointing the barrel downwards as its trunnions had long ago rusted solid.

All of the crew stood about looking splendid in their monkey suits, along with several dignitaries in period dress. A TV crew waited expectantly while the barrel was cleared of foreign matter. The cannon was being lowered onto the foot of Sergeant 'Fick' Fred, a cockney whose nickname referred to his physical characteristics rather than his mental capacity; he was in fact a very skilled engineer artificer. He managed to partially clear his No 12 foot, avoiding serious maiming at the last moment as the two ton monster thudded back into place.

"F--k," he screamed in true Anglo-Saxon fashion.

"Double F--k," he shrieked in pain and hobbled off out of sight.

The crane driver wisely drove off immediately and the embarrassed crew swarmed around the gun to prepare it by placing the charge at the base of the bore and taping electrical leads out of site underneath the barrel. The touch hole having long ago rusted closed meant firing the beast electrically. The ammunition technical officers prepared to crank the generator on 'Fire'. The crew took up their positions, the civilians tried to look important, and the cameras started to roll.

At the last moment Fick Fred reappeared looking like a casualty from Waterloo, but determined to carry out his duties as gun sergeant.

"Keep clear of - ouch F--k - the muzzle you lot," he yelled at some over-curious bystanders.

"F- all civilians." He hobbled back to the rear like Long John Silver.

"It's all f-ing ready, sir," he said to the officer, pain causing him to forget himself.

"About f-ing time," replied the officer, getting caught up in the occasion.

The cannon finally roared again with an impressive 'crump' and covered the area with dense white gunpowder smoke. The crew stood like rocks while the TV cameramen finished their work. Afterwards the person in charge of the TV crew came up to thank us, but added,

"I'm afraid this will have to go out mute. With sound, no editor would pass that atrocious language of your sergeant."

HMS Tiger, a light cruiser, but classed as a heavy cruiser because of its powerful armament at that time, automatic water-cooled 6 inch main armament that could fire twenty rounds a minute and 4 inch secondary armament with a rate of fire of forty rounds per minute, sailed into Wellington harbours and signaled the end of my career in the NZ Army.

After being shown over the ship and noting, among other things, that the most dangerous place for the crew to be near was the chutes where the empty shell cases flew into the sea when the guns were on automatic. Returning afterwards to work and inspecting NZ's answer: World War Two 3.7 inch anti-aircraft guns redesignated coastal defence, I began to plan for something other than a career in the NZ Army. I was limited by lack of funds, but the answer came in a suggestion from Corporal Price, who had served in the Canadian Air Force. He pointed out that the Canadian Army served in many places in the world as United Nations forces. This convinced me, and, on receiving advice from Canada that although one cannot transfer between Commonwealth armies, they would look favourably on me should I apply on arrival, I completed immigration procedures and sailed for Vancouver aboard the 'Oriana'.

Chapter Two

In the early 1960's it was still cheaper to travel by ship, than to fly, if we avoided the multitude of social occasions on board devised by a high ranked professional martinet cloaked under the name of "Entertainment Officer".

I came from a country that retained a patriotic tradition, dating back to the First World War that was designed to keep the breadwinners home with their families: six o'clock closing of all pubs. The bar hours on ship were very tempting indeed. At the rare times when all the bars were closed the two ships resident drunks could be found in the aft lounge viewing the collection of clocks mounted on the wood-panelled bulkhead showing the different times of the major cities around the world.

"If we were in Honolulu we would only have to wait fifteen minutes 'til the bars opened," breathed one.

"If we were in Vancouver the bars would be open," burped the other. They would then wander off, consoling each other.

I don't remember them ever taking time off for sleeping or eating.

The entertainment officer also shared their lack of need to eat or sleep and, like authoritative figures everywhere, had the knack of catching you when you were not obviously doing something. He was a large florid-faced man with an endless supply of bouncing energy and would swoop down on you in places like a companion-way where there was no escape. Clipboard in hand, he would stand over you to plead, implore or even threaten you until you capitulated and signed up for the "B " deck starboard side green team shuffle board competition. One quickly became adroit at avoiding him.

First port of call was Suva, Fiji. Ships were always met and welcomed by a band, in this case the Royal Fijian Police, resplendent in their red coats and white Sulu.

"Fighting your way through the lines of hawkers on dockside was as bad as the Normandy landings," a veteran told me when we had made the Suva shops proper. It was here that I received my first lesson in the strange art of bartering. I needed a new electric shaver. Having nursed along my old single-headed relic for the past year, the duty-free prices seemed attractive. The Chinese owner-salesman had been lurking spider-like behind his wares and scuttled out to drag me into his shop. Without waiting to ask if I actually wanted something, he launched into a complex behaviour pattern based on unloading unwanted stock. I wandered over to a display of electric shavers and he immediately switched to extolling the virtues of the many different brands, some of which I had never heard of. I pointed to a well-known brand model and enquired the price.

"3.10.6 Fijian pounds," he beamed. This was 10% below New Zealand retail; he knew his trade.

"1.0.0," I countered, "New Zealand ". His face took on the pained expression of someone who had hoped for a skilled barterer but had to settle with a novice.

"3.0.0, special discount for you," he began again and so it went on. Finally we settled at 2.10.6. I was surprised to see a gleam of satisfaction in his eye; I had thought Orientals were inscrutable. I needed to save face but lacked the nerve to reopen the deal.

"I demand a guarantee or the deal is off."

He finished me off in style: "Of course, what would you like: a two year guarantee, a five year guarantee or a ten year guarantee?"

He opened his drawer and displayed an array of guarantees for every occasion. I retreated back to the ship and the safety of fixed prices.

After leaving Honolulu I was introduced to the wonderful flair of the British understatement. A cultural voice on the ship's communications system intoned that we could expect some inclement weather as we sailed north-east and might experience some discomfort. A short time later, crewmen were to be seen shutting watertight doors while dressed in life jackets. The "Oriana" was then a modern vessel with all the latest technology which caused one to wonder what it would be like in a smaller craft. The waves seemed enormous, running at the ship and either destructing on the hull with a dull bang or attempting to undermine it by lifting and lurching. A ship's routine for the passengers always revolves around meal hours, with every other activity subservient to eating. With the rough weather only the strongest of stomachs presented themselves at mealtimes. The waiters were not much better off. I would have thought it impossible for most of them to look more pasty-faced than they were but they managed to.

The beautiful calm entrance to Vancouver's harbour was a welcome contrast to the heavy weather of the North Pacific. Pine tree covered islands slipped past in silence as Oriana marred the ironed flat surface of the water making her way towards Vancouver docks and the beginning of a new life for me.

Over the noise of everyone trying to disembark at once, I heard my name being paged to go to the lounge on "B "deck. I presented myself to two very polite officers of the Royal Canadian Mounted Police force and, like most people who meet the Mounties for the first time, I was a little disappointed: they were dressed in field uniform and not their famous red coats and scout hats. They politely but very thoroughly went through my immigration papers and asked for details about my background in explosives. They seemed satisfied that I intended to immediately join the Canadian army and wished me luck.

I wondered for some time why I had been singled out of all the passengers for such individual attention and it wasn't until several months later when a series of bombs rocked Quebec and the separatist movement, the FLQ, claimed irresponsibility that I appreciated their thoroughness.

New experiences come one after another. I had never seen unemployment lines. When paying cash for clothes and accessories I was asked:

"What's wrong with your credit, buddy?"

Identification was demanded by barmen needing proof of age and some of the drinking laws were archaic, even by New Zealand standards. One drink in front of one person at one time. Although you were allowed a shot of spirits with a beer chaser, you couldn't shift your drinks to another table; a waiter had to do that. When I asked why several bars had organs in them I was told that pianos were illegal: they might encourage singing.

I walked into an empty Armed Forces Recruiting Office and an army sergeant started to shake his head; the armed forces were not recruiting. After passing over a letter from the Canadian army implying they would treat my application favourably, I was treated entirely differently; I was one of "them".

CHAPTER TWO | 27

I was taken through joining procedures very quickly and sent to the army establishment in Vancouver where I marvelled at the excellent food and facilities. There were three young soldiers in civilian clothes who were kept segregated from me and ordered not to even speak to me. I found out later that these lads were being discharged for being a "problem" and they were not to contaminate me in anyway. I realised then that the Canadian army did not mess around trying to correct bad behaviour; they throw you out. There were too many keen young men wanting to join up. I was quickly passed through the initiation ceremonies and issued a ticket to Shiloh Manitoba. I was impressed that there were two trans-Canada railways; I was to travel on the Canadian Pacific. This must be one of the great train journeys in the world. The Canadian Rockies, the food, (I was not allowed the steak meals, officers only) and to go to sleep looking at the prairies and to wake up still in the prairies. I was well looked after by the first Negro that I had met and when he jumped down off the train with my bags I slipped some dollars into his unobtrusive hand.

I had become accustomed to gratuities and waved as the train pulled out, leaving me in complete silence. I was not alone, an olive-drab Canadian army jeep waited for me on the other side of the track. I humped my gear across to it, said 'Hi' to the driver who grunted and I was driven quickly but safely to camp HQ.

Basic Training was longer and harder than in the NZ army. I was put into the artillery; no more making the ammunition and letting someone else 'fire' it. I was to be a 'real' soldier. I was careful to keep my previous training to myself, but most of the recruits were younger than me and often asked advice. Many of the instructors had served in Korea with New Zealanders and I suspect had a soft spot for a Kiwi but they concealed it well. The three months basic ended and I was awarded 'best cadet'. I thought this a little unfair given my head start but it seemed a popular decision. We had now graduated. We were allowed to wear insignia and, more importantly, anolised buttons which did not receive daily cleaning. Our training in artillery began.

If we thought the worst was over we were wrong. Training was rigorous and very physical. Throwing a two ton, 105mm Howitzer around was not easy; all of us wished we had joined the armoured corps where hydraulics did it for you. The sergeant drilled two maxims into us:

"There are no excuses!" and

"Don't be last!"

The last often meant having to push your howitzer over a bank and watch it career down into a marsh. While everyone else went back to the barracks for a shower and a meal, you had to drag the gun back, clean it again and arrive back very late.

To remind us that on occasions we had to operate on our own or in small groups we were often given tests. One such test was to drive out miles into the wilderness and be dropped off without compass or equipment other than water. We were expected back at camp by a certain hour. My three companions looked at me. Helpfully one suggested:

"Why don't we split up and see if we can find a trail?"

A rare original thought came to me:

"There is a jump tower at the camp."

The jump tower was a huge structure, several hundred feet high and used for initial training for parachutists. They had the lovely experience of being hoisted up slowly, thus gaining a very real impression of height, then released and stopped from impacting into the ground at the last moment by a welcoming open parachute. Paras have told me that this is more terrifying than jumping from an aeroplane. Most ground troops shared the idea that jumping out of a perfectly serviceable aircraft was lunacy. It was good old terra firma; the more firma the less terra.

"What's the jump tower got to do with us getting back?" My friend shared the prefix SK in front of our service number which indicated we both joined in British Columbia but he always seemed to be half a pace behind everyone else.

"The jump tower has night lights on it as a warning to aircraft." I waited expectantly but had to reveal the complete plan.

"We wait until dusk, the tower lights up and after our nice rest in the shade we head straight back as fast as we can."

"Yeah." two of them said in tandem.

"Wow." from my faithful British Columbian friend.

We waited until dusk in the shade of stubby mutated pine trees, drinking our water sparingly and telling lies about sexual contests. Canadian sunsets on the prairies are simply awesome. The huge, magnified sun slowly rippled below the horizon, changing the pale blue sky into brilliant blue, pale yellow and finally into a deep red. It seemed to last forever.

Right on cue the jump tower tunnel turned on its lights. To the south with a light step and even lighter hearts we jogged towards comfort and success. We soon found a secondary road. This was becoming too easy. Where else would a road being going out here but towards a civilization? After a half hour of jogging, headlights appeared behind us and slowly gained on us, illuminating the surrounding countryside. We checked with one another and nodded and the vehicle was flagged down for a lift.

The driver was a jovial staff sergeant cook; his waistline proclaiming his love of his trade. He agreed to take us back and even joined in with our singing. As the camp lights drew nearer we relished the success of being amongst the first back.

"Every year you wiseacres think you can put one over us." He didn't sound like a sergeant cook anymore and we shared an uneasy feeling.

"We know all the tricks because we tried most of them ourselves." He sounded much more like a drill sergeant and our spirits fell further.

"You Bo hunks keep your butts glued to the seat I'll say when you get out." With grim satisfaction he drove up to the camp, bypassed it and drove a further fifteen miles out the other side. He let us out with a word of advice,

"Use the jump tower lights to guide you back." He drove off laughing and left us to a long march back. We arrived to find the kitchen closed and lights out. For a week after, nobody spoke to me.

The routine of eating, sleeping and training was broken tragically during live round firing on an exercise late one morning. Our battery was in line. Number one gun had a premature explosion: the 105mm high explosive round detonated immediately after clearing the barrel. The double explosion cut through the bustle of a battery in action; everyone froze. We on No 2 gun suffered no injuries but No 1 lost one dead and three wounded, one seriously with shrapnel wounds. Due to the strange way of an explosive pattern a lad on No 4 gun, the furthest away, also suffered minor injuries. The battery responded like a well-oiled machine: all firing was cancelled, ambulances called out and we were sent down from the guns, back to camp and kept busy. It took a long time for our spirits to recover. Fortunately, perhaps, at the parents' request the burial took place in the young man's home province.

CHAPTER TWO | 31

Six months training was coming to an end; we had one last exercise on the prairies. It was high summer and the giant mosquitoes of Manitoba used insect repellent as a 'pick-me-up'. They could sting through a summer uniform shirt leaving large painful welts that would last for days. It was here that we found that basic infantry tactics actually work. After being marched around in all directions for a suitable time, a machine gun firing blank ammunition opened up from a ridge in front. We all managed a disappearing act while the front soldier on 'point' duty was pronounced 'dead' and happily retired to the rear for a mug of tea. Incensed by still being 'alive', two of us used natural cover to work our way quickly to the flank of the machine gun position. Our speed surprised them as we had the satisfaction of emptying our magazines of blank rounds into their midst and waiting to be told what good boys we were. Our speed also surprised the rotund sergeant umpire who had two great loves in life: making life miserable for recruits and Molsten beer. He arrived late and the sergeant in charge of the machine gun, with a wonderful sense of tactical timing, threw a thunder flash at us. This oversized firework exploded with an impressive crump and, when the dust settled, we were declared 'dead'. Our indignation was tempered somewhat by the tea and biscuits in the rear.

That last night I was on guard duty and a cheerful corporal told me to watch carefully for the, 'Wolves'. "Wolves?" I didn't intend to take chances and secured several live rounds of ammunition from an understanding quartermaster clerk for my rifle. I was the most alert guard on exercise that night: ears tuned to the most distant howl and eyes peeled for any sign of grey shadows moving amongst the brush. It was much later that I found out that the last wolf seen in southern Manitoba was in 1928.

The end of corps training was decision time for me. I was allowed the chance to attend a regular officer selection board. This would have meant a commitment to a career in the army, something I was not ready for. My original reason for joining the Canadian army was to travel and I decided to stay with that. I was posted to the Second Royal Canadian Horse Artillery Regiment based in Winnipeg, Manitoba and scheduled to join the Canadian Brigade attached to the British Army in the Rhine in Germany.

During the months of preparation for the move I was given a plumb posting in Revelstoke National Park back in British Columbia, shooting down avalanches with a 105mm Howitzer. Once again I felt someone was being benevolent; such postings were rarely given to newcomers.

To celebrate my good fortunes I took a taxi for the first time since arriving in Canada. I was not aware of how the 'flag fall' system worked. After being deposited outside the Winnipeg railway station I paid the exact fare. The driver was a little put out.

"You know, buddy, we drivers have to exist on tips to make a living?"

"Don't give me that line, I saw you start the meter at thirty-five cents, do you think I am that gullible?"

I walked away with what I hoped was a man of the world manner while the taxi driver drove off, channeling his exasperation into his gearbox.

Revelstoke National Park in British Columbia is traversed by one of the most expensive roads in the world with a large percentage of it covered by concrete shelters to protect it from avalanches. Our job was to bring down the build-up of snow with artillery fire before it became too dangerous. The road maintenance crew would then clear it away with their machinery.

The brilliant Canadian fall was over. The deciduous trees' leaves had finished turning all shades of orange to burgundy at the embarrassment of having their sap flow reduced. In Revelstoke in November it was all conifers packed in deep snow.

CHAPTER TWO | 33

The lance sergeant in charge of the gun was a very large Indian with a Zapata style moustache. He was reputed to become very nasty after imbibing even a small amount of alcohol.

"If you guys think you are going to sit around on your butts all day waiting for a snowfall I've got news for you all." He produced a battered clipboard.

"Those that want to do snowshoe training line, up over there." He waved his clipboard towards a storehouse badly in need of paint. I made up my mind quickly. There was no ski lift here so gaining the high ground would be physically demanding and the resulting lack of control and attempt to come back to where you started from would probably break bones. There would be no sitting around a large stone fireplace with your leg in plaster, chatting up young ladies and sipping mulled wine. You would be sent back to camp and replaced.

To my surprise, only I and one other gunner trudged over to the shed, the snow squeaking in protest at being compacted underfoot. The rest of the team avoided eye contact and we were soon to find out why. The ski instructor was the National Park Ranger, a sane man with a quiet manner who obviously enjoyed teaching trainees. Our Indian sergeant turned out to be a maniac who in my carefully suppressed opinion should have been confined to a reservation, preferably in Mexico.

"You think this is cold?" His breath sent up clouds of steam as he struggled to lace his snowshoes on.

"Up in the Arctic we keep the vehicles running twenty-four hours a day so they don't ice up and if you go outside; lower than minus forty degrees your breath freezes up!"

I felt relieved that we were not posted to the Arctic but to Germany, surely the weather would be more 'ordered' there?

Training with snowshoes was a painful and frustrating exercise. The trick was to move across the snow fast enough so as to avoid sinking into it but not so fast as to bring on a heart attack. While the sergeant scuttled around like a boatman insect on water we tried to kick the shoes wide to avoid stepping on ourselves. This unusual action played havoc on your hip joints and the inside of your legs. The sergeant was finally satisfied when we were complete physical wrecks and we followed him back to camp looking much like Napoleon's retreat from Moscow.

A few days later the smug look on my fellow gunners' faces was replaced with envy. The park ranger was going out into the ranges to look for a reported mountain lion that had been sighted too near several small communities. Skiing was not an option; on the dense tree-clad slopes you needed snowshoes. He chose me to go along with him.

The landscape was literally breathtaking. The dry crisp air stung the nose and throat and the steep pine-covered slopes caused us to stop often to rest and admire the views. The silence seemed perfect for in the mountains no sound was needed; everything was stated visually and the only noise was the sound of human interlopers slowly winding our way upwards.

We had traversed several small range tops when the Ranger called a halt.

"It's now mid-afternoon and we are both worn out. I don't think we'll risk trying to get back before dark."

He read my feeling of panic at having to camp out overnight.

"Don't worry, there is a hut not far, just for this type of situation, we'll spend the night there."

We trudged the last kilometre to a snow-covered but very substantial hut, fully equipped with food and cut firewood. It even had a radio to inform the camp we would not be back that night.

The warming of the hut with the stove, and of our bodies with hot food, on top of the day's exertions, caused both of us to start nodding off.

"I'll take the lower bunk, old bones after all." said the Ranger.

I managed to clamber into the top after two attempts. Almost immediately I fell asleep, only to be woken what seemed to be seconds later by a loud thump inches from my head. I didn't know where I was and my brain was in overdrive trying to sort out reality.

"What in God's name was that?"

I was glad the Ranger couldn't see my face. Another thump, this time followed by a scuffle.

"It's the mountain lion, I guess," the Ranger sounded tired," It's probably attracted by the heat, just go to sleep. You're safe enough inside and we'll track it in the morning."

Thump again. This was too much.

"If you think I can calmly go to sleep with a wild beast, that I've never even seen, inches from my head, you're crazy!" I had never been more awake.

"O.K., O.K."

The Ranger, kind man that he was, struggled out of bed. I was out and dressed in a flash. The Ranger took his rifle out of its cover. It was an old, but beautifully maintained, Remington 30.06. But his next words were less reassuring.

"Take the lantern, open the door for me and when I run out into the snow hold the lantern above the door. The cat will be blinded and I'll shoot it."

His look left no room for argument.

Feeling like a party to suicide I did as I was told. The door opened, dropping the temperature inside immediately, and the Ranger, working the bolt on the Remington and flicking off the safety with a practiced action, ran out into the snow. Fortunately the snow was still packed down by our feet previously. The ranger took three fast steps as I held up the lantern above the door, fully expecting to see a great cat leap on his back and knock him to the ground. What would I do then? The Ranger spun around and fired at the same time. There was a satisfying slumping noise on the roof. The Ranger hustled me inside and slammed the door.

"Did you see it?" I had to ask.

"All I saw in the light was two large yellow eyes. I hit him right between them."

"Now can I get to sleep?"

The ranger ran a pull through the Remington but left it handy, I noticed. We both climbed back into the bunks. I expected to have nightmares that night but instead fell into a dreamless sleep.

I awoke early before the ranger and could hardly contain my excitement as I pulled on my clothes, rushed outside and climbed onto the roof to see my first mountain lion. It had snowed during the night and there was a large hump covered in snow one side of the gabled roof. I kicked off the snow and there it was. It was huge. It must have been shot between the eyes because the eyes were gone along with the whole head. It was a barn owl!

I don't know to this day if the Ranger knew all along and put the display on for my benefit but, if he did, he took a lot of joshing from the locals.

"Shot any barn-owls lately, Pete?" Followed by a chuckle, would be around for a long time.

After a heavy fall of snow we were at last called out for some action; the weeks of waiting were over. The 105 mm howitzer was towed by a heavy four wheel drive truck with us inside. Already the heavy snow was causing the vehicle's snow-tyres to spin occasionally and it continued to snow heavily. The gun was towed into a rest area and positioned over a concrete platform nearly swept clear of snow. Lines engraved in the concrete enabled us to position the gun for pre-determined trajectory; the sergeant called out the bearing and elevation and, as a double check, looked through the open breech at the target ridge.

Then we carried out the army's favourite activity of, "hurry up and wait," while the park ranger closed off the western end of the park. When he came driving past following the last car we were able to fire. The eastern end of the park had been closed sometime before.

"Fire."

We were only using a light charge. The range to the ridge was not far but the noise seemed reaching deafening. A plume of snow exploded on the ridge; the sound reaching later.

"Reload!"

We waited. There was not a sound or any sound of movement. Suddenly the whole sides of the ridge seem to move downwards towards the road curving away below us. Trees were snapped off like matchsticks, bare black patches of rock exposed, yet there was no noise. For all the power and destruction of the induced avalanche, its own snow muffled all sound.

"Fantastic," someone breathed.

An all-clear was given and it was the road maintenance crew team with snow ploughs bulldozers and graders. They soon cleared the road for use with tyre chains. We repeated the exercise twice more that day with varying degrees of success but none were as spectacular as the first.

It was Christmastime. My first white Christmas and everyone in the community was involved. The food at the camp had always been superb as part of the contract for the maintenance men. Food at all meals was served up at the tables until there were leftovers; all the military put on weight. Nothing was spared with the track-trained Christmas turkey feast but first we had to visit all the houses in the community offering a small gift and receiving hospitality. It was a wonderful experience and even the snow stopped so that we could all imbibe somewhat without the threat of being called out that day.

On my final day at Revelstoke I witnessed for the first time the power of rumour. The park had been closed and we were waiting for the last cars to clear before commencing firing. An out-of-province driver wound down his window and, braving the temperature, asked,

"Why have you guys been called out, what's up?" He couldn't take his eyes off the gun and readied ammunition. One of the wags in the team answered spontaneously.

"The Dukhabors have gone too far, we're going to blow them out of the mountains!" Wide-eyed, the driver took a last gulp of cold air and rewound his window. He drove off in heated conversation with the other occupants.

CHAPTER TWO | 39

The Dukhabors were a strange sect believed to have escaped persecution in Russia last century and settled in various parts, usually secluded ones in Canada. From time to time they had claimed persecution in Canada, demonstrating against this and had, on one occasion, gone too far by blowing up a power pylon. The RCMP had got their men and incarcerated them in a jail near Fort St. John, far to the north of the Selkirk Mountains where we were.

The Dukhabors' method of demonstrating took Jesus' teaching literally.

"If a man takes you to law and would have your tunic, give him your cloak as well." For the Dukhabors this could mean parading around the court naked. Although I suspect Jesus' intentions were to humiliate the court through laughter, the Dukhabors usually managed to channel the laughter back on them.

A community of them had arrived at the town where two of them were jailed and duly paraded naked in the streets. The local RCMP officer in charge of an area roughly the size of England could find nothing in his manual on how to deal with scores of naked men, women and children. He decided to improvise. Evening was approaching and he suggested that they stay overnight in the local barn and discuss the matter rationally in the morning; they agreed. After securing his charges, he padlocked the door and nailed up any other avenue for escape. The inhabitants tried several means of breaking out, and then retired for the night. The RCMP officer then clambered up onto the high-gabled roof and hung a gas lantern above the air vents near the peak of the roof that are a part of all North American barns. Northern British Columbian mosquitoes are cousins to the Manitoba ones but with added suicidal tendencies. Attracted by the light, they swarmed into the barn and feasted on naked flesh. The RCMP officer ignored screams, pounding on the doors and appeals for mercy. He slept contented. The next morning the Dukhabors were released, subdued and covered in bites. They dressed and departed, leaving the small town with another part of Mounties folk law.

The driver of the car must have taken our mischief seriously and probably exaggerated on it as well. Several reporters arrived, looking for action, and the office phone took a year's phone calls within a few days. People in charge were not impressed. Some of this frustration filtered down to me. I was dumped unceremoniously at a small station, with my kit bag, to await the C.P.R. back to Winnipeg.

'Station' was too grand a word for it as there was no platform, just an open shelter. Bored, I went inside to look around. On the back wall there were two red flags and two lanterns and a sign that read: TO STOP TRAIN IN DAYLIGHT WAVE A RED FLAG. A LANTERN AT NIGHT. With a satisfying feeling of Canadian Pacific Railways power, I stopped the large train.

In Winnipeg the regiment had some time on its hands before departing for Germany. The routine was relaxed somewhat and many soldiers took early embarkation leave.

Apart from the drudgery of guard duty, which was stepped up, not to protect us from Canadians, but in preparation for Germany, we had time for my friends to introduce me to Canadian football - a slightly more barbarous form of American football, (never called it gridiron). At first I thought it boring, too stop-start with huddles to decide what to do, several seconds of mayhem then a host of umpires whistling and giving post mortems. The linesmen resembled Sumo wrestlers in space suits but, as I came to understand the plays and the moves, I became a fan and still coach a schoolboy version of it today.

Ice hockey was exciting at all levels, the speed of the players and the contrasting cold atmosphere and hot tempers. Sin bins were new then and some stadiums had not built animal proof screens between the boxes. The players often carried on their fighting in the sin bins. I was introduced to the fickleness of spectators during one match when a famous veteran goalie's head, scarred from blocking countless pucks, skated on wearing protective headgear for his last season. Doctors had insisted he wear the headgear or not play. He was booed roundly by the crowd.

Several of my friends were French Canadians. This was rare in the services; at that time both English speakers and French Canadians tended to keep to themselves. French Canadians were often given the derogatory term of 'pads', indicating something that was below a 'frog' and, on one occasion during basic training, they would be put on a charge if found talking French. This, in a bilingual country. They tried unsuccessfully to teach me that old style French which mainland Frenchmen find so amusing. However the 'swear words', all of a religious nature, came in handy more than once.

During a going away party in our canteen I witnessed a fiery little corporal from the Royal 22nd Infantry Regiment, often called the corrupted French, vingt deux, go into action. He had been drinking with friends and felt the need to use the plumbing. As he walked towards the toilets he found his way barred by a squat, pink-fleshed gunner. His close set eyes were dull and flat.

"Where are you going, pad?" he slurred. He had lent across the passageway, putting his hand on the wall opposite. The little corporal would have to duck under his arm to get past. The gunner was relaxed and enjoying this; the corporal a little ball of energy about to explode.

"To the crapper, I'm sure." His accent caused the gunner's lip to curl. With a sharp slap with his right hand, the little corporal knocked the gunner's hand down off the wall. His leaning body already falling towards the wall was given a helping left hand by the corporal behind the gunner's neck. The gunner's head hit the wall with a dull wet noise and he slumped to the ground. The little French Canadian continued on towards his ablutions.

42 | KUROSAKI KILLED THE CAT

My turn for embarkation leave finally came around and I decided to travel east to see Ontario and Quebec while I had the opportunity. A close friend of mine, David Jantzi, lived in Kitchener, Ontario and invited me to stay there for a few days. Kitchener, despite its very British name, was home to a large German community. Its name changed from Berlin during the First World War for patriotic reasons. I found it a lovely town and, using it as a base, I made several forays out to view Niagara Falls, Buffalo and Detroit. To avoid passport problems on the border I was told to say I was born in Canada and was going to the States for shopping. It worked on what must have been one of the most relaxed borders between two countries.

Kitchener was on the Canadian National Railway network so I took this route to Montreal. The city was buzzing when I arrived. John F. Kennedy had been assassinated that day and the respect for that man was reflected by sadness and a sense of loss that the French Canadians revealed. This sad event clouded much of my sightseeing and I travelled further east to Quebec after only a few days.

Quebec had a sense of history about the old city. The only walled city in North America, strategically overlooking the St Lawrence River, moved at its own pace in time. It was off season and I invested the last of my dollars in a small attic room in the Hotel Frontinac, a huge Gothic structure with verdigris-covered copper roofing. Inside was very olde worlde.

Counting my last change, there were no credit cards then and I had prebooked my train ticket back to Winnipeg, I had enough for a light meal in Frontinac's impressive restaurant. Dressed in blazer and grey flannels, I was the sole diner at 6.00pm. I was to find out later that the place really got into gear after 10.00pm. The French waiter had no excuse but to give me his undivided attention and he even managed to keep his eyebrows from elevating when I ordered a beer and a sandwich from the menu. This was after all a sandwich North American style, complete with salad and chips.

As I sipped on the beer to make it last, the waiter returned, smiling, and placed before me a sizzling dish of garlic prawns. I checked around to ensure that there was no other diner and pointed out to the waiter,

"There must have been some mistake, I ordered a sandwich." The waiter smiled, shook his head and faded into the background of pot plants. I felt I had done my duty; the mistake was theirs; I demolished the prawns. The waiter appeared, cleared the plate of devastated prawns and set down half a bottle of French white wine.

"Is this all complimentary for the first diner of the night?" I enquired. The waiter still refused to speak English, I enjoyed the wine.

There was more to come: the chef himself appeared at the table followed by a brood of underlings.

" For you m'sieur," he beamed and began ladling on to a huge warmed plate, steamed fish in a white wine sauce, sautéed vegetables and deep-fried potato balls. Amid a final clatter of cutlery and porcelain the quartet marched back to the kitchen, leaving me temporarily speechless.

This was now getting serious. I had $6.78 in my pocket and, mistake or no mistake, if I was presented with a $30 bill I would be washing dishes for a week, miss my train and the army would throw me so deep in jail they would have to pump sunshine to me. I left the meal and approached the waiter standing at attention beside the dessert trolley.

"I can't eat this meal unless you tell me what is going on. Remember, I only ordered a sandwich ". The waiter relented; they had had all their fun.

"Your meal is with the compliments of the gentleman at the bar," he indicated, " and he would be very disappointed if you let it get cold," he finished politely.

Relieved, but still confused, I returned to my table and finished what must have been the best meal in my life. The waiter parked the dessert trolley beside me and left me to make my selection while he brought the coffee. After packing in a delightful cheesecake I took my coffee over to the bar; it was introduction time.

My patron was drinking a cocktail and reading a French language newspaper.

"Excuse me, sir, but I believe I must thank you for a wonderful meal." I sounded very English and very formal. He spun around on his stool. He was in his thirties, black haired and well-dressed. He was also well on his way to being intoxicated.

"I saw your blazer badge." He exuded good will.

"We don't get many New Zealand soldiers here in Quebec. I want you to enjoy your stay." His English was excellent.

"Have a liqueur with your coffee, you choose." He indicated a bewildering array of strange bottles.

I don't know how I found my way up to my attic room later in that large, near-empty hotel, but the next day I learned that my benefactor was the brother-in-law of the hotel manager and always put everything on account which he never paid. He was a well-known local character and had once challenged the Premier of Quebec to a duel on the Plains of Abraham. The Premier declined.

On the trip back to Winnipeg I could not get interested in my book. There was too much to reflect on.

The camp outside Winnipeg was in orgalised turmoil; we were moving to Germany. We were trained in batches down to Trenton RCAF base and packed into Yukon aircraft, a military version of some passenger aircraft. The seats all faced rearwards and we were assured that in the event of a crash we would have a greater chance of survival.

We flew the Atlantic and landed in Germany on a cold grey morning. The difference between the dry Canadian cold and the damp German version did nothing to raise our spirits. After a cursory inspection by German customs we were repacked into military buses and driven to what was to be our new home for the next two years.

One of the young soldiers who had never been outside of Canada before gave us a good example of unconscious humour:

"There are more Volkswagens here than in Canada!"

Chapter Three

The Canadian Brigade was part of the two divisions that made up the British Army on the Rhine. On the Rhine sounds very romantic; in fact I suspect that when Germany was divided after the World War II the Soviets took whatever they could, the US the best of what was left, the French the wine and food growing areas and the British were left with the destroyed industrial ruins and the Ruhr valley. Obviously the British saved the best quarters they could for themselves and the Canadians, being the last to arrive, were given what was left.

Driving up through the Ruhr valley the German Wirtschaftswunder was very much in evidence. Germany was becoming prosperous in the early 1960s; new and carefully restored buildings were everywhere although regular gaps of bombed out sites was a reminder of the extent of destruction of carpet bombing.

Our camp was near the small village of Deilinghofen, the nearest town was Iserlohn, some twenty kilometers to the west. The barracks had been temporary quarters for the Wehrmacht

- one could understand why. We were packed eighteen to a room with compacted earth floors and cockroaches big enough to be given right of way. The living conditions were the worst I had ever been in. Next door, in similar barracks, was a regiment of the Princess Patricia's Canadian Light Infantry, and behind us were a regiment of Bundeswehr Panzer Grenadiers who annoyed everybody by having their tape recorded bugles blow at 0515 hours each morning, on purpose, I was sure. We were not alone in our camp; we shared with a surface to surface battery of Honest John missiles. The nuclear warheads were guarded by triple barbed wire, mean, half-starved Dobermans and even meaner US infantry. The duty free beer helped. Becks and Carlsburg were 40pf - 5pf's cheaper than Coke. We settled in to enjoy life.

Settling in lasted twenty-four hours. We were introduced to a new word of American origin: 'bug out'. 'Bug out' meant that everyone threw whatever was necessary for fighting, eating and communicating into vehicles and drove madly to an ever-changing pre-determined spot to await orders for deployment. This always happened at night-time or when it was raining, and was a wonderful way of destroying routine, all in the name of combat readiness.

Those who did not drink or were light sleepers suffered. The 2230 hrs lights out was never adhered to.

"Lights out men," the bombardier would call out happily - he could afford to be, having the only private room in the barracks.

"Good night, dearie," someone would imitate a person with expanded tendons in their wrists. 'Bang', the door would fly open a few minutes later.

"Where's the bloody light switch?"

"Shaddup and hit the sack," from several voices in unison.

CHAPTER THREE | 49

"And 'f...' you all too!" Mutters, curses, the sound of boots falling, the squeak of bed springs as someone got up to the toilet, snores, farts. 'Bang', the performance was repeated several times over as individuals arrived back from the canteen. A 'bug out' in the early hours of the morning made one think of a transfer back home.

The Canadians had a somewhat better relationship with the locals than did the British. One incident near Hertford did nothing to improve the situation. Hertford had been turned into a car-park by the Royal Air Force during the Second World War. One of the few remaining original buildings was a fifteenth century double-storied structure near a bend in the road. The locals were rather fond of it.

British tank regiments, stationed on a hill nearby, were equipped with the massive sixty three ton 'Conqueror'. It stood almost 4 metres high and was in fact a test bed for the 120mm gun. The regiment sallied forth one morning down the road, approaching the bend where the ancient building had stood for almost 500 years. The first tank approached the bend and the driver, who could barely see out over his hatch, applied the brakes to one set of treads. The Conqueror, unlike more modern tanks with rubber pads attached to treads, had only steel tracks. One side of the tank locked, biting into the bitumen, while the other tread relentlessly ground on, slewing the armoured monster slowly into the ground floor of the old building.

The result was something akin to a Mexican chicken coop, with Germans falling out of windows and rubble everywhere. The old building sighed, and settled timidly on top of the intruding tank. The dust slowly settled. The whole town would have been up in arms if they had any. The British tank regiment, sensing this, churned around and clanked back up the hill to their base, leaving a twenty-four hour guard on the tank. Who would want to steal a 63 ton tank?

Reparations were quick but expensive. The old building was jacked up, the offending tank extracted and the lower walls rebuilt with the same materials. 'Conqueror' was later withdrawn from service. It was considered too heavy, especially for the local bridges.

An opportunity that came my way was taken up at once. Our battery commander asked us at parade.

"Does anyone here want to assist with the regimental canteen?"

"Sir," I came to attention and caught his eye.

"Can you do the job? It's permanent, you realise?"

"I have worked in that position before," I said quite truthfully, knowing the advantages that would go with it.

"Very well," the commandant appeared satisfied. "Report to the staff now." The staff sergeant was an older and very relaxed N.C.O. He was also an avid left-hand golfer, and was ecstatic that Bob Charles had won the British Open that year. We hit it off immediately. Running the Regimental Canteen Services meant very few parades, no guard duty and flexible hours. We operated like a separate capsule within the regiment, carrying and stocking up stores, arranging sales and running the local sports stadium food stand. It also meant a lot of local travel and I began to enjoy Germany.

I got to meet several other British soldiers in similar positions. One of the advantages in the job was that we did not take part in manoeuvers, busying ourselves with the supply of goods to the troops.

A British friend of mine was to deliver stores to a guard's battalion on manoeuvers near the training area of Sennelager. One of the few large open areas in Northern Germany, Sennelager had been used for the same purposes by the Wehrmacht. Concrete copies of landing barges used in training for operation 'Sea Lion' were still there. My friend was cleared by military police and allowed to proceed up to headquarters unit which was completely dug in and camouflaged on a hillside. While deciding what to do next, he noticed a bright yellow Mini wind its way unconcernedly from the direction of the 'enemy' lines. It stopped near the brow of the hill and a tall, thin British full lieutenant unwound himself out of the car with some difficulty. He was not in combat gear, and obviously unaware of what he had driven into. A guard's sergeant major disguised as a bush approached him, unsure as to whether a bush should salute.

"What an absolutely brilliant day," the lieutenant took a deep breath of fresh air. "You can even hear the birds singing." At that, a patch of tussock grass rose up out of a foxhole. Underneath the tussock was a private, his face covered in camouflage paint.

"Tweet tweet, sir". He saluted and dropped back into the countryside. Immediately several other patches of tussock concealing N.C.O's rose up, trying to locate and identify the smart arse.

I was at this time meeting and dealing with more and more Germans, and felt the need to learn the language. I enrolled at a private school in Iserlohn, run by a Dr Voight. This proved to be a good investment; I was exempted from all manoeuvers so that they would not interrupt my studies. The camp became quite bearable when it was almost empty.

Fourteen days leave was an opportunity to see more of Germany. Strangely, most Canadian soldiers were content to go either to Copenhagen or Amsterdam, settle into bars called 'Canada' or 'Ontario Rose', listen to American and Canadian songs on the juke box and chat up the local females.

I managed to convince a group of friends that this would be good opportunity to see what the rest of Germany looked like.

We booked the train to Wiesbaden and tickets back down the Rhine to Cologne on the ferries. We could get off and on again as many times as we wished. To save money we decided to be the original backpackers, taking our packs and equipment so we could stay one night in the rough and the next at a modest Gasthof.

At Wiesbaden we became aware of American influence. The local army Post Exchange was huge and on the car lot outside was the sign "American cars, all makes, 24 hour delivery." Mindful of the NZ situation of a two year waiting list for restricted models, I was impressed. One American officer was not. We overheard him ask,

"What da mean, tomorrow; why can't I have it now?"

At Rudeshein we were introduced to German wine; we had no choice. There was a wine fest on at the time and we didn't want to get off on the wrong foot by ordering beer. It took about an hour to become a life-long addict, learning that the '57 and '59 Rieslings were the best. Everyone was pleasant and helpful, and gave us contacts further down the Rhine.

That set the pattern for our trip: visiting castles and vineyards, saying how much better they were than ones previously visited, making friends, and drinking wines with names we couldn't pronounce.

One castle we visited towered over its section of the river and had a secret tunnel connecting it to the vineyards and winery. The builder was a person after our own hearts.

By the time we reached Cologne we were not in much of a mind to appreciate it. The huge Gothic cathedral, with its famous twin towers, had recently completed its repairs and made a deep impression on us. We slept on the train all the way back to Hemer.

CHAPTER THREE | 53

Meanwhile the British were continuing their tank-terrorizing activities against the locals. An elderly Comet tank had broken down and the crew had departed for reasons best known to them, leaving one behind to await recovery by Royal Electrical and Mechanical Engineers. By the time the recovery vehicle arrived, a tank transport with crane and winch, the crewman was bored stiff.

" 'bout time," he grumbled.

"Fix me shackle on for us, matey." The REME corporal began unwinding the heavy winch cable. The tank trooper fixed the shackle onto the recovery ring on the front of the tank, and double checked the gun was locked into the rearward position.

"All clear," he waved to the recovery crew.

"Stand clear, you lot," the corporal said to a few locals who had come to watch. They stood fast.

"Clear off!" he screamed, obviously believing that if you screamed loud enough in English you will be understood. A few shuffled back. The winch was engaged and the empty tank started slowly up the extension tracks towards the transport's deck. At this stage a Volkswagen, engine clattering, drove around a corner and, ignoring the keep clear signs in English, parked right behind the transporter.

"Ere," the tankie gestured. "You can't park here, piss off." The driver, obviously proud of one of the few lasting successes of the Third Reich, looked even further down his nose, straightened, clasped one hand behind his back, presumably to support an old war wound, and stalked off into the Gasthof for a beer. The onlookers, in a show of solidarity, joined him. The Comet had just reached the point of balance at the top of the run-on when the shackle pin broke. The cable scythed around with a hiss, cutting the top of the transporter's cab off as clean as a knife. Fortunately there was no-one inside.

The Comet trundled back down the tracks and over the top of the Volkswagen, squashing it almost flat. The owner came out of the Gasthof, sat down, and cried. The REME crew felt genuinely sorry for him and brought him a coffee.

Later, the tank crew member filling the inevitable accident report in quadruplicate came to the box marked 'damage to other vehicles'. He wrote himself into history: 'tread marks visible on roof'.

The Brits were not averse to going to the locals when short of marks. Toilets in the local bars were used as target areas, and many a local was relieved of more than he intended after being thumped from behind. A friend of mine, attentive to his personal security, always used a cubicle where, standing side on, he could watch the door. On one occasion as he was finishing the lights went out. Zipping up and wishing that he hadn't had those extra beers, he worked the latch open and waited. The outside door opened and shut and there was a scuffle followed by the sound of two bodies hitting the floor.

"Piss off, you berks, I'm English." Muttered apologies as the light came back on.

One British regiment was blessed with a thinking commanding officer who took it upon himself to raise the level of culture among his troops. This always seems to be a contradiction in terms where you train young men to be homicidal maniacs and culture them at same time.

The RSM was a character of what everybody expects an RSM to be: vertebrae fused together, used turpentine for aftershave and sprinkled gunpowder on his cornflakes. He had a voice that could stall a tank. Once, during a church parade, when an unfortunate recruit had unknowingly left his hat on inside the church the RSM had loomed over, bent down, and whispered reverently in the recruit's ear.

CHAPTER THREE | 55

"Get your 'at orf in the 'ouse of the Lord, c——-t'

The CO explained what he wanted.

"We will spend some time on promoting culture among the ranks." The CO considered for a time.

"Yes, we will start with poetry, Keats, I think."

"Sir." At the next parade, after the officers had fallen out and gone to whatever duties they could find, the RSM addressed the ranks.

"You will be studying poetry during lecture time and, to start with, hands up who knows what a Keat is?"

Not all duties could be avoided. NATO manoeuvers involved everybody and, prior to that, our regiment ensured that all ranks requalified on the small arms range. One group was advancing down the range with orders to fire five rounds at various distances from the target. During the advance, half a dozen crows flew in noisily and settled on the mounds of earth behind the target butts. The reaction was inevitable. All weapons were retrained on the intruders and the mounds erupted in a cloud of dust as all magazines were emptied. When the dust had settled, all the crows flew casually away, their 'caws' seemingly disdainful. So much for the combined firepower of automatic rifles and sub-machine guns.

NATO manoeuvers were vast. One a few years previously had been stopped; they had run out of land space.

When our battery stopped for the night, guns had to be dug in, slit trenches, latrines dug, guards posted, and when everything had been secured, you might be allowed a few hours sleep. One night even that precious sleep was shattered as another 'friendly' unit moved onto a ridge beside us, lights full on, radios blaring, and everyone shouting orders to everyone else. Mercifully the noise died down after several hours. Finally there was absolute silence on the ridge.

At first light, several of us strolled over to see who they were. They were an American supply unit; their vehicles were scattered everywhere. A few soldiers were sleeping in the vehicles; the rest were residing comfortably in the nearest farm building. There were guards posted and, when we asked them if they had to dig trenches and so on, they looked surprised.

"Hell no, this ain't for real, we just mark on the ground where they would be if it was the real thing." They gave us Hershey bars to make us feel better.

One of the advantages of being in the Canadian forces was that we were often chosen as umpires for war games, being somewhat in between the US and the Brits. Umpires would give a decision as to who was dead and why, and refer any disputes up through the ranks if matters got heated, as often happened. Nowadays it's all done by computers.

One of our bombardiers because of his lowly rank was stationed at a lonely fork in the road, a place of no strategic value with only a few trees and a dummy tank to cover the Y section. The dummy tank was made up of sheets of roofing iron, boxes, and a stovepipe for a gun. A crisp new Union Jack flew over this sad reminder of Britain's dying empire.

After a long wait, the sound of a motor woke up the umpire. As the motor got louder, other sounds filtered through: music, cuss words and laughter. A US army jeep, filled with immaculately clad military police, complete with uniform dark glasses, transistor radio and Coke cans, slowed down at the intersection. The fifty calibre machine gun was uncovered. Seeing the umpire, they waved.

CHAPTER THREE | 57

"Hi, how's your arse?" they laughed.

"Lemmy, note one dummy tank, see ya". The jeep slew around the bend, its inhabitants masticating on gum in unison, and resumed breakneck speed. The umpire resumed his lonely watch, but not for long. A full convoy of US army supply vehicles, some twenty vehicles in all, approached the Y section in the wake of the all clear from the preceding jeep. The 'dummy' tank started up, fumes rising like angry breath, pieces of wood and iron scattering like discarded scales. The stovepipe clattered to the ground, leaving the convoy looking down the barrel of a 120mm gun. This was 'Chieftain', Britain's new main battle tank, previously kept under wraps. It was considered to be the best defensive tank in the world at the time. The new Union Jack looked decidedly more fitting.

The Americans fumed, raved, and attempted to intimidate the umpire, but he was not having any of it, and proceeded to declare the convoy 'captured'. It was the British tank commander, a slim figure with a moustache as black as his beret that surprised everyone by disagreeing.

"No, no, we are not capturing it, actually, just asking for a ride."

"A ride?" spluttered the convoy commander, seeing all hopes of rapid promotion in jeopardy. "Waddaya mean a ride"?

"We shall just join in the middle of your convoy, old chap, and go along with you." The convoy commander desperately tried to think ahead.

"Now don't do anything stupid, will you, like trying to give us away, or call in an air strike on yourself. We are loaded, you know." The umpire duly noted and, after a lot of slamming of doors, the convoy restarted, and crawled away like a line of sheep with a wolf in their midst.

We heard later that the tank had got itself well behind 'enemy' lines and caused all kinds of havoc, including taking a full colonel prisoner. Our American cousins denied this vigorously.

Our groups of umpires were in the midst of more action. An American infantry group, supported by armoured personnel carriers, was making short work of advancing towards their objectives. We never learnt what their objectives were. A ridge in their path was occupied by members of the Bundeswehr, who annoyed the Americans by firing machine gun blanks at them, simulating mortar attacks by igniting pyrotechnics, and generally making a nuisance of themselves. The American reaction was rapid and copybook. The APCs went to cover and began spewing covering fire; the Americans were not known for stinting on ammunition. An air strike was called in, and appeared within minutes, dropping imaginary napalm on the ridge, and disappeared, leaving everybody partially deaf. For dessert, artillery fire was targeted on the ridge. The APCs raced to the textbook flanking position, and disgorged their troops who professionally 'took' the ridge. There was no-one there; the place had been abandoned. Then all hell broke loose on the next parallel ridge; the Germans had dug in there and poured imaginary fire into the flank of the out flankers.

The US were to experience similar tactics soon after in Vietnam, where the fire would be very real. The US air force was called in to save the situation, but appeared to be busy elsewhere.

The NATO air forces played a dangerous game of 'chicken' at that time. Flying down just inside the border with East Germany, the pilots would streak across the border and time how long it took for the Warsaw Pact aircraft to detect and attempt to intercept them, dodging back across the border at the last moment. Both sides unofficially played this dangerous game. It was to have tragic results. An unarmed passenger light plane lost its bearings in poor weather, and strayed across the border.

It was pounced on, and shot down by Migs before it could be identified. The game ceased.

My time for leaving came far too soon. I had the choice of a paid fare back to my point of joining, Vancouver, or to any army institution that could process discharge that was closer. I chose London, England.

I took a few days leave, visiting a local bierfest that was a poor imitation of the Munich Oktoberfest we visited the year before. We drove on the dodgem cars and were astounded to find that, unlike on the roads where Germans attempted to kill themselves at random, in the dodgem ring everything was sedate and 'ordnung'. My companions soon got bored with following each other slowly around the circle.

"Let's have a smashing time!" said one.

"Way to go," said the other, spinning the wheel hard down to the right and crunching into a startled local.

"Nein, nein."

"We're not nine, we're twelve." Crunch, another local gentleman had his vertebrae rattled.

"Too easy, let's go back the other way." Absolute chaos with local patrons abandoning cars and fleeing us madmen, at great danger to themselves. The power was abruptly turned off, and a squad of heavy Teutons advanced towards us. We joined the exodus.

The last few weeks in Germany were a dream. I was officially struck off strength, so did not exist, but had to wait until CALE were ready to process me in London. The most common thing said to me was,

"You still here?"

Finally I was issued with travel vouchers and NATO travel documents to Hook of Holland, and London. NATO travel documents sped me unchecked through all customs. I continued the habit of arriving in cities on sad occasions. This was the day of Winston Churchill's funeral.

Chapter Four

I had met Jim Berry, a Londoner serving in the Canadian army, in Germany. He was the only person I met in the Canadian army, who had been to New Zealand. He had been on a working holiday several years previously. We had struck up a friendship and when he was discharged a few months before me we arranged to meet up in London.

Arriving at Waterloo station I piled my kit bag and gear in the space beside the driver of the utilitarian London taxi and climbed inside. The driver swivelled in his seat and opened the sliding glass partition. Seeing I was in uniform, he refrained from telling me I should have given him my destination before getting in.

"Where to, Guv"?

"Grosvenor Square please," I pronounced it with the "s". The driver shuddered and drove to the address of the Canadian Army London England opposite the American embassy. I accepted the flag fall.

At CALE it took only a few minutes. I signed for my discharge papers, was wished well by a contented looking sergeant cutting a white owl cigar, and walked outside a civilian.

On instructions from Jim Berry I booked into the Union Jack Club, a low priced establishment for servicemen and was given a cell on the top floor.

Most of London had stopped for the funeral of Sir Winston Churchill; I joined them and watched from the TV room. It was a very moving occasion, one of which the Duke of Edinburgh was to say much later,

"The sort of things we British do very well". It was a moving sight to see the Dockers, who could not have been further away from Churchill politically, lower the gantries of their cranes as the barge carrying the entourage sailed slowly down the Thames. There are many sayings of the great man and I recall my favourite on that day: : Churchill had been informed that a seventy-five year old man had been surprised in a compromising position with an eighty-six year old woman in Hyde Park in the middle of winter. Churchill paused for a while then said, "It makes you proud to be English doesn't it?"

James Berry knew all the angles and had everything organised. First up was a good address and I found myself in a cramped attic room at No. 1 Ovington Square, Knightsbridge, an elegant house for gentlemen run by a Colonel Kyle, Retired, who shared my interest in white wine. Ovington Square was only a few minutes walk from Harrods and it wasn't until I had worked out the exchange rate compared with the local pay structure that I realised how expensive it was.

"Now you must get the right threads," said James taking me to a small shop near Trafalgar Square that sold cancelled orders from Saville Row. I soon found several suits that fitted well without the need for adjustments and at a fraction of the cost of ordering direct, if one could do so.

CHAPTER FOUR | 63

Snobbery costs," James smiled approvingly.

On Jim's advice I had transferred my account from Bank of Montreal's military branch back to Canada and then onto London. We arrived at the Bank of Montreal, a crusty old building in Threadneedle Street that looked like it had never seen a mortgage in its life and proceeded inside. We approached a superior looking person behind a massive counter marked New Accounts.

"I would like to open my account please." This banking assistant had the ability to sound as polite as to be mildly insulting, a trait I was to notice in the Japanese later in my career.

"I regret, sir, that that may not be possible; we would require several references," he replied, showing disinterest.

"In that case you had better give me the balance of my money and I'll go elsewhere." He was starting to get up my nose.

"Make that cash unless you can give us some references for your cheque!" James added beginning to enjoy himself. The assistant allowed a look of annoyance to flicker across his face, excused himself and retreated behind large pillars to check. A pleasant faced young lady saved some face for him by completing documentation and issuing a cheque book.

It was sometime later, when making a purchase at Harrods, that I appreciated the value of the account. Not having the full amount in cash, I produced my cheque book and asked,

"Can I pay the balance by cheque or will you require cash?"

"Cash please, sir, if you don't mind." He then noticed the Bank of Montreal cheque book.

"That cheque will be entirely satisfactory, sir." In London even banks have a social status.

James, because of his age, had a position as a security guard at the National Portrait Gallery in Trafalgar Square. He would often bemoan the fact that buses of tourists, mainly American, would arrive, the passengers rush to see Goya's 'Duke of Wellington', made more famous because it had been stolen then recovered, cast a quick glance at it from behind sunglasses then return to their bus. He expected me to try for something better.

I presented myself to a well known and respected employment agency, immaculately dressed. Gentlemen in those days didn't require CV's. I was sent to Firestone Tyres in Brentwood, interviewed and offered the position of assistant public relations officer in advertising. My newly acquired Canadian accent may have helped: most of the executives were American.

The careful presentation had paid off and I sailed into a career of commerce. The position was interesting but poorly paid. I escorted tours around the factory, explaining how tyres were made and, on occasions, accompanied the advertising team to the motor racing tracks at Brands Hatch, Crystal Palace and others. It was at these exciting places that I met the drivers who used Firestone tyres at the time: Clark, Bruce McLaren and another young New Zealander on his first circuit: Chris Amon. That lifestyle was also very expensive. Having no expense account, I found my savings were being eroded and I felt concern for the long term future.

'England swings like a pendulum do', went the lines of the song and London in the 1960's was doing just that. The Beatles reigned supreme; Carnaby Street was the place for young people to buy clothes; the Kings Road in Chelsea the place to be seen in them. A property boom saw Meccano-like cranes guarding foundations holes like birds of prey. The Barbican, after serious war damage, was being redesigned and rebuilt and the highest building in London, the Post Office Tower, was causing concern. People might be able to peek into the grounds of Buckingham Palace.

My bank balance was also causing concern: it was almost nonexistent. A financial rethink was necessary. There was no chance of promotion at Firestone: the advertising budget for Britain was limited and there was only one manager not near retirement. The Americans loved promoting people with grand titles, but little if any money.

I answered an advertisement for Securicor who were expanding and needed security officers for their armoured car network that was competing with an American company. There was little choice: the salary of 20 pounds a week plus overtime was double what I was on at Firestone. I departed my short career in commerce and began work at the Securicor depot in Vauxhall. This also meant a shift in rooms to Wandsworth Common at a much more common rate. My financial swing had been reversed.

The landlady of the modest, but large, terraced house where I had a bed-sitter, kitchen and shared a bathroom reminded me of the actress Margaret Rutherford. She sat me down for tea in the parlour and noticed me looking at the 1948 map of the world which showed the glorious British Empire in red all across the globe.

"What do you think of the national debt?" she asked.

"Umm, it's not too bad is it?"

"It is," she insisted, "we British should not be in debt, it's disgraceful." I could only nod agreement.

She was married to a Polish ex-air force officer who seemed to be more British than she was. He had anglicised his name but I noticed the dinner-ware and cutlery behind the glass door of the cabinet were embossed with a family coat of arms. He used to meet his old comrades on Friday nights in the lounge while his wife went off to play bridge. I often tried to sneak past the lounge door so as not to be noticed.

"Ah, John, come join us for a nightcap." Polish vodka is not for the casual drinker, especially when dispatched neat and fast. He and his friends would talk of the old times and make grand plans for their return to the old country; it was all a little sad. I didn't think any of them believed they would ever see Poland again. I used to sleep well on such nights.

They had a little dog, some sort of terrier that resembled a rat. Contrary to belief, not all dogs resemble their masters. This caracal canine was sneaky and mean tempered. It used to chase me upstairs, nipping at my heels, then race back to the protective skirts of its mistress.

"Don't worry, John, he will get used to you in time." She would pat the little monster lovingly.

One day the dog made a tactical blunder: pursing its usual performance when the Mrs. was not at home. Waiting until it had reached the top of the stairs, I turned and gave it a swift kick between its set of legs. It flipped a somersault, bounced down the stairs and disappeared with a squeal. The next day it stayed by its mistress' side, eyes staring at the floor.

"I see he's got to know you now."

"Yes, we managed to come to a little agreement."

Working at Securicor was similar to being in the services. The staff was mostly ex-policemen or ex-servicemen and was a good team to be with. Staff, for security reasons, was never permanently given a route or services of pick-ups and deliveries. The changes meant you got to know greater London well and my driver, being cockney, prided himself by showing me the real London and all its songs as well.

As is often the case when living too close to events, you can miss them. Once, when driving past the houses of Parliament late one night, I remembered:

"The MP's are working late tonight."

"'ow you know that then"?

"The red light shines on the top of the tower at night; they fly the flag during the day."

"Bloody 'ell." I mentally thanked my social studies teacher who, along with most others at the time, was an Anglo maniac.

My driver now and then needed to increase his fat intake; he would become morose and edgy if he didn't receive a daily ration of grease. It was against regulations to frequent places like transport cafes where we stood the risk of being contaminated by 'undesirables'. Ignoring this, my driver would often stop at his favourite, off the Edgeware Road. The Luftwaffe must have concluded that this cafe assisted their war effort by damaging the health of the locals: they left it intact but badly shaken.

The door shuddered open and the wooden floor screamed in protest as you made your way past heavy tables with cracked curling lino tacked on top. The counter had cracks in it large enough to swallow up any loose 'bobs' and a large chipped enamel teapot sat stewing on it. A large teaspoon was chained to the counter. The proprietor was a pear-shaped creature with hair sprouting out of a stained tee shirt and black fingernails. I suspected he was a failed truck driver inflicting revenge on the industry.

My friend gave his order and it was repeated by shouting through the service hatch.

"Bacon, fried eggs, tomatoes, beans, two fried slices and sausages." The order was repeated back through the hatch like a naval speaking tube.

"What's yours moosh?"

"Tea and toast, please," I said in my best antipodean accent. I didn't have the nerve to look through the hatch. The proprietor didn't give the order the dignity of being repeated but slapped two thick soggy slices on an even thicker plate marked with the old crest of British Railways, and charged me 9d. My driver's congealed compilation arrived and disappeared, aided no doubt by its accompanied lubrication. I threatened to turn us both in if he ever brought us there again.

"Got to 'ave a fry up," was the reply.

Thursdays and Fridays, being pay days, were the busiest and part time staff were brought in to make up the crew numbers. Some of them who worked a few hours a week were not issued with uniforms. The entire fleet of armoured cars would assemble outside a hall in Chelsea and from there would be given their work routes and supplementary crew members. It was often a scene resembling a slave auction rather than an organised dispatch and sometimes crews left shorthanded. The managing director did not help the situation by insisting on helping out at ground level to show that there was no 'us' and 'them' situation at his firm. He would often rush around, fill up a vehicle and send them off with a thump on the side with his fist - something that did nothing for the blood pressure of the more keyed up crew members. In one vehicle, just after driving off, the driver, not recognising his crew member in the back, said through the grid,

"You're new here, aren't you? How long have you been working for Securicor?"

"I don't. I was walking along the road when some strange twit grabbed me, insisted on giving me a cup of tea then he pushed me inside this van." The managing director was seen less at the dispatch site from then on.

One of the heavier duties was the collection of coin from the London Transport buses. The depot weighed the coins into different coloured bags for denominations which we collected and delivered to the nearest bank. Each bag weighed around 20 lbs. One driver, who played rugby for the London Welsh, was about 6 foot between the eyes and should have been caged when off the field. He liked to practice his passing with the coin bags. This was mainly wishful thinking because I doubt that he had ever touched a rugby ball while playing, but I ended up on the receiving end of the bags to be loaded into the van. There was no escape as the bags came right at me like cannon-fire through the front door. Behind me was the steering wheel. In desperation, I reversed a garnet ring on my right hand; the next big bag ripped open like an over-stuffed sausage scattering copper from the van to the nearest drain. The velocity decreased to an acceptable level.

One van, when loaded, was about to be locked when the crew were astonished to see several West Indian immigrants, armed with pickaxe handles, come over a wall and rush at the van.

"What the 'ell?"

"Inside - fast - lock." The driver was a man of few words. Inside, the crew pulled pickaxe handles from their clips. In those days these were the favourite weapon of bandits. They also saved on a heftier sentence for armed robbery.

"Buster, Buster, Buster," the driver called on the radio. This was the distress call that would be picked up by both the police and Securicor. The driver gave time and location; the crew checked the sealed air-conditioning and waited like a submarine crew for the attack. It came with a flurry of blows of good English hickory denting and rocking the van. The coin vans, because of the weight they carried, were the biggest and strongest of the armoured cars. The onslaught continued as the crew wondered:

"Who the hell would try to steal coins?"

"You saw who." The radio squawked but was ignored because of outside interference.

"You can't bust into a van with a pick axe handle?"

"Perhaps their planning was faulty?" The radio was muted as the broken aerial clattered off the roof. A side window starred and went opaque.

"Why don't we just drive off?"

"Because, because......" The driver started up and drove off with the bandits still attached to the sides and roof of the van.

"Now what do we do?"

"Watch this." The driver had regained control of events and aimed the van at the doors of a wooden garage - obviously an ex-tankie, trained in Germany. The bandits dropped off like fleas off a dog and disappeared. The police found no trace of them but the driver received a commendation.

Following this incident, it was decided that for both public relations and self preservation reasons a Securicor self defence club would be formed using the initials SSDC, which sounded very secretive. Most of us had done some sort of unarmed combat in the services although my instructor had stressed:

"There is no such thing as unarmed combat - you can always find something to use: your tin helmet, knife or a hunk of wood."

"Or fossilised bully beef!" someone added under their breath.

Our self-proclaimed officer was a brown belt in judo. Showing his certificate, he glanced around to see if anybody could do better.

"Did a bit of boxing, man," said a quiet man from South Africa who later turned out to be the ex-army middleweight champion.

"I come from Glasgow," Jimmy, a hairy Celt, mentioned, needing no further comment.

The club was not a great success. Those who could handle themselves dropped by to have a look then decided it was too 'set piece' for them. This left the rest of us feeling we were not accomplishing much. I decided to check out the local judo club to see if they had anything better to offer.

The London Judo Kai in St. Oswald's Place, Kennington Lane was run by G Chew and a well known judoka and author, Eric Dominy. They told me that there were judo classes regularly but also that there was a karate beginner's class starting with a Japan-trained black belt instructor. I decided that this was for me. I would be a James Bond in six weeks. I did not realise it would be the beginning of a twenty five year study and career.

The training was exhausting, but relaxed. We were taught one technique during the beginners' hour lesson. This was repetitious and a little frustrating for the quick learners but everybody had the correct technique before progressing. I was later to realise that this was innovative compared to some traditional martial art systems that expected students to take a year to learn how to punch.

The system was Kyukushinkai, which meant little to us as karate was just beginning to make its presence felt in England. The arrival of Sensei Susuki and his Wadu Ryu gained much publicity. The publishing of Oyama's book 'What is karate?' followed by 'This is karate', gave more prestige to our class of thirty members.

It was a fun time as well. Like most trainees we found there was a gap between learning basic techniques and trying to use them in a free fighting situation. At that time there was no such training as one step sparring or randori, free fighting at a slower pace. You just learnt how to punch; kick and block then were thrown in at the deep end to get on with it. The drop-out rate was accordingly high.

One of the club's characters was a resident of deepest Lambeth. He was a nightclub 'doorman' without the use of his left hand which had been amputated when he was a child. When working he had a chrome steel hook attached. There were never any serious punch-ups at his club. For free sparring he had two hands made of plastic: one 'tsuki' or fist and one 'shuto' or open hand. Often during sparring he would call an illegal time-out and elaborately change his hand before re-entering combat. I decided that, handicap or no handicap, I was going to neutralise this appendage and, after we had taken up a stance, I grabbed it to see what he would do. He looked nonplussed for a second, and then twisted around. There was a ratchet sound from his hand as it came off, leaving me holding his artificial hand. It was my turn to look nonplussed before he whacked me in the side of the head with his good hand.

"At least you had a piece of me," he chortled.

Then, as now, pretenders got 'into the act'. The BBC presented a small item on the new art of 'karate'. The announcer made his introduction:

"In my book there are only two sports: running and fighting, and if you can't do one, you must do the other". He paused to give the audience time to appreciate his wisdom. The camera switched to a thickset individual with a sallow complexion and dark hair. He could have passed as part oriental. He proceeded to grunt, shriek and throw punches and kicks in all directions before attacking and demolishing stacks of clay roof tiles. When the chips had stopped flying he turned to the announcer, his accent giving himself away.

"I will now attempt the 'ardest 'it of all in karate." He narrowed his eyes for effect.

"I will attempt to break a two inch board wiv me 'ead." He imperiously picked up a piece of lumber with grain as thick as he was, scowled at the camera, and, grasping it on each side, brought it down on his forehead with all his strength. His attacking scream was cut off as he staggered off-camera, which quickly switched back to the presenter. The sound system picked up the sound of a crash. The announcer was looking appalled as to the cause of the noise but quickly faced the audience and controlled himself.

"Yes, well thank you very much for that, we will now take a small break for a commercial." I was sure there was no pun intended.

Securicor was asked to provide a team for a film company making a private commercial on security. The team would act out an attack on security men when leaving a bank. It would be by masked bandits armed with the inevitable pickaxe handles. The team was the self defence club instructor and me. We were dressed in full uniform: helmets with a long neck protector like a seventeenth century Roundhead and goggles in case the bandits went up-market and introduced chemical warfare in the form of acid. The metal case containing the money was chained and locked to my waist. This always caused me some concern because veterans told the story from the days where the cases were chained to the wrist. Bandits simply chopped off the hand of the unfortunate guard and made off. If they extended to this tactic it would be embarrassing.

We practised until we had it perfect. I blocked the first strike of the pickaxe with the metal case - no sophisticated karate techniques here - I then rammed the case into my attacker's face and kicked him on the knee cap. (Control was essential). My guard stepped to the side of his blow and threw his assistant in a classical hip throw. His assistant was once a professional wrestler and managed to land with a sickening thud and scream but remained unhurt. The third attacker, after this pitiable show of inadequacy by his team, was to have second thoughts and flee.

The film team came to the depot to set up. The director was a flighty character with a long thin neck and protruding eyes. His hands flapped continuously as he darted around the set delaying the long suffering film crew with constant adjustments.

After hours of waiting we were finally ready for a dry run.

"All right, dearies, let's see what you have for me." He stood arms akimbo one hip protruding. My partner stiffened like a dog smelling something strange.

"Quiet everybody............y now!" He clapped his hands together with a limp flop. We went through our routine; it was over in minutes.

"No, No, No," he shook his head vigorously and my partner stiffened further. I sensed he was about to tell him to try and do better (or worse).

"Far too fast, dearies." He advanced on us with small deliberate steps.

"I want you to do it all again at this pace." He walked us through the routine at an amazingly slow speed; we gained the impression that anyone could have performed the routine, leaving us somewhat miffed. We shot the scene over and over again from different angles and heights until we were all bored to tiredness. Finally, after four hours, he pronounced himself satisfied and gave the order to pack up. We were left with the feeling of dissatisfaction.

It wasn't until months later when we received the completed film that we realised the director's and editor's skills. Simple music built up the atmosphere to one of tenseness. Close-ups of the stocking-covered bandits even gave us a start and sound effects as the pickaxe handle caved in the metal box emphasised the moment. Slow motion showed flakes of paint drifting down into my face and a final shot of a discarded pickaxe handle rolling after the fleeing third bandit was a masterpiece. My partner was suitably impressed.

"I didn't know that we were that good." I had to agree.

The relaxed attitude of the renamed London Karate Kai changed with the arrival from Japan of our new instructor Steve Arniel. Steve simply appeared at the club after a long journey across the Soviet Union and began practicing sanchin, a breathing kata, or form that stopped all the members from their lukewarm warm-ups. We stared at this strange ritual and wondered if he had caught some strange respiratory disease in Siberia.

Without any noticeable change we became aware of a different atmosphere. The clubrooms changed from being a 'training hall' to becoming a 'dojo'. Almost overnight we had become a dedicated group of students. We had found a cause.

Steve Arniel made no adjustments to the Japanese training system to cater for local standards or attitudes. The programme, standards and gradings were the same.

A bond formed between the early members to take whatever was thrown at us and see it through. Only a few gave up and most are still training in one form or another today.

For the first time I became aware of similarities between the British and Japanese. Not only are they both an island people with a love of tea and poets, but they also share a martial tradition and a similar history of conflict between King - Emperor and the military. The Japanese martial arts had a base in Britain since the 1920's when kendo was introduced. Judo and then karate were then well received.

Raising the profile of Kyukushinkai meant going public. Karate demonstrations were expected to show breaking techniques. So we privately practised long and hard on makeshift striking posts to develop the technique and power for a variety of strikes and kicks. The pain of failure we kept to ourselves.

One demonstration for charity was at Lambeth Palace no less. Whether the Archbishop was opposed to lethal martial activities at his residence was not known. My attempt at Tamashiwari was to shatter a stack of roof slates about 6 inches thick. I had done this successfully before but what I did not know was that the slates had layers of dirt on them that would act as a buffer and absorb any penetrating power.

"Next, a demonstration of breaking techniques using impi, the elbow." Sensei Arniel nodded encouragement. I checked the distance again and with a hearty shout, kiai hit the stack in the centre. Pain shot up my arm as the first two slates begrudgingly split.

"Once more," Steve ordered. Thinking I had misjudged the focus I re-aimed and struck again; more pain as four slates parted company. My assistants supporting the concrete blocks on which the slates were stacked brushed off the broken slates, dust rose with the swelling on my elbow.

"Once more," repeated Steve, "or you will be replaced." The final indignity.

Ignoring everything, I threw myself at the stack, body weight following the strike. The stack broke with a noise like flatulence and a great cloud of dirty grey dust rose up, obscuring me and my assistants. When it settled we looked like the black and white minstrels. The crowd, thinking it was all part of the act, were very appreciative; my elbow wasn't.

Much later, at a cost of several pints of Royal Toby and bitter, I secured the negatives of the debacle from a grinning fellow club member.

Training on smooth surfaces all the time was not good enough, we were told. A weekend visit to the seaside was planned.

For the first time some of us were reminded that discipline in karate was extended beyond the dojo. Expecting to be allowed to make our own arrangements to drive to the seaside, we were rebuked in front of the class gathered to depart.

"We travel together and arrive together," said Sensei and that is what we did.

If we expected to find children making sand-castles, city dwellers paddling with their trousers tucked up and a knotted handkerchief for headgear, we were to be disappointed. The beach had been chosen for its isolation. In English terms this meant less than one hundred people per square football field; in reality it was where young and not so young lovers met. I don't think it even boasted a name.

I don't believe southern England was quite ready for scores of shouting pyjama-clad figures punching the waves, kicking the sand and generally destroying the environment and its tranquility. One local advanced on us with evident courage.

"Are you karate?"

"No, Church of England!" He withdrew suitably confused.

Running through the sand dunes three abreast and chanting,

"OO - SAH," sent local lovers ducking from cover and trying to replace clothing at the same time. I'm sure the sand we kicked around helped check the population explosion by preventing several contacts. The local dialect interestingly consisted mostly of Anglo-Saxon adjectives beginning with 'f'.

Thoroughly exhausted, we staggered to where some of the wives had set up a tent and prepared food and drink. Standing around with our hair full of sand, salt-encrusted skin and waiting to fall upon the food, we noticed the arrival of Her Majesty's Police Force. The portly constable leaned his 1920's bicycle against a sign forbidding something and marched towards us leaving his bicycle clips on to keep the sand out of his number twelve's. By the time he reached us, his ruddy face was shining with sweat; he produced a standard issue notebook.

"Right, who's in charge here?" he sounded almost friendly.

"I am, constable." Sensei was a model of co-operation.

"You will have to remove that." The constable waved his notebook at the tent. The atmosphere relaxed a little as we had all thought that the locals had complained.

"Bylaws forbid the pitching of tents, parking of caravans, and sundry vehicles on the foreshore." The food and drink was hastily handed around and the tent collapsed. Satisfied, the constable stamped off. He couldn't resist a parting shot.

"Remember, no erections on the beach." The wives joined in the laughter as the constable made off, the back of his neck reddening.

"Hadn't we already done our bit on that one?" The dojo clown had to have the last word.

Word soon got out that we were to have a visit from Jon Blumming from Amsterdam. Blumming Sensei was a fifth dan - the highest Kyukushinkai grade outside Japan. He also held dan grades in judo and a little known martial art both in Japan and overseas, jodo. He had a simple philosophy: size and strength were everything. He also had an effective way of dealing with any critics during his demonstrations: he simply ordered them to come up and do better. There had never been any takers.

The London Karate Kai was a gloomy place at best but when Jon Blumming arrived, training stopped to acknowledge him and didn't continue because he and his equally large henchmen were blotting much of the light from the door and several windows. Fortunately he didn't take part in training. He was here for the filming of 'Modesty Blaise' where he was playing the part of a Dutch heavy (what else) and to discuss with Steve Arneil the bringing over from Japan of Kyukushinkai No.2 man, Kurosaki Kenji. Kurosaki Sensei would take Jon Blumming's place while he was absent filming and he had expressed a desire to visit England. Rumour had it, that Jon Blumming and his partner in anti-crime had an out-of-jodo-training-hour's activities when in Tokyo. They would use an old car stocked with stealable "goodies," park it beside the road and wait for the inevitable robber(s) in the bushes.

When confronted by two super heavyweights in top physical condition most would-be robbers fled, those too slow were subjected to randori until they were thrown senseless then delivered triumphantly to the police. On one occasion a robber carried a club but after one look at Jon handed it to him but received a beating with it in return.

After several of these "instances" the police had had enough and gave both a gold medal for outstanding community service along with a solemn warning against any further activities. Now days this would be called entrapment.

Sensei Blumming and Arneil seemed to get on well; both had Japanese wives and as Steve could speak Afrikaans, communication between them was good. Arneil Sensei knew Kurosaki Sensei well and arranged to train with him at Jon Blumming's dojo before bringing him to London.

There was a new 'spirit' in the dojo; we were now going to have one of our own top instructors visits us. He would appear on national television to demonstrate how to demolish bricks with his famous head butt. Training intensified.

Kurosaki Sensei arrived and expressed the desire to see the Tower of London, the Queen and Soho, not necessarily in that order. He had only two priorities in his life: karate and socialising. He had only enough time to take one training session. The entire dojo was running on nervous energy but Kurosaki was relaxed and told Steve to take the session while he went around, smiling and correcting the students.

The time towards the end of the session that we had all been dreading arrived: free sparring. We all sat down in the formal position on our knees. Kurosaki, like an executioner offering the condemned a concession, invited us to sit cross legged. Kurosaki homed in on the biggest, ugliest member of the dojo, a green belt, and said the fatal word,

"You!" The poor man lumbered about trying his best to land something, then attempted a frantic kick. It was smashed away by Kurosaki's shin; the man hobbled off to the side and collapsed.

I then witnessed the best demonstration of aggressive blocking I had ever seen or would see again. Kurosaki Sensei blocked everything that was thrown at him with his fists, elbows, knees and shins and in the process turned most of the dojo into cripples. Finally, Arneil Sensei pleaded in Japanese,

"Please, Sensei, could you demonstrate some attacking techniques; they would appreciate it." Appreciate indeed! A green belt was plucked from the line to fight; I was next. The green belt threw caution to the wind and attacked with the subtlety of a kamikaze pilot. Kurosaki gave himself space then landed a sizzling round house kick to the neck. The green belt dropped like a counterweight and I wondered if I should ask permission to change my library books. Kurosaki Sensei had had enough; the session was over.

The Hollanders had just enough time to recover from their aches and pains when Kurosaki returned to inflict more of the same on them. Determined to show Sensei some of the local wonders and to avoid training non-stop, they decided to take him to the tulip festival.

The tulips were beautiful at that time of year, presented in colour coded ranks, each plant perfectly planted in line, not a petal out of place nor the merest suggestion of non-matching colour. A perfect place for Sensei to relax and indulge in Zen. They lost him. One senior rank said to another,

"Where is Sensei?"

"I thought he was with you!" a surprised reply.

"God - ver - damme." A club member foolish enough to be standing nearby was summoned,

"Have you seen Kurosaki Sensei?"

"No, he's with you isn't he?"

"God - ver - damme." Heads started to turn as members rushed off in all directions to find Sensei. Sensei was found sleeping peacefully under a tree, unaware that a search party resembling the Keystone cops had been scouring the tulip park. He said he wasn't very interested in flowers.

Sensei was invited to one of the instructor's house. The family had spent hours in preparation: cleaning, selecting local food that Sensei might appreciate, the children wearing their best clothes. After the meal they sat around in a cosy family circle to listen to Sensei expound on training methods. The children's kitten jumped up onto its customary place on the arm of the chair where Sensei was sitting. Absentmindedly he stroked its fur and was rewarded by a purr like an outboard motor. Sensei was emphasising 'kime' (focus).

"If your techniques lack focus you are just imitating." Sensei cracked his knuckles and made a fist.

"You cannot succeed without focus!" He brought his fist down with lightning speed to make his point. Unfortunately, he forgot that the cat was between his fist and the object of his focus, the arm of the chair. The cat had no chance, and expired with a small sound such as you get when squeezing a teddy bear. The children started to cry; Mom and Dad were understandably furious but dared not say anything. A contrite Sensei, not knowing what to do, handed the limp bundle of fur to the father. The smallest child wailed,

"Kurosaki killed the cat!"

It was decision time for me. I had always been interested in individual activities rather that team sports and I found karate offered a personal challenge at increasing levels. I also appreciated the fact that most of the training could be done on your own and that failure could only rest on yourself. I began to realise that this builds character as well as physical advancement; the open-ended training system appealed. I made the decision to travel to Japan to train and, if successful, become a professional instructor. I had no idea where I would teach if successful but I knew that New Zealand had no professional karate teachers; that was an option I would leave open.

The decision meant an increased commitment to training and saving money and I found, like so many students do, that the two are not always compatible. An increased workload means less time for training and vice versa.

I began to take two one hour private lessons a week with Steve Arneil; an obliging Securicor arranged work schedules to fit. I also began to save money by exploring and enjoying all the free activities that London offered at that time. All the museums were free and it took ages to see them properly; a seat could always be found for 2|6 up in the gods in theatres and all the top stage personalities of the time were available. One could stand outside the railings of the embankment and listen to the bands playing without being charged for a deck chair and a few of the state owned stately homes were still free. Each payday my armoured car driver would detour through Threadneedle Street so I could deposit my savings into a steadily growing account.

I have always been a slow starter and the private lessons gave me the sound basics on which to build during club nights. Although control was insisted upon, contact was often made and my colleagues at Securicor used to shake their heads when I would appear in the mornings with signs of battle damage.

I began to view other martial arts for comparison and found the simplicity and aggressiveness in kendo appealing. kendo was one of the earlier martial arts in England and there were several clubs practising in the traditional way. One such club trained in the upstairs ballroom at the working men's club in Coalville. The members were all fitted out in full armour, waiting to begin the sparring part of their session. As they stood there, Darth Vaderish, the fifteen year old son of the instructor sped up the stairs and scuttled into a back room. He was a known 'pain'. There was a loud pounding on the stairs and a great 'yobo' rushed into the room and stopped abruptly at the sight of a score of armed and armoured kendoka, rattling their bamboo shinai like insects' antennae.

"Er, I'm not going to cause any trouble," he told the club, blinking in surprise.

"I am sure you won't," replied the Sensei and mayhem resumed as the yobo fled back down the stairs.

A local character and author had built himself a house that was in fact a minor fortress. He had been interned by the Germans in the Channel Islands during World War Two and, to avoid boredom, joined the Waffen SS. The Russians were not impressed and threw him into a gulag after Germany's surrender. The approaches to his 'house' had a series of level areas that any sane person would have used to set a park bench or a fountain for the visitor's pleasure. These areas were used instead for training spots and one would have a makiwara (punching board), another sandbag for kicking, and yet another, various weight training devices. I suspect the owner wanted his visitors exhausted before they arrived in order to give him an edge. Inside the house it was rumoured that behind curtains, under couches or just in plain view, various weapons were scattered throughout, all within an arm's length of the occupant. He was not a person who took chances.

A friend of mine was invited to the house but never made it past the front gate. As he was about to enter, the owner appeared with a double barrel shotgun and blew the neighbour's rooster, perched innocently on the fence, into a mass of airborne feathers.

"He can't wake me up in the morning now!" My friend quickly and carefully made his exit.

CHAPTER FOUR | 85

In London, kendo was undergoing the beginnings of change. Knudsen Sensei, otherwise known as the Mad Monk, ran his dojo in an ultra-conservative manner. The bringing into the dojo of his helmet was something of veneration and he would never speak directly to his students - this was always done by a Sempei (senior). He did, however, train traditionally. His students always took at least three shinai (hollow bamboo swords) to a Shiai (competition) knowing that they would break at least two on each others' heads. When 'competition kendo', disdainfully labelled 'Zip Zap Do' by the traditionalists, began to gain ground and take over the organisation, the Mad Monk retired in a huff with several adherents loyal to his way.

Later, a Japanese teacher Otani Sensei was to insist on instilling Zanchin (alertness) into his students. In one incident he dismissed his class who, after they had found enough energy to get off the floor, wearily made their way downstairs to undress for a shower. As they were about to, the shower door burst open and, with a kiai (shout), Otani Sensei charged naked into his students flailing his shinai. He had crawled out the top floor window, jumped down to the next floor and slithered through the shower window. I doubt if London was quite ready for him.

My time in London was ending. I spent several wonderful weeks in a converted oast-house in Tunbridge Wells, Kent with a fellow karate student before leaving England with another student to drive from Paris to Rome. From Rome he would return to London; I was to travel onto New Zealand to see family and friends before going to Tokyo to train with Oyama Sensei at Kyukushinkai Kan.

There was a surprise in store for me. The pub next to Securicor depot in Vauxhall was frequented by most of the staff. I had trained the bar staff to always serve me ice cold bottled beer, even in mid-winter, and told them stories they never believed about how beer was delivered to pubs in New Zealand in petrol tankers and served in a similar manner. It was a real London knees-up; all the locals attended and I paid for nothing that night. All the old songs were sung and for the first time since I had left New Zealand, I felt the sadness of leaving a second home. Those wonderful people are in my thoughts often.

We spent several days in Paris before hiring a car to drive up through Belgium, Holland, and Denmark to Sweden. There we met a New Zealand girl our own age who was travelling to Berlin. She asked for a ride; it was a favour we were to regret.

Using a map, we found a road that led to the German Democratic Republic's border and drove through a wooded landscape for several hours. It was night-time when we arrived. All was closed. A local kindly informed us that only three main autobahns to Berlin issued visas. We drove all the way back and found the autobahn. When we arrived at the border again it was two o'clock in the morning. We were treated to an incredible sight. The East Germans were having a periodic purge on all crossings; light blazed everywhere; lines of cars stretched back from the borders for kilometres; trucks and heavy transports even further. Every vehicle was being systematically searched by truculent guards. We were kept waiting for hours in a line waiting for visas. In front of us was an American family of four. The husband was unmistakably military but was in civilian clothes; the wife was losing patience.

"Honey, why do we have to put up with all this, we won the war didn't we?"

"Yes, dear, but we have no clout here."

"I want popcorn," complained a freckled faced boy of about ten with stains around his mouth. "Double butter, have they got double butter?"

"Shush, junior."

"Mommy, I'm tired," a little girl was tugging at her mothers dress. Dad's blood pressure increased to the point that when it was his turn at the desk he exploded.

"What kind of crap outfit is this? You goddamn square heads couldn't run a party in a brewery; no wonder we kicked your goddamn arse in the last war!" He slammed four American passports onto the table. The official at the desk was a thick set woman with close cropped hair and shoulders like an all-in wrestler. This likely candidate for a sex test in the next Olympics casually flicked through the passports without even lifting a dense eyebrow.

"There is an irregularity; you will wait at the end of the line!"

"Next." Her breath smelt of testosterone

"Honey, how many times have I told you not to lose your temper?" The wife's voice augmented by the crying children faded towards the end of a long line. We fell over ourselves to be polite, wincing as we paid an outrageous fee for our visas. Gratefully we got back into our Volkswagen and drove carefully off.

However we were given no instructions and unknowingly drove straight past the post where we were supposed to stop and present our papers. Everything erupted around us like a Hollywood set: flood lights came on; barriers slammed shut; dogs began barking in German and guards armed with sub machine guns ran towards us. We began to wish we had stayed in the other Germany. Strangely we were not taken and shot; it was worse. A border guard who looked as if he had two glass eyes made the most of this moment.

"Are you stupid?" he asked.

"We are not used to such excellent security where we came from," said my friend. I thought he was pushing it.

"Get out!" The car was searched and we could feel the eyes of the people behind us looking at obvious candidates for incarceration. Our punishment was swift: we had to drive back along a narrow road through mine fields and sour faced guards to come back again properly.

We arrived in Berlin at 8:30 in the morning and had breakfast in a noisy all- night and day bar near the zoo. It was another world. I remember East Germany by the colour grey. Grey cars, grey skies, grey industrial towns and grey people - it was a relief to drive back over the border into Bavaria. It was like changing from black and white television to colour.

The next part of our journey seemed to be taken out of a fairy tale book. Castles, churches and villages passed by as we drove through Austria, up over the passes into Switzerland and down again into Italy. I found that Rome was a city much like New York in that you had to be 'in the know' to appreciate it. Rome was not a place where you can just arrive, move into a room and feel comfortable; you needed help to get under its skin.

After a few days my friend and I parted after returning the faithful Volkswagen car. We had paid an all up front fee but we were still charged extra by the local Avis mafia and were inexperienced enough to pay it. Naturally there was no receipt.

I had a ticket on BEA to Athens and found that city very different with people going out of their way to be hospitable. I took a taxi up to the Parthenon and avoided the guided tour. It was an experience just to sit under the ancient columns and imagine what had once happened there.

Afterwards, with time to spare, I wandered down the streets away from Athens and found myself, hungry, in a back street, well off the tourist circuit. A homely cafe with outside seating announced itself with the sign of the local beer; I ordered one. Beer, beera or beeru is understood everywhere. A young lad sprung out to take my order.

He spoke in Greek which I obviously didn't understand but I pointed to an old man eating a dish of spiced mutton; it looked and smelt delicious. The lad shook his head and disagreed; I wondered if the dish was too spicy for a foreigner. A large man with a jet black moustache came out; he was obviously the owner.

He paused after a further barrage of Greek, his eyes twinkled. I pointed to the dish again; both looked unhappy and disappeared together. What was the blasted dish anyway? The cook himself came out.

More Greek, then a few passers by also joined in to help, Laughing they all helped me up and escorted me to the kitchen. The cook took all the lids off the pots, gave me a plate and said what could only be

"Help yourself!" I did and, many more bottles of beer later, realised that you don't need to understand the language when you find hospitality like that. I still don't know what it was that I ate.

If I had told my Greek friends that I was going on to Istanbul they would not have been so happy. Even after five hundred years they were still mourning the loss of Constantinople and the Byzantine Empire. I spent three days in Istanbul, staying with an American Air Force captain whom I had met on the plane. He insisted on my staying with him and his wife.

I marvelled at the still standing parts on the walls of old Constantinople. Much of it had been destroyed earlier in the century by an earthquake but, that which remained, was impressive. There were only five thousand defenders on the walls in the fifteenth century but it was still a wonder how the Ottomans had breached those massive fortifications. The great church of Santa Sophia, now a mosque, still gave some hint of the grandeur of the culture.

There were only eight passengers on the BOAC night flight from Istanbul to Hong Kong and the stewardess invited us all up to the first class so we wouldn't feel lonely. We had a party and the co-pilot came back and joined in drinking fruit juice. They did things like that in those days.

I don't remember much about Hong Kong on my first visit. I think I overdosed on culture shock and my stomach rebelled against any further exotic intakes.

It was a relief when I walked out the door of Sydney's airport and flopped down in the back of a taxi and heard:

"Gidday, mate, where're ya going?"

The flight home to Wellington seemed humiliating. When called, I looked for the gate number but there wasn't any. I was directed beyond the last gate to a fire exit and followed a few fellow passengers down the outside staircase to the tarmac. We were further directed past the rows of large 707's and there, hidden in their shadow, was a Lockheed Electra turbo prop which probably had a top speed of 200 knots in a screaming dive. The flight to Wellington was four and a half hours and I asked if I could buy duty free goods for my family.

"Sorry, we don't carry any; we don't have the room." We arrived in Wellington on an unusually fine and windless day. We were surprised when we landed with a severe jolt. The captain explained over the intercom,

"Sorry about that, folks, I'm not used to landing in Wellington without the wind."

Chapter Five

Immigrants had introduced judo into New Zealand after World War II and by the 1960's judo was finally established with several Japanese-trained instructors.

A few karate instructors had a small but dedicated following with some clubs eager to gain knowledge from whatever source available. These sources usually meant going down to whatever Asian ships were in port, finding out, often through sign language, if any of the crew practised a martial art and, if successful, spiriting their friend back to a hall somewhere to drain him of whatever he had to offer. The result was that there were many local karate clubs practising a pot-pourri of systems and styles without structure or a defined direction. Many believed that they were adopting the best of several systems but just how the best was identified was not clear. Later, most of the clubs either amalgamated with a recognised system or faded away.

Judo, being organised with its own Federation affiliated to Japan, was by far the strongest martial art in the mid 1960's.

Many dojo's had a small karate club attached. In Wellington the judo Club travelled in style in a black 1927 American model hearse. This gave the tournaments at the time a real status: a hearse parked outside while the hall rocked to falling bodies, grunts and screams; the locals would often hurry past.

To boost my funds further I took employment with Sterling Security and found myself on night shift at a local factory most of the time. To avoid falling asleep and to prepare for Japan, I set up a series of training stations around the factory using heavy boxes for weight training, metal supporting bars for chin-ups and sacks of various substances for striking. I was followed around these stations by my faithful German shepherd bitch. She was the complete fraud: vicious looking and sounding, but being in fact a softie. The local cat fell asleep on her for warmth. She would look at me with cocked eyes as I huffed and puffed around the circuit, obviously wondering why any animal would go to such exertions when they could sleep. I often wondered why too.

At this stage I was not certain that I would return to New Zealand permanently; there were many opportunities overseas for qualified karate instructors.

I packed up all my modest belongings into a wooden trunk and booked a passage on the P & O liner, Chusan, to Sydney, Brisbane, Darwin, Singapore, Hong Kong and Yokohama, price: 105 pounds. Chusan was a one class liner and one of the older P & O vessels. She showed her age by breaking a driveshaft just outside Sydney. This meant an extra week's stay in Sydney while a new shaft was flown out from Britain; it also meant being shifted from the overseas terminal on the Quay to an ignominious berth deep in Darlington.

Before departing Sydney a quiet Chinese teenager made up the foursome in our cabin. He declined to join our sightseeing excursions in Brisbane and Darwin. In Singapore when the most wayward of our group suggested we visit the red-light area (for sightseeing only, of course) he smiled and politely declined again. When we returned on board and the most gregarious of our group were exaggerating their experiences he said quietly,

"When you come to Hong Kong I will show you some good places to go." We soon forgot about his promise.

When we arrived in Hong Kong and cleared customs we noticed a long wheelbase Mercedes 600 waiting outside.

"Come and have lunch with me and my family." He invited us all. Stunned, we picked our way into the limo, fearful of scratching something and were whisked away up towards the peak. Halfway up, the limo stopped.

"I'll only be a moment, please, to pay my respects to my father." He disappeared inside a Victorian-facade building with the name Hong Kong Tennis Club engraved in stone. It looked ultra-expensive.

"Your father is a member here?" one of us asked, impressed, when he returned.

"Oh no," said our friend smiling, "he owns the club." I made a mental note never to underestimate the quiet unassuming type; true to his word he showed us some 'very good' places. The restaurants were an eye opener when compared with the local adaptations in New Zealand or even London. In Wellington the Chinese immigrants were mainly from Canton and the food reflected this but watered down to suit the local Kiwi palate. Buttered sliced bread was always served first and whatever you ordered whether served on a base of noodles or rice seemed to taste the same, heavily laced with cabbage. There were no licensed Chinese restaurants and everything was washed down with tea (acceptable) or coffee made from essence (undrinkable). The restaurants our friend introduced us to were well off the tourist track, and full of Chinese. The meals chosen by him were a stunning array of taste, texture and temptations. The local beer was not bad either. We were coached in bargaining, "if he does not hesitate and reach for his abacus you are too high." We were shown where the best bargains were to be had, the Chinese mainland department store had leather trunks and the best shirts at a fraction of the price paid in London. As the Chusan sailed out of the 'Fragrant Harbour' we had a collective feeling of debt.

Most of the passengers crowded the rails to get a glance of 'the horned isles' as Chusan sailed into Yokohama harbour. All were disappointed: it was still early winter in 1967 and Yokohama and the countryside beyond were shrouded in grey cloud. This had no effect on the endless fishing boats of all sizes that came and went, ignoring the foreign passenger vessel.

Customs was thorough for those landing with visas issued for other than holidays. On completion of this close scrutiny, I took the luxury of a taxi to a Ryokan, or Japanese style inn, recommended in Tokyo. The hospitality was everything expected and more and, after the relaxing bath, two housemaids brought a traditional meal to my room and, on entering, burst out laughing. While wondering what social blunder I had occasioned on my first night, the girls pointed to my two hairy legs exposed by a short kimono and rushed away to look for a larger one. I slept well that night in a warm futon with the sweet smell of new tatami (mats) and the tinkle of a small waterfall in the garden outside.

The next morning I presented myself at Kyokushinkaikan; the old dojo had been tucked in behind Rikyu University. It had holes in the floor, walls covered with newspaper articles of Oyama Sensei's career and his daughter sat at an office desk by the door. Foreigners were allowed to train free to encourage expansion of the organisation overseas, but were discouraged from some cleaning duties. They tended to lean too hard on the windows and break them. There were no showers.

CHAPTER FIVE | 95

The new dojo was a four-storied building that at first looked impressive until a hospital was built across the narrow road later that year. The architect either had no idea how a dojo should be designed, was given conflicting orders by Oyama Sensei, or was a snakes and ladders addict. The ground floor consisted of an office, a small dojo fitted with judo mats and only suitable for private lessons and large glass display cabinets filled with Sensei's trophies. A large staircase, taking up far too much room, lead down to the basement containing showers, lockers and a lot of empty space, then up to the dojo on the second floor. A balcony and a huge shrine squeezed the floor space to accommodate thirty students. The staircase swept on upstairs to Sensei's office, a conference room and secretary's office. On the fourth floor were Sensei's living quarters. Linking all the floors and balconies were concealed stairways that looked like they were designed for both fire escapes and police raids.

Getting past the office girls on the ground floor was the biggest battle but finally, after showing memberships cards and letters of introduction, I was ushered into Oyama Sensei's office by a brown belt obviously taken out of training by the appearance of his sweat-soaked gi.

"Welcome, welcome to my dojo." Oyama Sensei stood up behind his desk and eased his powerful bulk towards me, extending his hand for a shake; he had a powerful grip. He read my letters of introduction, nodded and spoke in rapid Japanese, summoning his black belt instructor from the dojo, his secretary and a girl to prepare tea.

Sensei spoke very highly of Steve Arneil, calling him 'my son'. I was to find out later that he had three levels for foreign students: 'good student', 'very conscientious' and 'my son'. I did not know it at the time but it was not my destiny to ever rise above 'very conscientious'!

Formalities over, he assigned his secretary, who spoke excellent English, to me to arrange a room close by. I was very fortunate to have her assistance; she found me a small four and a half tatami room with a sink and a gas-ring, within ten minutes walk of the dojo at a very reasonable cost per month. Key money was expensive but the agent's fee was waived. Converting the currency was easy: one pound sterling equaled a thousand yen. I spent the rest of the day buying sleeping gear and food and settling into a new way of life. Training was to commence at 10am the next day.

To my surprise I found the next day that I was the only overseas student training at the dojo. There were a few foreigners who were living in Japan more or less permanently; I was to meet them later.

On my first day I found the dojo was neither friendly nor unfriendly; I was just another student, though as a brown belt, I was not at the bottom of the pecking order. I was to find out later that I was the first foreign student to come to Japan and hold his grade; everyone else went back to white belt. I was thankful for Steve Arniel's promise that any belt that he awarded would be equal to the Japanese standard.

The training pattern was lengthy warm-ups, forty minutes of basic techniques, half an hour of kihon - moving across the dojo in different stances and using a variety of techniques. This was followed by kata practice - forms of predetermined patterns starting with simple forms and advancing through to very complex ones. The advantage of being a lower rank was that you could rest when the seniors were practicing the more advanced. 'Rest' was a relative term when you had to sit in the formal position. Sometimes a kind-hearted senior would invite you to sit cross-legged which merely transferred the pain from your legs to your hip sockets, but usually they forgot. Two and a half hour sessions twice a day, six days a week. There was training on Sunday morning but I pretended to be religious to allow my tortured body twenty-four hours to recover.

CHAPTER FIVE | 97

During my first training session a young white belt asked:

"What is that awful smell?"

"Just the smell of a new gi, concentrate on what you are doing." The senior slapped the white belt's face for being distracting. This was still common in a dojo at that time although I never saw a foreigner treated that way. We were, however, subjected to being hit with a shinai to 'toughen us up'.

Months later, when two Dutch students arrived and commenced training, I too noticed an awful smell. Having been on a Japanese diet with no dairy produce, the best way you could describe the smell was 'rancid'. Mindful of the slap I kept quiet but I wondered if the answer was to sell the Japanese more NZ dairy products which would help NZ's balance of payments and we could all smell the same.

After completing the first training session I limped home for some food and rest. The hardest decision I had ever made was to drag myself back for another dose of the same at 4.00pm.

For the first few weeks I was sore and lonely. Had I not made it very public that I was going to Japan to train for a year I could have quietly packed up and slipped away. Pride and fear of failure kept me going through those early months.

The news spread quickly around the dojo and was translated for my benefit: we were going into the mountains for a weekend of training in the snow. Time-Life magazine reporters would be covering the event; an article on Kyokushinkaikan would be published.

"We are all fortunate," the dojo Sempai told us. "Winter training camp (Gasshuku) is usually five days long, and many students do not make the finish." I began to like Time/Life magazine.

Early on a Saturday morning, we were stacked into two buses and set out for the mountains of central Honshu. I began to understand why most Japanese travel by train: the roads were atrocious and got worse as we travelled further inland. I tried to concentrate on the scenery and not the deep ditches that indicated a very high rainfall as they flashed past, inches from the bus's wheels.

The mountain ranges looked similar to New Zealand's from a distance, but as we came closer the difference in the trees was obvious. Unlike the wide variety and colour of the New Zealand bush, the Japanese hillsides were covered in giant grass called bamboo. The bamboo mirrored Japanese society: ordered, all growing the same way and very little personal space. Large native trees and conifers filled many valleys and were topped of with a layer of mist.

We arrived outside a monastery of rambling buildings untouched by paint; the road tiles were covered in moss. The smelly, noisy buses were quickly ordered away, and we were invited in for a prepared lunch.

The dining room was unheated and unadorned, but did provide wooden tables and benches. We sat, and waited to be served by white belts and novice monks. My bowl of food arrived, and I looked around to see everyone fall on theirs with a clatter of hashi (chop sticks) and throaty noises of approval. I looked down at my bowl and saw a mound of cold, glutinous rice. Embedded on the top was a fish, half the size of a sardine, intact with its glassed over eyes staring reproachfully at me. I turned to the young man next to me and asked him,

"Would you like my bowl? I'm not very hungry." He looked like a dog that had just been praised.

"Domo, domo." The food disappeared and I had made a friend for life.

After lunch we changed for training - outside. Surprisingly our feet did not fall off after half an hour in the snow; we were kept moving and our circulation kept pace. The cold did not affect Oyama Sensei who stamped around, correcting students and instructors alike.

Later the Time-Life magazine reporters arrived. For some reason I had been expecting Americans and the chance of some English conversation; I was disappointed to see that all the reporters were Japanese.

Only brown or black belts were to be used in the photos and about twenty of us set off in single file along narrow paths and over rock faces to reach the area where the photos were to be taken. Oyama Sensei led the way like a good British officer and several white belts struggled along in the rear carrying food and equipment. The photographers, dressed in suits, looked very out of place.

Oyama stopped briefly at several places he had used before but moved on. It was late winter and the thaw had caused the waterfalls to become gushing torrents, smashing themselves on the rocks below. I thought they would have made a great backdrop; I did not realise what we would be required to do. Finding a suitable waterfall with several flows measuring a meager fifty litres a second, we had to take up positions on the slippery rocks while the cameramen set up. The white belts made and lit a large fire some twenty paces away. It looked very inviting.

At a nod from Sensei the senior black belt began counting.

"Ichi, Ni, San, Shi..." We had to kiai (shout) on each count and several crow-like birds flew away in disgust at being upstaged.

The senior black belt then took off his top and picked his way across the rocks to stand under the waterfall in the standing mokuso (meditation) position. He stood there for several minutes, impervious to the freezing water while the cameras clicked and then staggered off stiffly to thaw out by the fire. The next most senior took his place and we all moved around clockwise.

It came to my turn. Being the only foreigner there, all cameras trained on me. I reasoned that I had more body weight than any of the Japanese students so should be able to withstand the cold better. With confidence boosted by this 'edge', I took up my position. I had anticipated the freezing water but not the small chunks of ice that tried to beat their way inside my skull. Mercifully, pins and needles were followed by complete numbness as I stood there, expressionless, while the cameras clacked and whizzed, deliberately I suspected, longer than for any of the others.

At last it was over and I made my way towards heaven in the form of hell's fire. I appreciated the look of respect in the senior black belt's eyes, but was stopped in my tracks by a polite but insistent voice.

"Excuse me please, gai gin san, but two of our cameras have used up all their film." Two poker-faced cameramen nodded in agreement.

"Please go back for one more time." It took reserves I didn't know I had but somehow I managed an encore. I had to be helped away afterwards to the fire, a shivering wreck.

I never bought Life magazine again, and was delighted when it went into receivership and folded for the last time.

Winter training was continued the next day with long sessions of meditation in the cold hall. No instructions were given on what was expected of us and it was debatable which was the more painful: standing outside in the snow and freezing from the soles up or kneeling inside to obtain the same lack of circulation. If this was Zen training it could only have one object at this level: discipline of the body.

The trip back to Tokyo resembled a busload of prisoners released from jail: songs were sung and stories told. There was camaraderie amongst all the groups. Something difficult had been attempted and accomplished; we shared a feeling of team success.

This team spirit was carried over into dojo training. There were now two factions in the dojo: those that had been on the winter training and those that had stayed behind. The distinction was more than physical. Those that had been on the Gasshuku were fitter and harder; there was a mental edge as well; the others were a little overshadowed.

A Spanish student who trained at the dojo on occasions gave me good advice on living in Japan. He was a gregarious character, much loved and respected by the Japanese. I never did find out what it was that he actually did in Japan and why he had stayed in the country so long.

"Do not stay in Japan longer than for one year, you may end up going strange," he began.

"What do you mean by 'strange' and haven't you been in Japan for much longer?" I didn't understand him.

"I am one of the few survivors. I can show you many who are budo (martial way) bums who put themselves in a time capsule here, then are frightened to emerge." Even in my short time in Japan I had met a few of these characters.

"Spanish people have an affinity with the language that helps and, remember, we were the first Europeans here. I thought it was the Portuguese but felt it would be impolite to mention it.

"Second thing, while you are here always play the part of the foreigner, even when you have learnt the language and some of the customs." This was not what most people do when living in a foreign culture, I asked him "Why?"

"The Japanese are comfortable when dealing with a foreigner. They know he is not aware of customs and language and will guide him but if you know some of the customs they become hesitant and confused." He paused for a breath; I had never heard him give such a long speech.

"They will not know how much you know and if they anticipate and you make a mistake both of you will lose face; if they underestimate you they will also be embarrassed." I began to understand what he was trying to tell me.

"It even pays to exaggerate your foreignness; they love that."

I decided to put his theory to the test some days later. My apartment block was in a backstreet behind Rikyu University, away from the rush of traffic and people. It was a place of very narrow streets, local communities and small shops. Some of the bars could only seat ten people. At the small store where I bought my food I used to quietly slip in a few select items, pay for them and slip away. I was treated politely but without much enthusiasm.

Dressing up in the last of my English tweeds with cloth cap and walking stick that had been left behind at the dojo by some previously crippled foreigner I marched into the shop, spoke only English and began tapping the items I required with a walking stick. The young shop assistant's mouth dropped open before he scampered around trying to placate this stranger who was disturbing the harmony of his business. A few passers-by looked in on the entertainment and two of the shop owner's small children shyly poked their heads around a partition. I paid the amount owing with great gestures and, as I was striding out, I whirled around and gave the staring children a massive wink.

"Uwinku," they screamed and ran off, laughing. After that performance I was always met with smiles and fussed over; the children practiced their 'uwinku' on me; I had become 'their' foreigner and was always given special treatment.

A friend of mine had a similar experience on a commuter train. He and his friend who was a Maori with similar features to the Japanese tried to get off at their station. The doors slid open with a hiss and a barrage of businessmen assailed the doors from the platform allowing nobody on board the chance to get off.

"Orimasu," yelled my friend indicating he was coming through." Orimasu," louder this time and the Japanese, surprised to see that he was a foreigner, opened a narrow path for him to get out. His Maori friend attempted to follow him out but the crowd took one look at him, decided he was Japanese, and closed ranks, trapping him inside. He managed to get off, very disgruntled, three stations later and had a long walk back.

The combination of hard training and Japanese diet was having an effect on my body weight. I was no longer a big foreigner, just a tall one. I was down to 150lbs and started feeling that something had to be done.

Japanese restaurants were cheap but it was difficult to gauge your calorie intake. Western food was too expensive except for the odd meal. I found the answer at the 'Tonku' restaurant, a small place seating about a dozen people just around the corner from the dojo. The restaurant speciaised in pork dishes but the owner/cook had worked in some of the top hotels in Tokyo before buying his own business. He knew all about western style food. He came up with a compromise - part Japanese, part Western - and the prices somewhere in between. I went there most days after training and the meals were always varied. It was there that I had my first run-in with one of the black-belt instructors.

I had found that after a day's training I could not relax at night and go to sleep. My body seemed to stay tuned up and my mind likewise would not rest. Ideas and thoughts on training would keep me awake until late at night and I would feel tired in the mornings. I found the answer in one bottle (large size, please) of Suntory beer. Suntory was one of the new brewers of beer in Japan; they had imported experts from Denmark to oversee the setting up of their brewery and the result was a very acceptable Scandinavian-type beer. 1967 was the first year when beer consumption overtook sake in Japan. The one bottle of beer with my evening meal did the trick. I would wander home afterwards, unroll my futon, turn the radio on to listen to the news on the American armed forces network, and then fall fast asleep.

The only black belt I found at the dojo with a chip on each shoulder was a young Korean who took himself far too seriously. dojo rumour had it that any conversation with him would always get back to Oyama Sensei who was also Korean. He came into the restaurant and noticed my beer. Drawing himself up to his maximum height and sucking in air between his teeth, he advanced on my table.

"You will not drink beer when you are training at our dojo." His voice was loud enough to hear over the sizzling of pork cutlets and the conservation of the patrons. The small restaurant actually went quiet and I was reminded of the typical western saloon where the piano automatically stopped if anyone over 5 foot 6 inches pushed open the batwing doors.

"Why?"

"Because it is very bad for your health, you will get..." he was having trouble finding suitable English words," "Leprosy?" I suggested.

"Yes, leprosy, very bad and....."

CHAPTER FIVE | 105

"Ingrown toe-nails?"

"Yes, ingrown toe-nails also very bad!" Some in the restaurant understood English well enough to smile. I thought I had gone too far when someone pushed past my accuser and planted himself down beside me; it was Oyama Shigeru, the senior instructor in the dojo with the same surname as Sensei had adopted.

"Suntory biru kudasai," he called out to Mammasan. A bottle and a glass topped with froth appeared instantly; he drained the glass and smacked his lips.

"Oishi desu ne?" he said, confirming it as delicious. The patrons laughed and agreed. The other black belt's eyes went cold and he stalked out of the restaurant, smacking aside the colourful cloth fly protector that covered the top part of most Japanese doorways. I had gained an ally who was later to become a close friend but I had also made an enemy who was to wait his chance for retaliation.

My sojourn as the only foreign student of the dojo came to an end with the arrival of two Dutch black belts. They had their own dojo, had been graded by Jon Blumming and were to train in Tokyo for about five months. They also, at their own request, went back to being white belts. Despite having their own income and their accommodation closer and more up-market than mine, they were keen to join in with my modest social lifestyle to find the best value and avoid a drain on their funds.

They soon came to realise the difficulty of dealing with the Japanese. Both of them had been invited to the Netherlands embassy for a party celebrating their Queen's birthday. It was a black tie event and they needed suitable evening wear. One of them borrowed a tuxedo from me; it was a remnant of my short public relations career. The other had one packed in his suitcase but it was badly in need of dry-cleaning. To make absolutely sure there would be no misunderstandings we took an English speaking student from the dojo with us to the local dry-cleaning shop.

The owner greeted us all inside his shop, bobbing his head and smiling, showing a fortune in gold fillings.

" Please ask him if I can have this suit dry-cleaned and ready by Thursday night at the latest; I need it for Friday," my Dutch friend said. It was Tuesday. Our Japanese friend obligingly translated.

"He says yes, he can do that for you," came the answer. My friend was not fully convinced.

"Please ask him again; I don't mind if he can't; I'll manage somehow myself; I can't afford not to have it ready for Friday." The Japanese student spoke for some time to the owner who never stopped bobbing his head and smiling.

"He says yes again, he will have it ready for you." Relieved, my friend parted with his badly creased suit and received a handwritten ticket stamped with the owner's personal 'chop'.

On Thursday night we revisited the shop to find the owner still smiling but shaking his head. Exasperated, my friend asked me to bring someone from the dojo who spoke English. I persuaded one of the office girls to come and help sort things out. She questioned the shop owner.

"He says so sorry, but suit is not back from the cleaners, he is only the agent."

"But..." spluttered my friend.

"If he could not be sure it would be back, why didn't he say so in the first place?" There was a red flush starting to show on his fair-skinned face. Another exchange of Japanese.

"He says he did not want to hurt your feelings." The reply to that was mercifully in Dutch; I took him to a bar the next night to drown his sorrows.

Both my Dutch friends had entertained Kurosaki Sensei when he was in Holland and he reciprocated by inviting them to train at his dojo and go out for some entertainment later. I was invited along too so as not to be left out.

Kurosaki Sensei had his small dojo close to an American Army base. It was a very old kendo dojo with ancient kendo armour hanging petrified from the rafters. A student told me in a hushed voice that they had belonged to students who had never returned from World War II. Nobody felt they had the right to take them down. Photos of old kendo masters were on the wall alongside the shinden (shrine) and I was interested to note that the karate master's photo in pride of place was Miyagi Sensei, the founder of Okinawa Goju Ryu, not Oyama Sensei.

The dojo floor was a masterpiece made of that black native Japanese timber that had worn down over a century with the rubbing of feet. The lighter grain, being harder, stood out as though it was embossed; it made for both a beautiful finish and a good grip.

Kurosaki's dojo senior was Fujihira Sempei who had been a first dan for so many years because of his complete indifference to kata that in the end he was promoted without being asked so as to release the log-jam of students behind him. He was an extremely under graded third dan and, pound for pound, the best karate ka I have ever met. He later became the world lightweight kickboxing champion, fighting under the name of Ozawa. He used up so much energy, not only in training but in enjoying life, that he carried supplies of food around in his pockets and would offer you a leg of chicken or an egg as other people would offer candy or cigarettes.

His training philosophy was simple: you trained your arms and legs for speed and strength and linked them together with stomach muscles like steel fibers. One thousand sit-ups were common during his training sessions although new trainees were allowed to rest if they had to. Fujihira Sempei would move around the dojo, encouraging his students by jumping up and down on their solar plexus; I used to pray that Oyama Sensei would not adopt the same practice. The training system had advantages: Fujihira and his senior students could afford to hold their arms high, protecting head and ribs and use knees and shins to block kicks. It was no use hitting or kicking them in the stomach, the most you could hope for, was to push them backwards.

Sparring with Fujihira was like taking on a fox terrier: small and fast, he was never in one place. He was a master at eluding and ducking under your techniques to get in close and even behind you. Once, in desperation, I tried to grab him and fall on him but he wriggled away like an eel, delighted with the variation. One thing you did not do with Fujihira Sempei was not to fight him 100%. He considered this cheating him and he made you pay for it dearly.

After the training session Kurosaki invited us all round to the local night club. Many night clubs in Tokyo, then, were a strange mixture of American chrome and lights, crammed into the Japanese lack of space, with floor shows that copied Paris themes. There are not many big-bosomed girls in Japan and every one of them must have been pressed into night club service.

Despite being on leisure time, Kurosaki didn't relax completely and sat himself in a corner where he could view everybody and all the exits. One of his students confided in me that had it been a place visited for the first time, Sensei would have worked out where all the toilets were as well. None dared speak about it but it was rumoured that Sensei had once dealt fatally to an attacker in a night club. A patron had been foolish enough to challenge him brandishing a knife. Sensei was experienced enough to know that those skilled in the use of a knife kept it concealed until they slipped the blade under your ribs. He turned sideways to protect his vital organs, and then much to the surprise of his opponent grabbed the proffered blade in the palm of his hand. As the blade was on reflex action pulled back towards its owner Kurosaki followed the movement closing with a head-butt. A jail sentence was imposed for excessive self defence.

We were deluged with girls whose job it was to keep us happy, plying us with expensive drinks, laughing politely at even the most outrageous statements and letting their hands work under the table in the most unmentionable places. It was all expected behaviour, but I couldn't escape the feeling that it was like eating lollies with the paper wrappers left on.

When Kurosaki Sensei had had enough he stood up and walked to the door, signaling the end to festivities. The girls faded away, leaving the manager and his assistants to bow us out. No bill was presented; apparently this was one of several establishments that Sensei 'looked after', ensuring no one misbehaved.

The cool night air was refreshing after the air-conditioned night club. Sensei decided that we would walk to the train station. We were passing across a narrow street when a small Japanese car skidded to a halt, inches from us. We all stopped, a little taken aback. It was almost a toy car, made only for the domestic market with a two stroke motor and wheelbarrow wheels but the driver obviously believed that it gave him status far above lowly pedestrians.

"Oi Kimi Kurumu o, douro kara ugokase!" Sensei did not enjoy being spoken down to from below.

"Nan datte! Kimi no hou o ugokashitara dounan da!" To punctuate his message he smashed his hand down in a hammer fist onto the bonnet, denting the lighter gauge metal beyond repair. The radiator died with a sad hiss of steam and the motor bled oil onto the road, then gave one last rattle and died. I did not think it possible, but the terrified driver sank down further below the steering wheel to make himself less conspicuous. Sensei walked on as if nothing had happened; we followed quickly.

Two weeks later Kurosaki Sensei had left Kyukushinkai; Fujihira followed. It was not talked about openly at the dojo but, privately, seniors expressed the view that Kurosaki and Oyama had had a near friendly falling out and decided to go their separate ways.

Kickboxing, the Japanese version of Thai boxing, was starting to make its presence felt in Japan at that time. Kurosaki had gone previously to Thailand to fight Thai boxers as part of a Japanese three man karate team and had been knocked out with an elbow strike to the head. From that time, he had a healthy respect for Thai boxing and adapted his karate fighting style to accommodate it. The discussion at the time among the TV stations was whether to stage 'arranged' fights for their viewers - entertainment similar to professional wrestling or to have authentic fights like most boxing matches. Several TV stations opted for the arranged variety; one for authentic presentation. Kurosaki, not surprisingly, opted for the latter and went on to take his kickboxing gym to the top with Fujihira as a world champion.

One of the Dutch students had a letter that turned out to be the cause of a significant change in my training in the martial arts. It was a letter of introduction to Kuroda Sensei, a senior kendo instructor at the Tokyo Kidotai Riot Police. The Kidotai station was at Yotsua and some distance from our station at Ikebukuro. The fastest way to Yotsua was to change on the ring rail at Shinjuku but we preferred the longer subway ride that originated from Ikebukuro. We could always get seats and avoided the crush of changing trains. Over the next six months the Japanese could never understand this and would repeatedly explain to us how to get to Yotsua faster and cheaper.

CHAPTER FIVE | 111

It was also the first occasion where we came up against the Japanese trait of 'shutting the door' on their language. It was simple enough to learn to say "Yotsua Nimai" without an accent when ordering the tickets at the ticket office. If the ticket seller was looking down at his desk when we ordered he would automatically push the tickets through the grill and accept the money. If, however, he happened to look up and see that we were foreigners, he would automatically ' shut the door ' and ask once or even several times, where we were going.

It was a fair walk from Yotsua station to the Kidotai buildings. They were modern and had been spared no expense; the Kidotai were obviously a favoured unit. We were escorted to the dojo but it was unnecessary; the noise could be heard all over the complex. A kendo practice was in session and for the first time I saw a martial art, practising as hard, if not harder, than karate. All were in full armour and were practising cuts in the squat position: bouncing forward, cutting and backward cutting again, dragging the shinai well back over the helmet with elbows pushed out in the classical position. It was early summer and already very hot; pools of sweat were forming on the sprung floor and kendoka were falling over, not from fatigue but from slipping on the sweat.

"How long will they do this for ? " my friend asked in an awed voice.

"Until they are ready to drop," our escort answered, somewhat surprised at the question.

"What ranks are they?" I asked him; they all looked very competent.

"San dan or higher, all Kidotai police must be at least third dan in either kendo or judo." We watched the rest of the session in silence until the instructors were bowed off the floor and those remaining began the long process of tying their armour up and folding their hakama or split skirt.

We were ushered into Kuroda Sensei's room; green tea and cakes appeared at the same time. Kuroda Sensei was nothing like we imagined: short and squat with a ready laugh and humorous eyes, he put us completely at ease and called for an interpreter who first translated the letter of introduction, then the conversation. Kuroda Sensei spoke no English. The letter from Jon Blumming had asked him to teach iaido to my Dutch friend, Luke.

Sensei brought out several swords to show us. One of them, obviously very old, was curved much more than the others.

"For use by a mounted Bushi," explained Sensei through the interpreter." The bigger the curve the more contact it makes when slicing, just like a butcher's wheel. "It was a good analogy, being similar to a scimitar - another sword designed to slice from horseback.

The centerpiece was Sensei's own sword, made specifically for him. It was a no frills weapon with plain furnishings. Most of the cost, incredible for those days, - 400,000 yen - had gone into the blade, which seemed far too long for its owner.

"It is two inches longer than my old sword, and it took me two extra years to gain my 8th dan because of It.," Sensei said proudly.

He then took us out to the dojo and showed us what iai Nuki or iaido, as it became known to us, was. Placing the sword on his right side, the edge of the handle level with his knee, he bowed. The sword was then placed in front, handle pointing to the right. Facing the shinden, he bowed again. Picking the sword up with both hands, he deftly thrust it under his obi and out the side of his hakama.

What happened then was hard to understand by anyone with only a small knowledge of Japanese sword techniques. In a series of kata, the katana (sword) hissed effortlessly out of the scabbard and, after a series of parries and cuts, often in different directions, and from a selection of strokes, was returned in a sweeping motion back to the scabbard. All the movements had been slow and measured except for the cuts which were whip-like, the blood channels in the blade causing it to whistle through the air. One was left wondering how all Sensei's fingers were still in place.

"There are basically only four movements," explained Sensei. "Nukite, drawing the blade, Kuritske, cutting, Chiburi, flicking the blood from the blade and Noto, resheathing the sword. Unlike kendo, iaido is basically looking and cutting." He laughed and led us back into his room. He gave us his card and thanked us for coming to see him; it was obviously time to go and we left more than a little confused. "Would he teach us or not?"

The owner of our restaurant was very impressed with the card.

"Kuroda, very nice name."

"Muso Shinden Ryu iaido eighth dan"

"Shindo muso ryu jodo eighth dan"

"Zen nippen kendo renmai seventh dan"

"He is also shodo seventh dan," he added, surprised.

"Shodo?"

"Shodo is Japanese calligraphy, writing Japanese characters." We remembered that Sensei had told us that brush strokes and sword strokes were often very similar.

We were still not sure what to do next so at the same time next week we appeared again at the Kidotai. Sensei met us again, the tea and cakes appeared again and we went through the strain of polite translated conversation yet again. We watched a judo training session this time. Tatami mats were carried out by the policemen to be laid on the floor two at a time. Most of them struggled to hold onto the edge of the mats.

"Good practice for the wrists and grip," we were told. After watching thirty or so, heavyweights test the sprung floor's guarantee to its limits by throwing each other everywhere, Sensei politely thanked us for coming and we left, confused, for the second time.

We resolved to try one more time next week and if nothing eventuated we would take the hint. With some trepidation we approached the Kidotai for the third time. Sensei met us politely as before; this time there were no tea and cakes; we began to feel uneasy. We were then taken to a changing room; there, folded neatly on the floor, were two new dark blue hakama and gi tops. They were for us and we were shown how to put them on correctly. They fitted perfectly and our training began.

Luke was horrified to be told he could not practise left-handed. There were no left handed people in Japan. Left (heta) means awkward in Japanese; Luke had to practise right-handed.

After training had finished we went to the showers and were surprised that the blue dye had come out of the hakama. We stood there naked, looking like painted Picts. The Japanese laughed. We asked one why, in this modern age, hakama could not be made in colourfast fabric.

"Tradition." Many years later I learned a more logical explanation: the blue dye and sweat conceals any blood if you are cut in battle; a reddening stain on a white gi would give an advantage to an opponent. Payment for the lesson was refused but we were given a bill for the hakama.

CHAPTER FIVE | 115

Training under Kuroda Sensei opened another door: Sensei suggested we go to the Rembukan dojo near Shibuya and meet Shimizu Sensei; head of Shin do Muso Ryu Jodo, a martial art using the short staff. Rembukan was hard to find. We had to change trains - this time there was no longer more leisurely route - and take a bus from Shibuya station to a smaller suburb, then walk.

The dojo was down a back street and had been built as a dojo, not converted like many others. By Japanese standards it was spacious; the only problems being no showers and a long drop toilet. Sewerage had not yet reached all the suburbs in Tokyo and night carts still collected and transported to the outlying farms; the Japanese cynically called them "honey carts".

Shimizu Sensei was a small man with strong, thick wrists. We had been in awe of Kuroda's thirtieth dan, Shimizu Sensei held seventy. He was the master of shin do muso ryu, a school that taught seven different martial arts including the sword, kusarigama, long and short staff and even a martial art all but forgotten: hojutsu, the art of tying knots, made obsolete by handcuffs.

It was at Rembukan on that first night that I met another man who was to have a lasting influence on my future, Donn Draeger. Donn was a huge American with size twelve shoes. You always knew where he was by the crowd of Japanese gathered around the shoes by the door of a building; there amongst the tiny Japanese footwear would be Donn's great loafers, berthed like two great battleships among fishing vessels. Donn was also a tough customer: he had been a young Marine Corps major in the Second World War and had stayed on in Japan after the occupation force had gone home.

Training started that night without gear. We were given a short staff, about fifty inches long and one inch in diameter. These were not just sticks but were considered real weapons, made of Japanese heart oak seasoned outside for several years. The maker's name was stamped on the end. Basic techniques were difficult at first; thankfully there are only twelve of them. A new and heavier training schedule meant little time for leisure and the strain began to show.

Once a week, after finishing two karate sessions, we would wearily train to Yotsua for iai and twice a week to Shibuya for jodo. It would not have been possible had we not become, by this time, super fit from karate training.

We did have some free time and we usually spent this by going to 'Western' movies. I had never seen a 'C' grade movie before where the actors were mostly Italian with a token American. The films were shot in Spain to save money and the sound was dubbed in Japanese with English subtitles. We soon tired of seeing the same canyon in different movies with riders charging out the other end for variation and gallons of blood spurting from horrific wounds.

I preferred the 'chumbara', a sort of Eastern Western where the samurai engaged in 'land' wars, saving honour and painted damsels. The only difference was that the goodies all committed suicide while the baddies rode off into the sunset; all this for fifty yen.

Sometimes the strain of living in a society where if you elbow someone next to you it is felt on the other side of the neighbourhood, got too much. We had to find an outlet. One way was for the three of us to walk down the street with straight faces, one behind the other, left, right, left, right, then the crowd stopper: on the right foot forward we then placed it backwards then forwards again like an elegant dance step and carried on as if nothing had happened. The reaction from the Japanese was worth it: astonishment, polite indifference and smiling uncertainty. Did all the foreigners walk that way?

Bars were another way. We found that bars in a high-rise building were cheaper than those on the ground floors; they had to compete for custom. One we visited did not attract many foreigners; however they did have a menu in English and proudly presented it. We ran our eyes down the fare and there, listed under seafood, was - 'Cuddlefish'. We began to chuckle. Further down the list we came to 'curried lice'; the chuckles turned to splutters. Then came the one that opened the floodgates - 'Hambuggers '. We all exploded into laughter, tears streaming down our faces. One of the Dutch boys fell off his stool and lay on his back, helpless with laughter. The management was furious, tore away tear-stained menus and bustled us to the elevator. The next day it did not seem anywhere near so funny. It was pure release.

Oyama Sensei's attitude towards us changed when he found out that we were training in iai and jodo. He had made repeated promises to bring in a teacher to instruct us in bojutsu (quarterstaff). This had never eventuated. He was cool to the point of rudeness for some time until he either forgot about it or realised that it was not affecting out karate training.

The real thaw came when he decided to produce another karate book and needed foreigners to put on black gi and wince in obvious agony while Japanese black belts, in snow white gi, demonstrated techniques on us. Oyama was very efficient at producing books: he did it bigger and better than all the other authors and knew exactly what he wanted and how to obtain it in the studio.

One of the Dutch students did so well that he regained his lost position of "my son". The other Dutch student found the Spartan and celibate (at least officially) lifestyle too hard and fell in love with a Japanese girl who worked in a coffee shop. Despite warnings from senior instructors and throaty noises from Oyama Sensei, his training deteriorated, then fell off altogether. He decided to go home and take his Japanese wife with him.

A dojo party was held for him and we all sat round drinking beer, eating nibbles and singing a song when it came to our turn. Afterwards, he took us with him to go shopping at the Seibu department store. He wanted to buy presents to take back with him to Holland.

The advantage of using a department store was that you could walk around, select what you wanted at the right price, and pay for it at the counter and leave. No Japanese language was required.

I had already found that the reality was somewhat different. On the previous visit, I had chosen a photo frame and took it to a smiling young man at the counter; he spoke good English.

"Is that the type you want, sir?"

"Yes, that's fine." I put the money on the counter.

"Are you sure, sir, we have them in different colours "

"No, that one's fine."

"We also have this model on special." He rummaged around under the counter.

"No, I'll take that one," this time said between my teeth.

"Plain or fancy wrapping, sir?"

"Anything." I looked pointedly at my watch. He opened his mouth to say something else but looked at me and decided against it. I took the change and receipt and hurried away.

"Sayonara, please come again."

The visit with my Dutch friends was to become a classic. Two of the newer foreign students, a Chinese young man from Singapore and an American came with us. The Chinese lad spoke no Japanese; his American friend did, fluently.

CHAPTER FIVE | 119

We approached one of the counters for some assistance. An item that was wanted did not seem to be available.

"Excuse me, please. Do you have a black metal ashtray in stock?" The American asked in fluent Japanese. A shop assistant 'shut the gate', ignoring him and asked the Chinese lad.

"Excuse me, what is it that your friend requires?," also in fluent Japanese. The Chinese young man looked blank and asked the American.

"What did he say?" The American started to translate.

"He said _____, what the hell am I doing!" and turned back to the Japanese assistant and repeated his request in Japanese. The assistant fled to get help. He returned with a senior assistant with a lapel badge that read ENGLISH INTERPRETER. He asked,

"Can I herop you? " in reasonable English. The American, furious that he had not been taken seriously, repeated his request in perfect Japanese. The interpreter, who was paid to speak English, refused to lose face by speaking Japanese. Impasse. We gave up and went to look for a bar.

At Rembukan dojo we were given passes to a martial art demonstration held at the Hibya hall. Once a year, masters gathered from all over Japan to demonstrate their schools' techniques. It was a must for all serious students of budo. Donn Draeger took us under his wing to explain the finer points.

There was just too much to take in at one sitting. I wished I had seen it all much later in my career when I could've appreciated it a bit more. Masters of sword and weapons of every description including Naginata (a vicious-looking Halberd) demonstrated their kata. Our own schools, Shin do Muso Ryu, was well represented with Shimizu Sensei drawing gasps from the crowd with his adroit handling of the Kusarigama, the imitation lead ball at the end of a soft chain, striking his opponent or snaring and drawing them on to his sickle. Occasionally some of the older masters looked distinctly frail. Thinking this was ignorance on my part, I said nothing. Donn Draeger leaned over to me and said,

"If the old guy doesn't watch it, he will cut off a toe." I tried to keep a straight face.

Donn then went on to give graphic descriptions of the different martial arts, their strengths and weaknesses. If only I had had a tape recorder.

One master of kyudo (archery) had an imitation horse placed on the stage for him by scurrying assistants. It was designed, like a sophisticated rocking horse, to move the same as a horse at the canter. The master jigged up and down on this contraption, kimono flapping and knocked to his bow an arrow with a large bulb-like head. Donn whispered that this gave off a howling sound. The Japanese had long been aware of the value of psychological warfare. At a given moment the arrow was released it moaned across the stage, missed the target and carried on backstage. You could still hear the sounds of furniture being knocked over and screams of fright long after the howling missile fell silent.

There was now a distinct change in the way we were treated at the various dojo. After karate training the senior belts would tell me to stay back and they would go over many of the finer points with me. Physically this was the last thing you needed after two and a half hours of tough training but mentally things started to click into place. Shimizu Sensei took over my training personally and arranged for other senior ranks to give me extra lessons. Kuroda Sensei stopped teaching us iai kata from only the formal kneeling position that rusted up our knees and began the more advanced standing techniques. Donn Draeger explained the change.

CHAPTER FIVE | 121

"The Japanese get so many weirdos who join, waste their time and leave. What they do now is give everyone a hard time. After six months, those that survive are given everything they need."

We had survived; the period of testing was over; now the real work was to begin.

Chapter Six

One of the first difficulties that trainees of different martial arts face is adapting to the different maai or combative distances. A judoka operates within grasping distance, a karateka within kicking distance and a kendoka further away at sword striking distance. Learning motor skills in these disciplines is more complex because some of them have more than one maai; for example karate has three: long distance for kicks, middle distance for punches and close in for elbows, knees and head strikes. A complete karateka needs to be proficient in all three.

When I first began training in jodo and iaido my karate training was a hindrance, causing my movements to be stiff and inflexible; but after a time I found that I could switch from one to another without too much difficulty. Later I found my karate improved by being more skilled in different maai and timing.

Under Donn Dreager's tuition we began to understand the history and tradition of the martial arts. The word 'bugei' consists of two ideograms. Bu means martial (not military because Bu contains both military and naval aspects). Gei denotes skill and is synonymous with jutsu which refers to 'art' in an activist sense such as is made when referring to craftsmanship or technician-like ability. The word 'bugei' can be correctly translated as 'martial art(s)'.

'budo' is another word derived from two ideograms. The first connotes bu the same way as in the 'bugei' but 'do' is connoted as 'way'. The concept of do is a 'road' of life that is to be travelled over as the means of a discipline that leads to spiritual perfection of the traveler. The word 'budo' correctly translated means 'martial way(s)'

My initial more simple explanation made my teachers wince, but they did not correct it. "bugei means learning how to kill someone and budo means learning how to become a better person." 'Martial Arts' then is a much misused term: the only people that use them are the armed and paramilitary forces.

The bugei are also known as the jutsu forms. The budo, the martial ways, can be called the do forms. The bugei are identified by the suffix 'jutsu' which is usually added to the word which describes the weapon. kenjutsu can be translated as 'sword art', bajutsu - horse art, ninjutsu - stealing in art and jujutsu - flexible art. budo are identified similarly, the suffix 'do' is appended which indicates the weapon, the principle or the action and effect. kendo - sword way, judo - flexible way and iaido - 'instant strike' way, are some examples.

The knowledge we were gaining was like glue: sticking all the pieces together so they wouldn't fall away and be lost. Many of the techniques demonstrated at Hibya hall now made sense. Judo, a modern Olympic sport, practises a Koshiwaza, hip throw, that releases the opponent once he is thrown so that he can break-fall safely. The jujutsu master at Hibya slowly demonstrated how the opponent is held after the throw and thus falls on his head, breaking his neck. This was a good example of the difference between 'jutsu' and 'do' techniques.

Students who seek technical accuracy and a full understanding about the Japanese martial disciplines must clearly understand the differences between bugei and budo. The differences which lie between the martial arts and the martial ways are involved ones. They embrace philosophical, social and technical aspects, not easily separated from each other. To understand some of the major differences between the martial arts and the martial ways I was encouraged to study the purpose for which the martial arts and the martial ways were originally established. The first Tokugawa Shogun Ieyasu having won control of Japan at the start of the sixteenth century was faced with the problem of having tens of thousands of armed Bushi with hopefully nobody to fight. The move from bugei to budo had military as well as social advantages.

The bugei were developed by warriors for warriors who sought to consolidate their social class. In the bugei the individual is not important. The budo, on the other hand, was developed by warriors and commoners alike, not for a group cause, but as a means of individual expression; a means to be used in pursuit of a spiritual goal, that of self perfection. Here in budo the individual is all-important. The difference between bugei and budo contrast the purposes of self protection (the self being the group), and self perfection (the self being the individual). The bugei are totally combatively orientated. They are only concerned with the results in the battlefield and place great value in 'hit the target' or 'defeat the enemy'. They are the monopoly of professional warriors. The budo are to a lesser degree combatively orientated and in some senses not at all. They do not hold that 'hitting the target' is important. Instead, they stress no competition, substituting for it the need to respect one and all and to channel one's efforts into seeking self improvement.

What I was learning was the basis for long term decisions regarding classical versus sport martial arts, a conflict that is still going on today, although I suspect that the sporting aspect has won out.

I mentioned to Donn Draeger that I was surprised foreigners had access to the classical forms, mindful of their origins. The Chinese Wushu systems had long remained closed to outsiders Donn replied.

"Jodo, until 1956, was only taught to members of the police force. Because of dwindling support, Shimizu Sensei admitted foreigners in 1960. He was criticised by other masters because of this, but he has the vision to see that to survive, jodo must expand."

The classical forms of either bugei or budo that these critical masters taught were all founded prior to the Meiji era of 1868. Modern forms of both bugei and budo were founded in and after the Meiji era. With all disciplines, classical or modern, bugei are chronologically to the budo as senior disciplines; the bugei stand as ancestral sources from which budo derive. Traditionally the bugei are justified as the means by which the classical warrior met battlefield necessities. The budo are considered to be the mature forms of the bugei, the products fashioned from combative methods which serve under a veil of peaceful refinement, much like the bud which blossoms into a flower. Not all bugei forms have a corresponding budo form. The conversion of bugei to budo is not automatic; in fact most masters of bugei are not interested in making the conversion. There are far more bugei than budo forms and the development of a do form does not automatically extinguish its parent bugei.

Bugei are products of combative experience, largely that of a battlefield nature. The classical bugei were originated, developed and standardised as combative measures for use by professional warriors during the period in Japanese history when such fighting men ruled the nation. The classical bugei have literally been developed over the centuries and the bodies of the slain.

A warrior would know that if one combatant held his sword high over his head in jodan position and the other combatant held his low, in gedan position, the swordsman in the high position would be dead. A thrust to the lower abdomen would ensure the descending cut would never arrive; much like stepping barefoot onto a nail, the body's reaction would be to pull back. A warrior would also know that if the combatant in the lower position sliced upwards, cutting the wrists, the descending cut would still continue down. For that reason, and others, they were not 'sword happy'. They knew that if they drew their swords they would have only one chance in three of survival: they would either kill their opponent, their opponent would kill them or, as often happened, they would commit ai-uchi, strike and kill each other. Long before the invention of antibiotics the sword wounds often proved fatal.

The modern bugei forms have little battlefield experience, and most of the combative integrally comes from civil applications in modern law enforcement work. budo, classical or modern, are relatively untested on the battlefields and, at best, their relationship to combat derives from civilian scuffles. When the battlefields were serving the bugei, budo forms did not exist, and any combative experience passed onto budo would be small.

This lack of battlefield experience is not a serious defect for budo because the true purpose of budo does not involve battlefield combat. Budo is for self perfection, and those who use budo for the purpose of self defence cannot expect a fully balanced and sound efficiency from the budo forms.

The difference between classical and modern forms, either bugei or budo, rests on another important issue. Classical entities can be identified by the fact that they were founded and are being perpetuated by Ryu. The Ryu embodies the concept of preserving classical Japanese tradition, such as was founded in the feudal past by means of lineal descendants of the first founder. The descendants would either be a blood relation or a nominated successor. Classical Ryu seek to maintain a flow of traditional teachings developed and adhered to in the past and to be adhered to in the future. Change is not a part of a Ryu. All classical Ryu stem from feudal or earlier periods of Japanese history. Any bugei or budo which cannot document its founding in such a past is not a classical discipline.

Judo is an example of a budo form which fails to be, in the strictest sense, a classical form. Jujutsu systems are not classical entities: many were founded outside of the age which would classify them as classical forms. Kendo, as it is known today, did not exist in feudal times and must be regarded as modern budo. The many Japanese karate-jutsu are all twentieth century developments and are modern forms. Aikido has an unproven feudal age history in its ancestral form which is called aiki-jutsu or aiki-jujutsu. It is probable that aiki-jujutsu is mostly a product of the Meiji era. Modern day aikido must be regarded therefore as a modern form.

I could not help making comparisons between the Japanese Ryu and New Zealand Maori martial culture where many of the long and short club forms have been lost or changed. What would have survived today if the Maori had the equivalent of a ryu utilising kata?

Karate systems in the 1960s were at a crossroads. Many of them had to make decisions as to whether to include 'competition' into their systems and how much sport aspect should they introduce?

Traditional masters claim that once you introduce rules for safety, you weaken the system. Disallowing kicks to the groin, finger strikes to the eyes and attacks on knees limits combatants; worse, they would need to train on techniques that would 'score a point' rather than disable an opponent. Students would concentrate on 'winning' rather than improving their technique.

Because of their combative purpose, the martial arts, specifically the bugei, have no sports features. Bushi, or warriors, who developed the classical bugei realised that martial arts cannot retain full combative effect if at the same time they include the spirit of a 'game' and require all participants to abide by rules that are designed primarily to protect the participants. That these warriors were a very practical body of men is quite easy to see when it is appreciated that they were fully professional fighting men whose duty it was to be prepared for combat at all times. They expected to use their weapons and fighting arts against other equally professional and highly skilled warriors who were similarly armed. The Bushi could not afford to develop weapons and martial disciplines for other than a martial purpose. Modern bugei too have a combative purpose but it is highly dissimilar in nature to that of the classical forms in that it centres on restraint of an assailant rather than dispatch of an enemy. Several of these have been adopted by the Japanese Police force. Modern bugei also, because of their purpose, have no sport applications.

Only budo forms sometimes pursue sport features, but not all forms do. The classical budo, for example, absolutely shuns all practices that are sport orientated. On the other hand, modern budo forms in the majority accept sport features. Judo, kendo and karate-do are primary examples, though some types of aikido have sports features, including one devoted to sport competition. The Ueshibi style of aikido does not, and in spite of the fact that it is a modern form, adheres strictly to classical tradition.

The conversion of a bugei form to a budo form must result in the loss of the combative reality because the emphasis has changed from the combative pursuit to other ideals. Classical budo forms deal solely with the manner by which individuals may spiritually improve themselves. Sport is the opposite of such a spiritual purpose. Sporting aspects are concerned with champions, rewards, awards and entertaining an audience, with the recognition of and bolstering of personal ego. As such no sport can find a place in the classical budo scheme of tranquility and non-competitive harmony that all exponents of the classical disciplines are expected to follow. He who practises classical budo, is in competition with himself. Mastery of self becomes the contest; his opponent is the experience.

Modern budo, such as judo, kendo and karate-do, place great value on competition which is made under rules limiting both the application of technique and the performance of the contestants. Such rules also limit the range of techniques.

Classical forms of budo require the use of real weapons but do not permit the use of protective armour. They may be practised with or without an opponent under conditions of 'kata' or prearranged form, but they lose their classical status when they require exponents to exhibit technique for the purpose of comparison and evaluating mechanical and aesthetic form between competitors, who vie for a 'championship award'.

I have observed that some forms of iaido and judo were guilty of this practice.

An old Chinese proverb says, "There is no right and no wrong," and this applies when considering the purpose and the method of the bugei or budo in their classical and modern forms. Each type is orientated along specific and different lines, but it is the combative effect that the exponent is seeking when he or she enters into the study of either classical or modern bugei.

The problem is, as many overseas students here found out, these disciplines are not open to all persons to study. Being restricted to military, navy personnel or law enforcement officers. People from other walks of life will find difficulty when attempting to enter a classical Ryu or the martial disciplines in use by the Japanese armed forces which are usually closed to civilian members of society.

My military background helped, and it was Donn Draeger again who explained Oyama Sensei's negative attitude to me joining the classical Ryu.

"Oyama Sensei himself could never hope to join or be recognised by the classical Ryu. He was born Korean."

All teaching for classical bugei is conducted in the classical way which is conservative in nature, personally oriented between master and disciple and is to be intuitively learned. Students must adhere to practical lines which brought the classical bugei their combat correctness. All exponents train not for the purpose of changing tradition but for preserving it. The modern budo while exacting in nature are not as exacting as their classical counterparts.

Some modern budo are 'fun and games' types of activity social in nature and cater to individual tastes. The distinct voice of classical tradition is not usually heard by the modern forms and if it is, it is ignored.

Full dojo and big bank balances are more likely to be catered for and the ideal of 'bringing the budo down to the people', rather than the 'students up to the budo' pushed to the forefront.

Constant striving toward sports goals on the basis of mass popularity must weaken any activity.

Modern budo that emphasise sport goals cannot escape this influence and its many undesirable side effects. By taking the sensational approach to mass popularity through performances to audiences who came to be amused or entertained, modern budo techniques undergo considerable change, not the least of which, is further dilution of any combative effect they may have had.

I was to be faced with a conflict of conscience many times when called upon to demonstrate budo to audiences in New Zealand and Australia in the early days of my career.

Genuine fighting techniques are often quite subtle in nature, not showy by being direct action to accomplish its intended aim.

The untrained eye cannot see, understand or appreciate what is taking place. So to remain popular with the masses modern budo must please them by giving them more flowery but combatively useless kind of action.

The modern budo, appeal most to those people who place democratic procedure into every aspect of life. Lower grade 'kyu' ranks on 'committees' often have powers that far outweigh their technical abilities.

The classical bugei and budo, however, are supervised by an autocratic hierarchy of officials with whom there is no compromise.

It is the individual who must choose the bugei or budo, classical or modern as their preference, if it is available to them.

There is an ample check for those unsure as to the status of the budo or bugei offered.

The classical disciplines have no ranking structure, only a teacher and student situation although there are levels of teaching licenses.

Modern disciplines all use the dan, kyu ranking system.

I became aware that there was a status level to the various Ryu in Japan. Karate, not being Japanese was regarded far less than the sword arts. The Japanese Bushi had made the single-edged curved sword his central weapon, it became his living soul, an object of veneration and an integral part of Japanese culture, a position it retains in part today.

The style of iaido I was practising under Kuroda Sensei, Muso Shinden Ryu had been previously known as Aomori Ryu and is considered as the basis of training in iaido under the jurisdiction of the all Japan Kendo Federation. There are over 400 different styles of Ryu in Japan.

It was 'suggested' to me that if I intended to go further in my study of iaido I would have to have my own sword.

Buying a sword even then in Japan was expensive and difficult. A katana for a foreigner had to be long to balance his height and arm length and every inch of blade length over the average size meant thirty percent extra cost because of manufacturing difficulties.

The swords available at that time fell into three main categories. Old swords made before this century, copies of old swords, some of which could also be old, and modern swords made in or after the Meiji era. Army or Naval swords that had been mass produced similar to western swords are not 'katana' and although they are widely available overseas, these were and still are, illegal in Japan.

Another difficulty was that there were more Japanese katana in the USA than in Japan. A friend who was a soldier in the 'J' force occupying Japan after the war gave me a typical example.

"We were billeted in an old temple overnight far away from any town. I awoke in the morning stiff and sore from sleeping on the boards and looked up at the roof there, hardly perceptible in the morning light I could see many bundles tied neatly to the rafters, we soon had then down and discovered scores of Japanese swords, some of them obviously very old. We of course 'confiscated' them and dished them out as souvenirs."

To make matters even more confusing, some of the 'copies' of swords were more valuable than the originals. A Bushi might have fancied an older style sword and commissioned a contemporary sword smith to copy it; his copy would have included the name of the original sword's maker, quite acceptable at the time but considered 'a fake' by western standards.

In fact the contemporary sword smith may have had better metal to work with and possibly better techniques which would have made the 'copy' superior to the original.

For buyers of swords outside of Japan there is another possibility. Many Japanese officers during World War II, especially those of higher rank often substituted the pressed mass-produced blades with a genuine family heirloom. I was to buy such a sword much later in New Zealand.

When I enquired about the possibility of ordering a new sword, Kuroda Sensei replied.

"Not possible during your stay in Japan. It takes at least nine months for a sword smith to produce a blade."

Through our interpreter, Sensei explained how a Japanese sword is made.

Pieces of steel are heated and pounded by hammer lengthwise, then folded lengthwise. The sword smith then pounds the steel out into a wide piece, folds it in half then pounds it back into a long piece again. The process is then repeated many times over.

When folding the metal the smith must be careful not to include any air or dirt, this would cause the sword to break in combat. Enormous skill is required to produce the required degree of hardness, different grades of steel with varying hardness are used, and the result is a laminated blade with a hard cutting edge welded together. The cutting edge is tempered separately by attaching a paste made of clay, charcoal and powdered stone. The paste is spread so that the inside edge takes on an aesthetic appearance, often of clouds or waves.

After the sword has reached its proper temperature it is quenched in water, the temperature of which is often a guarded secret.

CHAPTER SIX | 135

I observed that even with this extended process nine months was a long time to work on the sword. Sensei explained.

"In each forge there is a deity on the shelf. Prayers are offered before and during work on each sword. The sword smith believes he has spiritual assistance and will not work on a sword when he is not feeling right, bad feelings might affect the sword."

I thought that a nagging wife could send a sword smith broke, but didn't dare test Sensei's sense of humour, good as it was.

The price of a plain sword long enough for iaido was about 200,000 yen. The average weekly wage in that time was around 15,000 yen.

I purchased a long katana with a heavy handle and tsuba (guard) at a sword shop in Asakusa for 100,000 yen. I preferred it over several others, it had the right feel about it and Donn Draeger agreed that it had a fine balance. Kuroda Sensei was not so sure.

Engraved on the tang inside the handle was the maker's name Yoshisada of Bizen province. Sensei produced several books listing Japanese sword smiths.

Yoshisada of Bizen lived and made swords in 1624.

I began to feel a little uneasy.

Sensei conferred with some other of the Sensei at the Kidotai and made a few phone calls. He then gave me the verdict.

"We are a little concerned if it is a genuine Yoshisada you have bought it very cheaply, if it is a copy you have paid too much." He noticed my unease and added,

"But don't worry, if you wish to take it back, I will send some of our big policemen around with you to the shop. They will soon refund your money.

I had no doubts about that at all.

It was decided that I should have the sword evaluated by an expert at the Ueno Museum that houses many of Japan's National treasures.

Ueno Museum has a system similar to the National Art Gallery in London where once a month it is open for hopefuls to have any masterpiece they found in the attic valued. Almost all of them go away disappointed.

One of the kendo instructors at the dojo laughed that he had taken a sword to the Ueno Museum, and had not got past the girl in the front office who told him it was a fake.

At the Ueno Museum an interpreter and I at least got past the girl in the front office possibly I thought because I was a foreigner and deserved more than an arbitrary decision. We were taken to a higher authority that examined the sword carefully then suggested we go to one of the curators, an expert in Japanese swords.

My hopes began to rise. Had I scored the buy of the century, an original Yoshisada?

We were ushered into the curator's office, a pleasant man with sharp eyes. His movements were very precise. He explained about the museum's history, asked where I came from, and then gestured for the sword.

It didn't take long; he knocked the wooden peg out of the handle, pulled it off, took a brief look at the inscription on the tang and put it all back together again.

"It's a copy."

I didn't take up Kuroda Sensei's offer to return it, after discussions with Donn Draeger and others we agreed it was an ideal sword for iai, if somewhat overpriced.

CHAPTER SIX | 137

Before I left Japan Kuroda Sensei sold me a katana that had been ordered previously by an Australian my size but not collected. I was to return to New Zealand in debt.

Before and after iai training the sword had to be cleaned. One had to sit in a Sezan position, withdraw the blade cutting edge upwards slowly and with the left hand wipe off any oil with cleaning paper. The strokes had to be made from the guard to the sword end, never in the reverse direction for fear of cutting your hand. After training, the blade was dusted with powder from an uchi-ko, a device that resembles a lollipop.

After removing the powder with cleaning paper the process is repeated several times until the blade gleams. It is then lightly oiled with a cloth, before replacing the blade. The scabbard is tipped upside down in a vertical position and given a light tap on a wooden surface to remove all small pieces of wood that have been removed from the interior by the action of the cutting edge of the blade.

Sensei would often be present during this stage, and if too much wood emerged you would be highly criticised for not drawing the sword correctly.

Carrying the sword to and from the Kidotai dojo was a problem.

In Japan a sword has to be licensed in the same way that a firearm is and anyone carrying one in its distinctive cover would be checked by the police. A foreigner carrying a sword would be double-checked and this happened to me on several occasions when passing the local police box and the policeman on duty did not know me.

The answer turned out to be quite simple, I replaced the distinctive sword cover with the common kendo shinai cover that was carried by Japanese and foreign students all around Tokyo. I was never stopped again.

During a kendo shiai (contest) at the kidotai I tried to gauge whether taller kendoka had an advantage with their longer reach over their shorter opponents.

"Sensei is the length of the bamboo shinai standard, or can it be any length?" I asked.

"No, the shinai can be made to any length you wish," he answered.

"Then why don't the taller kendoka use a longer shinai to gain an advantage?" I thought this would have been obvious, but Sensei gave me a look bordering on exasperation.

"Because that would draw attention to yourself."

I did not understand the lesson till much later. If you draw attention to yourself by using the rules to gain an initial advantage sooner or later someone will be sent to deal with you. The better way to improve is by perfecting your technique, not using short cuts for short term gains.

While I was in Japan, several black belts came to train at the karate dojo, who were physically very capable and showed it by defeating some of the senior belts. They stuck with their system and learned nothing, going back home happy at learning a few new kata to show their students.

Later I noticed that several of my own students had a natural advantage with a certain technique or timing, and stuck with it not expanding their learning and gave up when lesser talented students passed them by.

At Kyokushinkai, Oyama Shigeru was leaving to join Nakamura Sensei in New York, he had to complete the 100 man kumite (fight) before he left.

CHAPTER SIX | 139

I had heard of this grueling test of endurance. Both Steve Arneil and Nakamura had completed it, but this was the first time I was not only to see one, but to participate in it.

Oyama Shigeru had few difficulties with it, being the chief instructor, all his opponents and I were wary of him, knowing he was capable of holding something in reserve. His only problem was one of fitness, being an instructor meant that much of his dojo time was spent in teaching rather than hard training and this showed in the later stages of this marathon like effort.

Following the dojo party, where for obvious reasons nobody drank too much, he took me to a run down cheap sake bar well off the main roads.

It was an old tent, and patrons stood around wooden benches drinking cheaper grade sake at low prices.

We had a good night, vowed friendship and never to be forced to drink in cheap places again. The headache next morning reinforced that with more pain than I ever had suffered in the dojo.

It was summer training camp time and far more students signed up for them, rather than the winter version. I remember Oyama Shigeru's cynical remark.

"Only two ranks go on the winter camp, black belts because they have to, and white belts because they are too stupid to know any better."

The summer camp was held near a small village on the western coast of Honshu about six hours drive from Tokyo. We were billeted in an orphanage, and for the first time met many mixed race children, a legacy of the occupation and unwanted by either race. They could be pests when you needed to rest, demanding attention like children everywhere. After a few days I had grown a beard and the fascinated kids wanted to know what was happening to me.

"I am turning into a werewolf."

When this was roughly translated the children screamed and ran away, avoiding me thereafter, but watched me from a distance.

The food was down to the expected standard, and in order to retain some energy I brought a tin of honey to mix with the rice.

I had to wait until everyone had finished then scrape the unidentified materials into the rubbish tin and mix in the honey when nobody was looking. Later Oyama Sensei was giving a speech to all the students.

"This is a training camp, not a holiday camp, hard training and all the bad food is part of the toughening up. Take Jarvis for instance, he is a foreigner and would find the food even worse, but he is always last one out of the eating hall after going up for more!"

Some of the senior ranks who were aware of what I was doing gave me a baleful stare; I looked for a large crack in the floor to fall into.

Training began at 6:00 in the morning with half an hour's meditation. At least on the beach you could dig a shallow pit for your crossed legs to drop into, saving you the pain of legs going to sleep.

Luke had brought along an 8mm camera and had permission to film. This meant that whenever meditation was too long or the training got too repetitive, he would break off, run and get his camera and spend a long time filming. I offered repeatedly to do the filming for him so he could be in the frames, but he modestly declined. I swallowed more sand and continued on.

In the afternoon Sensei decreed,

"You will all go on a twelve kilometre run along the beach."

Sensei was not present when we assembled on the beach in gi. After a hurried consultation the senior belts told us we could take off our gi tops if we wished, and we started off up the beach, mindful of the 35 degree heat, so I decided to keep mine on.

If the sand hadn't been hard we would never have made it a kilometre, the run was a great leveler with skinny white belts gliding over the sand at the front, and squat heavy black belts digging the way through the sand at the rear.

After I reckoned that we had covered six kilometres, I panted to one of the senior belts,

"Isn't this half way, time to turn and go back?"

"We haven't run twelve k's yet."

"But six k's up and six k's back is twelve k's."

"But Sensei said we were to run twelve k's up the beach, and we will!"

The long walk back left me lots of time to reflect on the shortcomings of taking things literally.

My Dutch friend Luke was returning to Holland. He had to complete a third dan grading test and the 100 man kumite.

The third dan test was not a problem; it is always comforting to be invited to take a grading test rather than to just present yourself. Luke passed, and was scheduled the next day for the 100 man kumite.

It was still late summer and very hot in the dojo. All the windows were opened as far as possible.

Luke decided on wearing protective pads, the senior ranks shook their heads but there were no real rules, and he was allowed to compete with them covering his arms and shins.

The heat and Luke's style made it heavy going for him. Luke used sharp angular blocks with his arms and his shins to block lower kicks. It was not a style ideal to use over a period of almost five hours, and it wasn't long before Luke was in trouble from repeated hard contact. He began to go white from the heat and dehydration; a black belt threw a bucket of water over him while he was fighting. White belts scurried around mopping the water off the floor and avoiding the combat.

Somehow he hung onto the end, and was so worn out he could barely manage a smile when the dojo gave him a 'Banzai' for being the fourth person to pass the test.

It was not all over, in the changing room we found that his arms and legs had swollen up above and below the pads and below the pads was a mess of bruised flesh. The pads had to be cut off carefully with a knife.

My test was to come later in the year, and I directed my training towards Oyama Shigeru's sweeping style of circular blocks to avoid what happened to Luke. That style with some modifications for larger westerners was to be mine for the length of my career.

The Japanese have a wonderful system of parties where they stay at one place for an hour or so and then move on to somewhere else. These are called Nijukai (second party) Sanjukai (third party) etc. They allow participants to fall out at any stage without making fools of themselves by falling asleep or criticising the boss. They can also come back into the system later refreshed

– a tactic that has seen off many a hard drinking westerner not up with the score.

After Luke's dojo farewell party Oyama Sensei took us to his favourite Korean restaurant. We were all familiar with Korean food because it was good value for money protein wise as long as you avoided the spices designed to break down your immune system.

Two South Africans who had arrived that day and were passing through Tokyo had called to pay their respects to Sensei. They too were invited along.

We sat in the restaurant with its paper walls and hissing gas fired barbeques that would have given any fire inspector a heart attack and cooked the little fatty pieces of meat on the grill.

After several mouthfuls one of the South Africans gave a modest burp, nobody took any notice, suspecting the usual reaction to Korean food on untrained stomachs.

The first course was barely finished when the other South African gave a real belch that could hardly have been missed, still nobody said anything, and probably thinking it was a reaction to jet lag or something.

After the next course the first South African let go a ripper that would have done a camel justice. Paper lanterns swayed, and several other customers looked alarmed.

This was too much for Oyama Sensei who muttered something and headed for the toilet.

"Are we doing it right?" one of the South Africans whispered to me.

"Doing what right?"

"The belching, man, to show our appreciation of the food."

There was no way I was going to let them down gently.

"I'm afraid you have the wrong custom in the wrong country. Are you stopping by the Middle East?"

They sat there, mortified, all appetite gone. Sensei came back and grumbled something. The second party was over. The rest of us went on to a third party; I can't remember where it was or when it finished.

One morning at the Kidotai things were buzzing, with policemen in riot gear climbing into lightly armoured vans. Some of the vans had heavy wire mesh cages on top; others had film cameras mounted on their roofs with a 360 traverse.

Tokyo was to undergo the first of many student demonstrations protesting against the Prime Minister renegotiating the Japan/USA peace agreement and demanding the return of Okinawa.

Kuroda Sensei, at my request, 'arranged' for me to go along in private capacity. I did hold an authentic freelance press card bought from an entrepreneurial Hollander for an inflated price. It was in Dutch, which confused everyone, but the stamp over my photo was impressive.

Zenkaguren the Japanese Student Union claimed they could put a million students into the streets of Tokyo if they desired. A fraction of that would disrupt the city and did. The battle was well planned and organised by both sides. The students took over high rise roof tops and directed their protesters with two way radios; the riot police lined the streets, built up reserves and directed their men from the wire mesh cages on top of the armoured vans.

Large groups of students took over entire trains to get to their destinations, the public quickly vacated them. They carried picks and buckets to break up cobblestones; the police unfolded large nets and held them ready.

In Japan at the time it was legal for protesters to march in a straight line and that is how they set out, the front ranks about twelve people across, holding a long stout pole for strength. Behind them were held the colourful flags and banners, behind them again came the thousands of protesters wearing hard hats and 'Tenogui' scarves covering their faces.

The riot police looked vulnerable, two thin dark blue lines of officers several metres apart stretching down both sides of the street.

It had to happen. The students broke into the 'Snake' dance which was illegal. Using short steps in unison and the leaders chanting 'OOSSah' followed by the thousands responding 'OOSSah'. The line snaked 'S' wise down the street. The effect was medieval, with the sound delays echoing from the buildings.

The head of the snake then swerved and headed straight for the thin line of riot police. They were ready with a huge scrum-like reserve of heavies that had been shadowing the head of the procession.

They rushed in to bolster the line at the exact time the head of the protesting column hit.

In the confusion when the two lines had fused, heavies from the flying scrum rushed out, arrested the leaders of the column, bundling them into police vans and taking away their poles and banners. The snake stopped, headless, until new leaders, poles and banners were brought up to the front of the column. Once in place the protest started again legally in a straight line.

The process was repeated many times with growing injuries on both sides.

When several converging columns of protesters reached a large square area, order seemed to break down. New battle plans were drawn, rocks thrown, the police nets went up, and tear gas canisters were fired. The police charged repeatedly at the crowds, batons flailed and there were individual skirmishes everywhere.

At some stage a student was killed – run over by a police van. This was the first fatal casualty. After the demonstration had run out of energy and had dispersed, recriminations flew claiming police brutality.

The police were prepared, however. Film from the revolving cameras showed that a student had taken over the police van and had tried to back it out of the way, unintentionally killing a fellow protester.

Perhaps the final nod should go to the riot police; their casualties were far higher than the students.

The next day the Kidotai looked like a medical recuperation centre.

My training in jodo at Rembukan was further increased. Shimizu Sensei wanted me to attempt a grading before I went back to New Zealand. One of his dreams was to introduce jodo to all Boy Scouts throughout the world. He took personal control of my instruction.

I began to gain the greatest respect for this man whose father had been born a Bushi and had the right to cut down any commoner who showed insufficient respect, yet he had lived to see man land on the moon.

At 76 he was still setting examples. One afternoon when I arrived at the Rembukan for training he was atypically absent.

"Where is Shimizu Sensei?" I enquired after a suitable wait.

"He is at the local high school. Please [would you] go there and bring him back to the dojo?" a senior rank asked.

This little honour was in itself a sign of rising status.

I found the Sensei at the local High School not teaching judo as I had expected, but joining in an English class of fourteen year olds practising vowel sounds parrot fashion in the Japanese manner.

Sensei told me on the way back to the dojo that he had been invited to demonstrate jodo in the USA next year and was learning English.

"But Sensei, you will be an honoured guest, an interpreter will be provided," I assured him.

"I know, but I wish to honour my hosts by attempting to learn their language." At 76 Sensei was still a student at heart.

He was one of the last of the masters who had trained all his life in budo. An old photo in the dojo shows a young Shimizu surrounded by fierce looking warriors in traditional dress, all long dead. The photo is dated 1920. All his life he had only done one thing, train in budo. These men are gone now, modern life and monetary necessities mean no married man can survive financially, bring up a family and train full time in budo.

In training he was demanding and exact. In a jodo session you do not progress to your next kata until Sensei is satisfied with your previous one. On an off day you could be stuck on a lower kata for hours.

When you are introduced to a new kata you are not painstakingly taken through the movements as in other budo but quickly shown what is required then left to get on with it. A senior rank pressuring you with a wooden sword leaves no time for reflection, mistakes are many but the lesson is learned. This pressure system is designed to make you react, not think, the same as you would have to do in combat.

Techniques were never explained until you were ready for them.

Everyone who has practised a martial way will know that there is always at least one kata that you come unstuck on; one kata that the more you practise the worse it becomes. Athletes would call it a 'plateau'.

I struck such a kata in the second set of twelve. It required the judoka to swivel in the final movement underneath the swordsman and end up on one knee with the jo thrust up the swordsman's ribcage. Guaranteed to take his mind off sex for at least six weeks.

I was forever too late, leaving the swordsman ample time to lop off any appendage he took fancy to.

Once in frustration I said to Sensei that I doubted that I would ever master this technique and questioned its effectiveness anyway.

Sensei smiled and handed me the bokken (wooden sword) with his left hand, blade pointing down, cutting edge cutting edge facing towards him, our positions were now reversed.

In the final movement as I gleefully went to cut off whatever was available, Sensei stood on my hakama and disappeared out of sight. I ended up on the floor completely disorientated and at the mercy of a 76 year old. This was jojutsu, the combat side of jodo. The technique now took on a new meaning as I mastered it and moved on.

Jodo dates from the seventeenth century when the most famous Bushi in all of Japan, Miamoto Musashi lived. Musashi must have been very successful, because he died in his sixties at a time when the average age of a Bushi was twenty something. He was also a master of Shodo calligraphy and his artistry lives on today, long after his budo skills have gone. In his honour the largest battleship in the world was named after him in World War II. Musashi developed the Ni-to school of swordsmanship, utilising both the long and the short swords in a butterfly type action that defeated all his opponents but one. While in Japan we watched many films about him, Mifune Toshiro being our favourite actor.

The founder of jo was a Bushi called Muso, who unusually for the time styled himself much as Mohammed Ali the boxer would 300 years later.

He would wear a kimono with not only the eight mon or family symbols, but with the number one under the character for the sun.

He was in his eyes number one under the sun.

Muso was a master of the Roku Shaku Bo, the six foot staff similar to the English quarterstaff. When he came to hear of Musashi's skills he decided to seek him out.

He found Musashi gardening, and opened proceedings by mentioning that he had seen Musashi's father's skills.

Musashi, refusing to be drawn replied that if he had seen his father's skills then he had also seen his because they were similar.

Muso went all the way and asked if Musashi was frightened of demonstrating his own skills.

This was going too far, Musashi accepted the challenge.

A challenge in those days often used wooden weapons, but this only slightly reduced the danger of injury. Musashi had a reputation for using a wooden sword in battle preferring to skull his victims, rather than risk breaking a metal sword.

Musashi won the contest by catching Muso's Bo in the V of his cross sword block allowing him no chance of disengagement. He spared Muso's life.

Muso then retired to the mountains in the southern island of Kyushu to contemplate his defeat and devise a way to overcome Musashi's two sword technique. The cave where he lived in for several years is still there and pilgrims who visit it will see a shrine dedicated to him at the entrance. New Zealand is mentioned in the dedication. The Rembuden Institute contributed to the memorial in the early 1970s.

Muso came down from isolation with a new weapon and new techniques. The new weapon was the jo, shortened from the longer bo. The new techniques enabled the jo exponent to move both hands over each end of the weapon, making it more manoeuvrable in combat.

Muso rechallenged Musashi and defeated him in combat and likewise spared his life. They became if not exactly buddies, professional friends for life.

The training of high ranking jodoka from then to today gives some indication of difficulty of ever attaining the highest rank.

Every four years only the most senior ranks are taken away from civilisation for training as did Muso. Sometimes the training occurs near Muso's original cave in Kyushu.

On each occasion senior belts are introduced to three of the original twelve special techniques devised by Muso. The techniques are not taught, the senior ranks have them subtly exposed during training. If they are ready for them, they will understand them and adopt them. If they are not, they will have to wait patiently for another twelve years until they come around again. In case westerners are thinking that perhaps they could coerce a senior rank into showing a missed technique by offering to buy him a beer, forget it.

This insistence in excellence explains why a senior instructor was not considered suitable to train me during the end of my stay in Japan. Shimizu Sensei was looking for someone to take an extra session a week for me.

Hiroi Tsuneji, a seventh dan in jodo offered, but Shimizu Sensei decided to take the extra training himself. I had to ask Donn Draeger

"How could a seventh dan not be suitable?"

"Because he is also a seventh dan in kendo and iaido, and Shimizu Sensei feels this influences his jo technique."

We all attended a second large demonstration of bugei and budo on November the third, the anniversary of Emperor Meiji's birthday. Appropriately enough, the demonstration was held at the Meiji shrine, and it was larger than the previous one at Hibya hall. Everyone who was anyone attends this annual event. Kuroda Sensei was there very early, writing the names of the various Ryu in order of appearance on large pages of rice paper in large characters.

I have always regretted not having the temerity to ask for them after the demonstration, what a record of the event they would have made.

There were no humorous comments this time from Donn Draeger; he was part of the jodo team, the only foreigner at the demonstration. He took his role very seriously and explained afterwards why.

"Shimizu Sensei suffered a lot of criticism for teaching a classical Ryu to foreigners, so I, Phil Relnick, Quentin Chambers and others are determined to never let him down."

They never did.

Following the demonstrations, we were invited along with all the masters to a traditional meal. A famous Japanese singer would attend.

I had become well aware by now that 'traditional' meal meant 'inedible' and was not disappointed.

The famous singer was an elderly lady who sang traditional songs to an accompaniment of the traditional Koto.

'Traditional' music usually means unresponsive to the western ear.

When the famous lady had finished, she mingled with the crowd, talking to people here and there. She wore a kimono that could have cost somewhere near the NZ overseas debt.

Finally, she decided after the odd sake to sing a song in honour of the foreign guests. She began to sing in a high key 'Star Spangled Banner'.

Donn Draeger and the other Americans looked at me and smirked. As the great lady hit the high note on -"Land of the Free"- her top false plate fell out. All the Japanese looked somewhere else and all the Americans looked at me, daring me to explode in laughter. Training in budo does teach you control, and I must have used up several years worth, keeping 'bottled up'.

Later commuters wondered why several strange foreigners were laughing for their entire journey.

My time in Japan was coming to an end, and I was nervous as I came up for grading in jodo. Unlike other budo where you can make a mistake, recover and make it up somewhere else,

CHAPTER SIX | 153

in jodo because you opponent is a swordsman one mistake means in theory, death. You may come back resurrected next year.

Many of the jodo techniques cannot be mastered in one year, and I remembered being told several times when my frustration was evident

"Don't worry, that is a three year technique," or

"Don't worry, that is a five year technique."

Five years? I need to learn it now!

The moment came, and I selected a jo from the rack. We were allowed to select our own weapons and partners, Sensei would select the kata to be performed at the grading.

It was important to select a jo that was straight and heavy, made from seasoned Japanese white oak. There were older heavier jo made from Japanese Biwa, but older teachers would not use them, superstition was that they caused deep bruising which could lead to bone cancer.

A grading was a time to stay superstitious.

The kata were selected, they were fair and held no surprises. The one that had given me all the problems was included, but I was ready for that.

Once the kata started, there was no time for nerves, and suddenly it was over, my first black belt was a shodan in jodo.

A week later I was invited to the dojo for the presentation and a going away party. I was surprised to see that everybody was training, and I had not brought my gear.

I finished as I had started on the first day, training in street clothes, jo is to be practised always was the message.

Before the party started, Sensei gave me an insight in to the more casual attitude the Japanese have towards religion. Several bottles of sake had been placed on the temple shelf as an offering to the Gods. Sensei told me,

"Go down there and get the bottles of sake off the shelf before the Gods get drunk and fall off."

The iaido grading also went well. It was less nerve-racking; there was only Kuroda Sensei and me.

Afterwards he presented me with a grading certificate brushed by him. He asked apologetically for a fee, the grade had to be registered with the all Japan kendo federation. It wasn't until I got back to my room that a friend pointed to one of the characters. I had been graded a second dan.

One of the seniors at the karate dojo decided that I needed a break, and took me to watch a rugby training session. The Japanese thought that all New Zealanders are All Blacks, much in the same way that New Zealanders thought that all Japanese are black belts.

The training session was not one of rugby skills, but of fitness skills, and I watched amazed as the young university students were put through demanding anaerobic exercises. Shuttle-runs, power-ups, piggy-backing partners and sit-ups. This went on and on for over forty minutes. The coach looked on proudly and asked me

"Well, what do you think?"

I had to say something.

CHAPTER SIX | 155

"Ah — don't you ever rest them?" meaning that if he allowed some recovery time his lads might perform better.

"Rest?" he looked astounded. "They know how to rest. They need practise at carrying on!"

I had not yet come to understand Japanese thinking.

The day for my karate grading and hundred man fight drew near. There was much discussion on the reasons for the test.

Two black belts, who shall remain nameless, had got into an argument after downing too many Suntories.

"It is for inner strength," insisted one.

"No, it is for outer strength," insisted the other.

"Inner strength is more important than outer strength," insisted the first one.

"No, outer strength is more important than inner strength," insisted the other. By now they were walking across a railway station, fortunately it was late, and there were few commuters.

"I will show you outer strength," said the other, and landed a round house kick on a vending machine. The ruptured machine gurgled, spat juice in all directions, and then its lights went out. The police were discretely called.

"And I will show you inner strength," said the first one, and stepped onto the railway track. The oncoming train stopped just in time.

They were not so lucky with the police, who arrived like a swarm of angry bees, bustled them into a police van and took them away, still arguing.

Oyama Sensei had completed the hundred men kumite at the peak of his training, and although severely injured, defeated all his opponents, even though the dojo where his fight took place was noted for its strong fighters. He emphasises that,

"The essence of karate exists in kumite and the life of kumite exists in kihon. Therefore the person who has accomplished the 'hundred man fight' can be recognised as truly successful in karate, while a person who wins a tournament alone might do so by good luck."

The first time I had heard about the hundred man kumite was after Steve Arneil had arrived in London, and had fought the whole dojo (a mere forty-three students) during his first training session. When asked about it he shrugged the whole matter off by saying that this was 'the done thing in Japan'. He extracted a promise from me that I would attempt it myself at the end of my training in Japan.

The hundred man kumite is nothing new to budo in Japan. Kimura Masahiko, who held the judo championship for an incredible twelve years, had accomplished one hundred for two days. Yamaoka Tesshu, a very popular fencing master and hero of the Meiji Ishin also accomplished one hundred bouts in kendo while training to master the sword. He defeated one hundred opponents in a non-stop battle, and possibly was the first ever to succeed in this difficult performance.

Jo master Shimizu Sensei had also offered me some advice, reminding me of a saying of Miamoto Musashi

"When taking a long journey, think only of the next stopover, never the complete journey, or it may seem insurmountable. When fighting many opponents do the same."

I remember very little of the test, my grading for third dan had been much of a formality as had my friend Luke's, and I had pushed aside all other thoughts during the last few weeks. I kept reminding myself that I had not come all this way, spent all my money and suffered all the pain to fall at the last hurdle.

The hundred man fight seemed to happen around me rather than with me. I do remember the beat on the taiku (drum) announcing the start and the finish of each match, the marking of each fight on the blackboard and Oyama Sensei's critical eye.

There were around thirty in the dojo that night. Being a Friday, half of them were black belts and these were easier to fight than some of the white belts who lacked control and judgment.

I found that by using the circular blocking movement I avoided the severe battering that Luke had encountered and could take advantage of my opponent's mistakes to push through my own techniques.

I had to fight all those who were present at least three times It at came to the turn of my old friend the Korean who had lost face in the restaurant, he went all out to stop me. The rest of the dojo were surprised, but did nothing about it.

I survived his first bout, but had to pace myself before he came around again. Fortunately he was preceded by several lesser skilled ranks, which enabled me to ease off and reserve some energy to deal with the nerk.

During the later stages of the ordeal the fitness training paid dividends with a fresh burst of energy just when I felt near to exhaustion and finally being bounced in the air umpteen times by jubilant fellow students was not what an exhausted body needed.

Litres of beer at the local beer hall was a far more fitting finish.

The hundred men fight was not only a personal success, but a success of a training system that allows a student to push beyond the parameters of pain and uncertainty and experience the very depths of himself.

The official tests were over, but there was one more unofficial one to which Oyama Sensei turned a blind eye.

A walk through the park.

The park was at Ueno and several black belts would drop you off at one entrance of the park at dusk, then rush around to another entrance and wait for you to come put the other side.

The only problem was that between the two gates were an assorted bunch of weirdos that had their own little territories where they trained half for progress and half for show. They would delight in 'demonstrating' their techniques to anyone foolish enough to encroach on their personal training space.

I was given a period of time to make if through, then the black belts would come looking for me.

It was a complete non-event, I suspect they thought it was a set-up, a large foreigner, obviously trained, walking through the park waiting for something to happen. I did stop to watch a few of them training, but was studiously ignored.

My time in Japan was over. There was a lot of red tape to cut through to gain an export licence for my two swords, a final round of farewells, and then I sailed on a cargo passenger vessel the 'Eastern Queen' from Yokohama, to Kobe, Brisbane and Sydney.

Andrew Barber from New Zealand, who had joined me in the final month, sailed with me and provided an excellent training partner during the voyage, older passengers complained of the noise.

The ship had Australian officers and a Chinese crew. The officers were a great bunch and the crew very respectful to those who 'made the fist'. They refused to be tipped at Sydney, a sure sign of my new status.

A change at Sydney to the Italian liner 'Achille Lauro' for the three day journey to Wellington completed my sailing days.

Chapter Seven

If I had any misgivings about returning to New Zealand to start teaching rather than considering the more financial lucrative United States or Europe, they disappeared when Achille Lauro sailed into Wellington on a perfect summer's day.

The harbour was like glass and the sun reflected off the windows of the houses that cluttered the hillsides, giving everyone a welcoming glow.

I was to start work even before the ship had cleared customs. The T.V. crew from the program 'Town and Around' came on aboard to film the art of jodo.

After unpacking the necessary gear, we trooped up to the top most deck, away from passengers eager to disembark.

They shot several of the kata, preferring the ones that included a lot of action rather than technical expertise.

The now all too familiar ship's tannoy asked,

"Will Mr. Jarvis, passenger disembarking at Wellington please report to deck 'A' lounge."

I reminded the front man that this was me they were asking for.

"One more shot please, standing up there on the rail." The cameras ground on.

"Will Mr. Jarvis, passenger disembarking at Wellington report to 'A' deck now!"

I again appealed to the front man

"One last shot, standing next to me, looking at the camera, please."

The cameras worked away again.

"Mr. Jarvis, report to 'A' deck. No one can disembark until you have cleared customs."

The front man released me with a wave, and I rushed down to 'A' deck still dressed in hakama and carrying a jo. A crowd of impatient passengers crowding around the gangway gave me annoyed looks but said nothing; being armed helped.

The customs' desk on 'A' deck was deserted, apart from two customs officers; they were very understanding as they flicked through my documentation and cleared the ship.

Being last off worked in my favour, the inspecting officers impatient to go to lunch, gave my hand baggage a cursory check then waved me through. In two large trunks were swords, staves and an assortment of Japanese martial mayhem makers which would have taken a lot of explaining.

That night, watching 'Town and Around,' I was surprised to see myself appear magically out of no where to stand beside the front man. Later, due to slick camera work and editing I appeared to jump backwards from the deck to the rail, an impossible physical feat.

New Zealand Television had been showing 'Samurai', a program viewed by kids in Japan, but very popular with all ages in New Zealand. 'Town and Around' wanted to show a real live Samurai. Welcome to showbiz!

The task of beginning to build a national organisation from a position of debt was daunting. The majority of the independent karate 'clubs' welcomed and supported both physically and financially the system of a chief instructor. A few did not, preferring to protect their 'independence' and 'democracy'. This led to the first confrontations and endless meetings.

Professional instructors of any kind were not highly regarded in New Zealand in the sixties, coaches were expected to give up their time not for remuneration, but for the love of the sport, but for the smaller codes, much of their efforts went into fundraising rather than into raising standards.

Rowing was a typical example.

In karate, most of the clubs had been set up as sports clubs rather than dojo, and this led to a conflict between 'presidents' and 'committee members' who as often as not, had little or any technical skills and senior ranks who had little time for administration duties.

A typical situation was judo, where a yellow belt on a committee cast a deciding vote against a senior black belt being awarded a higher rank.

The only answer was to build a better and more efficient system, with control answerable to headquarters in Tokyo, and leave the back yard budoka to wither on the vine. Being in control of all, black belt promotions helped.

Before leaving Japan, Kuroda Sensei had presented me with a gift. It was a name for my new dojo, Rembuden, brushed in his famous style. The words Rem meaning to train with heart and spirit, bu - martial - and den a way of practice. The name was to place me once again out of favour with Oyama Sensei when the word Kyukushinkai appeared below Rembuden.

Rembuden's first training session consisted of eight members, some graded and some who had joined from local clubs. A few were new to training. Like the first group in London there was something special about them, three of them are still training today.

Noise, overheads and ventilation were not a problem; we trained free on Victoria University's Rugby field. Light was a problem, though, we had to stop at dusk. The students found it difficult to spar in the dark. Finding a suitable dojo was first priority.

It seemed all a little too much. Places available were either too big, too small, too far out or too expensive. Fortunately the weather was warm, and the nights began to lengthen.

Finally I found the ideal location, an ex-boxing gym at 131 Manners Street. The Boxing Association had gone to considerable expense building an office, changing rooms and showers, and then had to relinquish their lease. The skipping and pounding of punch bags drove the tenants on the lower floors insane.

Written into our lease was no training before 5:00pm, which was fine by us.

The new Rembuden dojo had several advantages. The building was old, an earthquake risk and the rent was low. It was centrally located opposite Wellington's Pigeon Park, and being on the third floor, getting up the flights of stairs was the first fitness test for new members. We were also high enough above the park not to terrify the pigeons or pedestrians with kiai.

We did not set off to a good start with our tenants downstairs. An over-zealous member threw buckets of water everywhere to clean the floor, and it soaked through downstairs spoiling design plans and estimates. I went further into debt. Later we would take over that floor as well as the dojo grew in numbers.

To build an organisation publicity was needed. Karate received far more media coverage than any other activity numbers wise, but the rub was the media was only interested in seeing bricks broken, people bounced and flying kicks.

One had to compromise, when you went public you paid your dues and gave them what they wanted, but when the public came to you either at the dojo or demonstrations you exhibited correct training methods and authentic technique.

November the third the Emperor Meiji anniversary was a special time for demonstrating; backyard budoka were not welcome.

New members joined in a steady stream, and came from as far away as fifty miles. One Chinese lad had come from the market garden area of Otaki, and paid his fees in cabbages and cauliflowers. He left when I increased the fees to zucchini and eggplants.

It was important to build up the hombu (headquarters) dojo first before travelling to provincial towns, or to open new branches.

Being a new dojo Japanese style training was introduced from the beginning. New members could view a training session, and then decide whether to join. This contrasted to introducing Japanese style training to existing dojo, where membership dropped alarmingly. Many of these amalgamated, disappeared or changed to a style more suited to casual training.

Kung fu, or more correctly Wushu, had not yet burst onto the scene. Bruce Lee was a few years off, but I did have a strange visitor climb the stairs one day when I was working in the office.

He was Chinese (not unusual) well dressed (not unusual) and spoke good English (not unusual). He was more than a little drunk (very unusual). After asking permission to come in, he told me

"I know the answer to karate." I was impressed.

"I am very interested to see it."

"But I cannot show you," he added smugly.

"If I attack you now, you will have to show me won't you?"

"No, even then I could not show you."

"Then what the - use is it?"

He declined to answer, and weaved his way back down the stairs. I have been wondering what the answer is ever since.

My first demonstration in New Zealand could be judged a success. It held at Victoria University before a positive audience, admission thirty cents. Time was well spent in explaining each art and technique before each demonstration. This set a pattern for future demonstrations, have a good front man who can speak well, explain the techniques in a way that is understandable to lay people and supply a touch of humour.

The newspaper article the following day made satisfactory comments such as 'not just breaking techniques' 'mental approaches' and 'character building'.

With the hombu club developing slowly but strongly, it was time to go public and take martial arts to the people. We started at Invercargill – the bottom of the country.

Invercargill had the nucleus of a good Kyokushinkai dojo.

Doug Holloway had introduced karate there after a study period in Japan.

The demonstration was at the Y.M.C.A stadium, before a near-capacity audience. Not being performers in a professional sense meant several cases of nerves before the start, but fortunately once started everyone was far too busy trying not to be hit to worry about an audience.

Another positive factor is that in almost all cases the audience is supportive, they want you to succeed, and this comes across to the demonstrators.

One of the audience was not so helpful, and lumbered out onto the floor during the breaking demonstration.

There are always two nerks in every crowd, and he was both of them, six foot two inches, no neck and a forehead designed to deflect armour-piercing rounds.

The audience fell quiet as he walked towards us.

"These are biscuits," he pointed to the clay tiles we had been demolishing. He wasn't entirely incorrect, old brittle clay tiles are far easier to demolish than modern concrete ones. A biggest danger with them is being cut by the shards. To be fair, we had been breaking those fifteen to twenty to a stack, any more and the stacks would have fallen over.

"I can break these too!" He was right again, if he leaned against anything it would break, but fortunately all the tiles had been destroyed.

"Would you like to break some wood?" I asked politely, and received an affirmative grunt in reply.

I selected the heaviest piece I could from a pile of timber already discarded for having little or no grain and large knots. I gave my partner the nod, he smiled in agreement.

The lout squared up, and unleashed a punch with the power of a bulldozer and about as fast. Just before he hit, we pushed the top of the board forward, his fist skidded down off the timber, taking the skin off his main knuckles and exposing bleeding flesh. The crowd yelled, enjoying this unexpected aside, he yelled in rage and demanded to try again.

This time, before the pile-driver landed, we tilted the board the other way, his fist scraped upwards, removing the skin from his fist knuckles and flecking us with blood.

The crowd had enough,

"Siddown ya bum," and other Southern niceties.

He wandered away, dazed, licking his hand.

We later found at out that he was a well known local character who had once in a fit pique punched his fist through the outer layer of a wooden railway carriage. Not a man to upset. I doubt that he learnt from his lesson; never rely on your opposition.

CHAPTER SEVEN | 169

Christchurch was the venue for the next demonstration, and this included one of New Zealand's first competitions.

My thoughts on competition at that time were similar to the breaking techniques, they were part of the price that had to be paid for exposure and interested new students.

Our hombu dojo had sent down a strong team.

One of the interesting aspects of the Southern dojo fighting style was that they loved to use yoko geri (side kicks) and at their level this necessitated the use of the straddle, or side on stance. Use of a side must be precise, if the knee is not locked on impact or the target is moving away, there is no focus, and worse, ineffective kicks can be charged down when the kicker is off balance.

That is what happened, the Christchurch students scuttled backwards and forwards, crab like, across and more often than not, out of the contest area, launching ineffective side kicks and were charged down or blocked by their opponents, who moved inside to punching range.

The rules were similar to now, no kicks to the groin or kneecaps, and no contact to the head, but unfortunately, being in a lower stance meant the Christchurch students' heads were at risk.

Later, with the introduction of leg sweeps and attacks, the side stance would all but disappear from competition.

There were a few disqualifications, but those did not affect the result; Wellington won four of the five events. The after match function in a local hotel was not a pleasant one with local supporters claiming

"But that's not karate!"

Hombu dojo was having women show a lot of interest. Some styles of Ryu had a separate training system for women and an adjusting grading standard, ours did not.

I did spend a lot of time promoting jodo as a classical art, perhaps more suitable for ladies as a discipline without the need for callous and strenuous exercise, but most of the young and not so young were not having any of that. They joined in the dojo work outs, demanding and getting their own changing rooms.

It was an honour to grade the first women and Maori black belt in New Zealand. Later, when western women trained in Japan they caused some consternation. The Japanese were not sure how to treat them.

We prepared for our first winter camp to be held at the Boys' Brigade site on the lonely coast road in Wainuiomata, east of Wellington.

The camp was spartan and unheated, there was no difficulty getting volunteers for cook house duty. It was the only warm place in the camp. A southerly wind blew in from the Antarctic straight up the valley, cattle sensibly looked for shelter.

The first camp set the pace for all those that followed; stories are still abound, some of them no doubt exaggerated.

Morning meditation started at six in the common room. Students sat in the formal kneeling position for about twenty minutes – long enough for all circulation to cease. It was not a success, students were asked to clear their minds and concentrate on nothing, imagine that their minds were a black board and every thought that intruded had to be erased. Easier said than done.

By concentrating so hard on controlling their minds, they neglected to control their bodies. A dawn chorus of flatulence drowned out the lone bird on the skeletal tree outside.

CHAPTER SEVEN | 171

Top left

Where it all started, wearing my Father's 'Truth' belt for the most scientific boxer.

Top right

The crew at Waiouru; the author is holding the gate open; the infamous Jim Price is on the far right.

Centre left

A Commonwealth affair Shilo Manitoba, Canada; the Lieutenant (left) is a Canadian, an Australian Captain, does the congratulations, the Sergeant Major overseeing everything is ex British Army.

Lower left

Kurosaki Sensei (centre) with Steve Arniel (right) and Bob Bolton (left).

Top left

The obligatory photo beside the mural at Kyokushinkaikan.

Top right

Kurosaki Sensei entertains Oyama Kancho (right) and everyone else at a dojo party.

Centre

Bugei in action Japan Cultural Day 1967.

Lower right

Sensei Shimizu and Hiroi.

CHAPTER SEVEN | 173

Left

Sword masters demonstrate kata at the Hibiya Hall.

Centre left

Kuroda Sensei in 'Haso Kamai' at the Yotsua Kidotai dojo.

Centre right

Oyama Shigeru serving food at a winter camp. Fujihira (later Ozawa) is packing up on protein.

Lower left

Quentinn Chambers ties up Shimizu Sensei with kusarigama.

Top left

Doshin-So, founder of Shorinji Kempo, preparing for Meiji Shrine demonstration.

Top right

One of the last photos of Donn Draeger.

Centre left

The new Rembuden Dojo 1974.

Lower left

Hospitality Aubrey Brooks style. Higaonna Sensei samples an Australian 'Barbee'.

CHAPTER SEVEN | 175

The morning run that followed was barefoot into town and back, a distance of about four miles. Students breathed a sigh of relief when the shingle road gave way to seal, and then to concrete footpaths. Their relief was short-lived; a light shower had dampened the concrete, which in turn moistened the soles of their feet. Mine were hardened by a year of dojo floors and remained intact, most of the students by the time they arrived back at camp found that their skin had peeled off. Only one unable to train went back home. They were a tough bunch.

Someone, unable to give them away to anyone else donated a large tin of prunes. These were served at breakfast and disappeared along with any porridge and toast. They were to further undermine the fortitude of the students. Two were overheard in the toilet.

"How are you enjoying camp?"

"I don't know, I have only seen the inside of a toilet door since I arrived."

For strength training, everyone was given a rock to carry around at all times, to training, to the showers, to bed. The rocks weighed about 6kg each, and if you found someone without a rock you could give him yours. Anyone found twice had to go home, nobody could carry three rocks. Some of the students, like hostages, became quite fond of them.

Formal morning training was outside in the fields. Stones were placed in rows like gravestones, while their owners moved backwards and forwards, in the endless routine of kihon.

Lunch was served by a student who had been a cook in the Territorial Army. He turned out to be more of a menace than any bleeding feet or rocks. The problem with any cook is that they can't conceal their failures; they have to be served up.

His failure was steamed rice that had to be chipped carefully into vulnerable crockery and crunched up along with exhausted cabbage and other unmentionable things. It was at least, hot.

Afternoon training was in the ice cold river which earlier had a light covering of ice in the still pools by the bank.

It had to be short, and the students, free for a few hours, wandered around the sleeping quarters with blankets draped over their heads, making it look like a M.A.S.H. unit.

We found at dinner that the cook had refused to admit defeat, and had redone the rice by frying it. This made no difference, except that each nugget was coated in fat. Morale needed a boost.

In the common room that evening, everyone had to present an item. Most of them chose skits, taking the Mickey out of martial arts. They were to get better and better over the years. Some regional dojo practising well before the camps presented very professional affairs.

My favourite, concerned a faithful servant Nigel, given a love letter by his master had to suffer attacks from every conceivable weirdo, defeating them all and arriving exhausted to hand the letter to his master's fiancée.

She read the letter and slapped his face.

Mindful of the ventilation, the next day's morning meditation was held in the frost outside. Rank has its privileges, and I chased away a cow and took up the meditation position on warm grass. Everyone else had to kneel in the frost. The lines were not very straight, due to the piles of cow pats around the field.

The second morning run was to the south, and with shoes on. When we returned, one of the students remained suspiciously fresh. He was called Ziggy, describing himself as a new breed of ultra long distance runner with a minimum effort running style. He remarked,

"This run is too short, I think. How far to the sea?"

"About seven kilometres." Someone deliberately fudged the translation from miles. 'Ziggy' trotted off happily back down the coast road. He arrived back in the afternoon, seemingly none the worse for his jaunt.

"It was more than seven kilometres, I think." It was more than twenty. 'Ziggy' later went on to warm up on runs around mountains and then the Sydney to Melbourne classic. He didn't need karate, he could run.

Breakfast found the cook still unable to give in. He had added milk to the rice and served it as a pudding.

Someone at last used their initiative and packed the remaining mess into a hole in the weir. I think it's still there.

As the organisation grew, we moved to larger quarters at the Wainuiomata Scout camp, then to Bridge Lodge in Otaki, fifty kilometres north of Wellington. Training camps are still held there.

Karate camps are a good for bringing dojo together and improving students' skills. Contact and comparison with others are essential. Visits to regional dojo were needed.

Wanganui, a small town on the west coast of the North Island, had a small group of dedicated karate ka. This was augmented by a large group of dedicated Maori karate ka from Ratana Pa. When the community at Ratana decided to do something, everybody joined in. Training sessions of over a hundred were not uncommon.

Once, during a break in training, one of our instructors took it on himself to coach them in American football. They all joined in with gusto, delighting in the blocking, screening and multi tackling. Their joy was increased when the coach produced the 'pig' or football.

"Gee, we get a ball as well?"

Hastings Highland Games was a surprise venue for our next and largest yet, karate demonstration and competition. I was more than a little concerned what Scotsmen at the Braemer of Australasia might think of Japanese martial art undermining this bastion of Scottish culture. Imitation Scotch undermining the sales of true whisky is not a thing to be taken lightly.

The Napier karate club, north of Hastings, was one of the oldest karate clubs in New Zealand. Members had to gain experience from exponents off visiting ships until one of them trained in Japan.

The black belts at the club provide local know-how and administration assistance to make the event, with over a hundred entries, a success. Later the club would become the second in New Zealand to build its own dojo.

The problem of allowing lower grades with little technical skill to compete became apparent when several of the matches degenerated into brawls. Senior black belts had to intervene on several occasions, and in one instance had to physically drag the contestants apart.

The questioning of decisions, sportsmanship parochialism, egocentrism and out and out tribal warfare was not what 'do' was all about.

Rembuden withdrew from the competition for a period that lasted seventeen years, although some members competed as individuals. I became a committed opponent of 'sport' karate and advocated an emphasis on traditional values until my retirement.

The Hastings tournament 'battled' on for several more years,

I had been appointed to the position of chairman of the South Pacific Region, an area that had the dojo stretching from Perth to Fiji. Visiting them threw a strain on the organisation financially and man-power wise. I suggested that well established dojo bring down instructors from Japan, but there were few available in Tokyo, and the cost was beyond many of the dojo resources.

Kato, a small but dynamic instructor was sent to Melbourne, Australia.

The Melbourne dojo was not quite ready for Kato Sempai, who introduced the Japanese way of training and sparring. Membership fell off, finances dried up, and Kato returned to Tokyo earlier than expected.

They were more cautious with me; I was invited to take 'seminars' in Melbourne and in Fremantle, West Australia.

I had thought that New Zealand was isolated from other countries and that this was effecting the growth of karate; Perth in Western Australia seemed more so. Singapore was the closest city with a growing martial art community, but with the Vietnam War over, many soldiers that had taken up karate and trained in Singapore would return to Australia and New Zealand to teach.

The dojo in Fremantle was a spacious affair on a first floor. The chief instructor proudly showed me his office first, then the dojo. Around the walls were racks of weapons of every description, including one with seven replica Thomson '45 submachine guns.

"What block is there against those, apart from a city block?" I asked.

"Erm..., those are just for show." He hurried me off to take a look at the showers.

Taking advantage of Perth's fantastic weather, we decided to hold an outdoor training session on the beach. We arrived at 9:30am on a sunny Sunday morning, and changed ready for training. There was not another student in sight. Their chief instructor seemed unconcerned. I wandered down and tested the water. In the middle of winter it was about fourteen degrees centigrade – warmer than Wellington in summer.

At five to ten there were still no students. I began to wonder if we were in the right place. Three minutes later, cars appeared from all directions, students jumped out already changed into gi and ready to begin. The session started on time.

After warm-ups and basic techniques, I lined them up facing the sparkling sea, took up a position in front of them alongside their instructor, and advanced towards the waves, pounding on each step.

"Ichi, ni, san, shi." The waves lapped around our ankles.

"Go, roku, shichi." We were knee-deep in the water, making movement difficult.

"Hatchi, kyu, jyu - mawatte" - turn.

Their instructor and I turned to see all the rest of the students stopped by some invisible wall at the edge of the water, punching but not moving. The sound of the waves drowned out their kiai.

"What are they waiting for, a written invitation?"

"Erm..., I think it is a little too cold for them."

By the time I had finished with them, they were only too pleased to throw themselves into the water.

Melbourne was well organised, although one of the dojo was run by 'show people' rather than physical trainers. The husband was renowned for pulling trams with his teeth, and the wife had a great difficulty in not making flamboyant moves in iai that were of no martial usefulness. Her husband went on happily grading himself each year until he became a twelfth dan. No one had told him that tenth was the highest.

Kyokushin in Melbourne had a strong following and trained well. Kato had made an impression there, and it was easy to instruct them technically without driving them into the ground physically. They were left in no doubt, however, as to what was required training wise for them to become effective. Afterwards, they took up this challenge and progressed well.

One student arrived from Broken Hill, a mining town in deepest New South Wales. Like many big men at the time in both Australia and New Zealand he was not completely convinced that karate was all it was said to be. In my experience such men never set out to blatantly 'take the instructor on', but never the less they needed to be convinced in free fighting.

They could not have been aware that the Japanese training system had been designed long ago to counteract any such challenges, however subtle. Free sparring always came at the end of a training session, and an instructor cannot join in for all the training, he must teach as well. This means that the students at the end of a session are always more tired than their instructor, who if he is a true professional should always be fitter than his students anyway. As an added advantage the instructor can always take his students through exercises that he specialises in, and in which, therefore, he is more proficient.

Even given these advantages, it is not an easy task; these were big, hard, no nonsense men. After training in Japan you end up thin, wiry and with a lot of training, but you tend to bounce off bigger and heavier opponents. I had already begun to use weights to increase upper body strength.

The great leveller then, was the round house kick. I had never considered mine to be particularly fast, and in Japan had only limited it to counter attacking, but students in these dojo had no defence for it, tending to hold their arms low. Time and time again, the instep would connect to the side of the head, sending even big men down to the floor, stunned but not damaged. They were street wise enough to know what would have happened had it been in real combat, and became convinced.

When students began to counter by holding by holding the arms higher and elbows outwards, it could still be a dangerous counter attack.

Taller students with slightly faster legs are very effective, provided they have the skills to handle closer infighting.

Sydney has always been a favourite city of mine, and I looked forward to returning there to teach.

Sydney was rich in the number of styles and colourful instructors proliferating there; many down to earth Sydney-siders felt some were a little too rich!

Sydney's Kyokushin dojo was on the second floor in an old building off Pitt Street. It had a lot of atmosphere and dedicated students.

Karate seemed to be a magnet to strange characters in Sydney. One masochist, appropriately nick named 'The Skull', and who was twenty percent of the N.S.W. National Socialist Workers' Party, had joined karate to learn how to beat up people scientifically in order to add a bit of class to the minuscule but well publicised Nazi rallies. This was of some concern to the instructors, who decided in the interest of martial culture to make life in the dojo very hard for him.

At first nothing seemed to work, he thrived like some vile virus on the hundreds of extra push ups and other penal exercises dished out to him for the most trivial mistakes. The harder he was hit in free sparring, the more he enjoyed it, wearing his black eyes and swollen flesh like iron crosses first class. Even a broken arm failed to stop him fronting up for further training in the cause of one party, one leader and one immigration policy.

The dismay of all the instructors was solved from a most unexpected quarter. One of the female students shouted a kiai that sounded vaguely like 'Sieg heil'. As his good arm shot up, she kicked him neatly in the side, causing him to fall on his rear. Laughter he could not take, and he was seen no more in the dojo.

Reports of his repeated arrests were heard of from time to time.

The Japanese Self Defence Force Naval Division, arrived in Sydney. A large demonstration and competition was arranged by the Japanese consulate in cooperation with local martial arts clubs. Good publicity by the news media ensured the venue was packed.

The event started well for the Japanese, but got worse. In Sumo, the several tons of collected flesh proved too intimidating for the locals, so they had to content themselves with throwing each other all over the place. The kendo standards of the Japanese sailors was far above the local practitioners, even though were instructed by a Japanese sixth dan living in Sydney.

Individual events looked more like target practice than free sparring practice.

An elegant aikido demonstration provided a less physical interval and, possibly, lulled the Japanese into a false sense of security.

The Japanese visitors had badly underestimated the growing strength of both judo and karate in Australia. To make matters more difficult, the NSW judo team had no scruples regarding the State of Origin. Several top judoka from other states joined the team; one was an Australian champion, several others Olympic representatives. Sydney audiences have the reputation of being the most critical in the world, but they warmed to the occasion of Japanese judoka being bounced on tatami. The Japanese, unused to such an unsupportive crowd, fared badly.

The karate was even worse; most of them were completely mismatched. I had a young lad half my size who, after a brief show of inadequacy, continually backed away. He was grateful when I didn't pursue him, and showed it by responding to my questions during a break when we were sitting side by side,

"How long have you been practising karate?" I asked.

"Only about one year, at high school," he replied.

"You got to become a black belt in one year?"

"Oh no, I am only a green belt, but before we arrived in Sydney, they asked how many had done karate, gave us all black belts, and told us we were the karate team."

By the looks on the Japanese senior ranks' faces, those days were obviously at an end.

One of the benefits of teaching in Sydney was access to the lucrative private lesson circuit. A group of about eight successful businessmen paid very respectable sums for me to teach them in their own homes. The lessons were held in a different home each week. It was a Jekyll and Hyde existence, with me living in a small bed-sitter off King's Cross, teaching karate at an old abandoned warehouse for most nights of the week, then being driven in very expensive cars to the near mansions of Double Bay and Vaucluse.

Perhaps not surprisingly, they trained as hard, if not harder, than the dojo students. Getting to the top of a profession, whether it's stockbroking or commerce, requires a single mindedness and toughness that was revealed in their attitude to training.

Afterwards, the lady of the house undid all the good work by laying on a spread of fine rich food and wines. They tried to outdo each other on successive nights.

Their previous private instructor had a reputation for being something of a tyrant. On one occasion he broke the sternum of one of his students by punching him too hard. Another member of the group didn't intend to be treated similarly. After changing into his gear at the next session he took from his bag a loaded large calibre revolver, and laid it on top. The fact that he was a secretary at the Philippine embassy with diplomatic immunity had the desired effect. Training was modified.

One Saturday morning after training, a barrel-like person presented himself to the senior instructors.

"I'm Aubrey Brooks." There was a delay while I thought of something to say, other than, "Who is Aubrey Brooks?"

"From Newcastle." I looked at the others, who signalled with their eyebrows that they had not heard of him.

"Are you Kyokushinkai?" Was all I could think of to ask.

"Of course, mate." He began to look more than a little annoyed.

"I am Newcastle Kyokushinkai." Later I was to find out he was not exaggerating. I must have looked unconvinced, because he stormed back down the stairs to his car, and puffed back up again holding two large photo albums.

"Take a look!"

We all gathered around the albums as he proudly turned the pages, revealing endless photos of himself, several of his fellow black belts and a few of his students. Most of them showing the destruction of building materials at charity of fund-raising events with important looking personages present.

"Very impressive." He began to look mollified.

"I didn't know we had a branch in Newcastle. Tell me about it." He did and several hours later left after securing that I would visit him in the near future. Many years later he was to tell me that the worst time in his career was when he realised that we had never heard of him.

Aubrey Brooks' visit showed the necessity of bringing together as many dojo in the South Pacific as possible. The only event that would generate enough finance to make this possible was an international tournament.

In 1970 this was a bold venture, but it was felt that Sydney had the population to support sponsors willing to inject money and a news media interested in providing coverage. The Sydney town hall was booked, invitations posted and fingers were crossed.

The event surpassed all our expectations. Teams from Perth, Melbourne, New Zealand and of course New South Wales attended.

The competition was of a good standard, the attitude of the competitors excellent, and the interaction between the different dojos positive. A near packed house ensured that half the air fares for the Perth, Melbourne and New Zealand teams were refunded. The Sydneysiders, not to be outdone, were generous hosts.

The only glitch in proceedings occurred during a break between competitions and the demonstrations of tameshiwari.

A well dressed person approached me.

"The person I represent wants to fight you and other senior black belts." The person he indicated had a prison haircut and matching prison complexion. I found out later that he had relieved the Australian Army of several machine guns, a deed that sentenced him to deepest gaol.

"If he wants to fight, let him work his way through the competition like everyone else, why should he be special?"

"He doesn't want to do that."

"He doesn't have a choice." I tried to make it sound final.

The tamashiwari demonstrations began with each dojo trying to outdo each other, bricks crumbled and splinters flew. At the end Aubrey Brooks and his bruised Newcastlers were the clear winners. The Sydney crowd was very generous with their applause. I looked around, but the lone challenger had gone; I didn't know if the breaking demonstration had caused him to change his mind. We were to meet again later.

I was to return to Sydney each year, the numbers in New Zealand were insufficient to support a full time instructor, so my time was split, nine months in New Zealand, three in Sydney. It was a satisfying arrangement.

Back in New Zealand I was to meet a student from the Wanganui dojo, Maureen, who was to later become my wife. This was <u>not</u> only a wonderful time, but an end to <u>not</u> worrying about bills, material possessions and where the next meal was coming. As every ex-bachelor has experienced, life, as of necessity, has to become much more structured.

The problem of balancing the responsibilities of marriage and a family with the demands of a professional instructor is not new. Records show that the success rate is not high.

My personal training alone demanded that I keep on a high level of skill in fifteen karate kata, thirty six jodo kata and twenty four in iaido. Just practising these alone took hours each day, and that did not include supplementary training for fitness, timing and power. There did not seem to be enough hours in the day.

It was over three years since I had left Japan, I felt it was time to return and invest more time in my own training.

Japan, like everywhere else, had changed. The noisy pachenko parlours, where devotees sat for hours pursuing the mindless activity of flicking ball bearings into slots, were giving way to the more sophisticated electronic games. Living costs had jumped dramatically.

I witnessed the social changes first hand when I booked into a new hotel in Ikebukuru.

I was informed politely that I would have to book out each morning and book back in again. I assumed this was due to high occupancy rate. I was wrong.

The room was unexpectedly small, with a bar stacked with every alcoholic goodie, all out of proportion to the other facilities. Other facilities included a closed circuit T.V. that played non-stop porn movies.

CHAPTER SEVEN

When I booked out the next morning, I was jostled by a throng of dark suited Japanese businessmen hurriedly paying their accounts and avoiding looking at each other or their girlfriends. The hotel was one of the new overnighters for 'businessmen' wishing to 'entertain' their clients. Reminding myself what I was here for and that I was married, I went to stay with a friend.

Training was a little disappointing, but still beneficial, especially spirit wise. Oyama Shigeru's brother was back training at Kyokushinkai, but many of the older senior belts had left. Kuroda Sensei had had a stroke, which limited his movements on his right side, but he was still as demanding as ever with my technique which had become rusty over the years. He also had training with him one Nakamura San, a famous kabuki actor, who was learning correct sword technique as part of his acting skills. His sword was very old and very expensive; he gladly allowed me to appreciate it.

Sadly, Shimizu Sensei had cancer and had retired from all training.

Kaminodo Sensei was acting head of the Ryu. Donn Draeger was overseas gathering information for his new book 'Asian Fighting Arts'.

There were also new laws. I was wandering around some back streets in Ikebukuro looking for a shop I remembered that sold 'tsuba' – iron sword guards. It was hot and I was dressed in shorts, tee shirt and sandals. A young policeman approached me.

"Excuse me, sir, can I see your passport?" I wasn't carrying it.

"I'm sorry, I do not have it with me."

"Do you know it is against the law for foreigners not to carry their passports at all times?" I didn't, but realised that ignorance is no excuse.

"I am sorry, I did not know this."

"Will you please come to the police station?"

"Am I being arrested?"

"Oh no, but you must still come with me to the police station."

So I did, and was ushered into the office of an inspector.

I knew what to expect. One of the reasons that Japanese people usually carry their cards is to ascertain on meeting someone their status in order to know to address them. It is no use saying you are a teacher, there is a large difference in social status between a kindergarten teacher and a university lecturer. I decided to inflate my status to gain some clout.

"Now, sir, your name please." I gave it.

"And now, your address in Japan." Again I obliged.

"Is that where your passport is?" I nodded.

"What is your occupation, please?"

"I am a teacher of the martial arts." The inspector paused, and looked at me as if making up his mind about something.

"Where do you teach these martial arts?"

"I am the chairperson of the Southern Hemisphere." The inspector spoke in rapid Japanese. Ten minutes later tea arrived.

"Who is your teacher?" The inspector smiled. I played my trump card.

"Kuroda Sensei, Kidotai dojo." I produced his card and offered it to the inspector; his smile faded and he fired off more Japanese. Biscuits were brought to accompany the tea just in case. The inspector would not touch the card, but looked at the number and dialed.

I could hear Kuroda Sensei on the other end of the line. So could most of the people in the police station.

The inspector looked very tired, hung up and took me on a tour of the police station while the officer was dispatched to my flat to pick up my passport.

It arrived and seemed to satisfy everyone.

"Do you promise to abide by the laws of Japan in future?" The inspector badly needed to save face.

"Yes, Inspector, and I want to apologise for all the inconvenience I have caused you and your staff." He smiled and escorted me to the door. He had one last card to play himself.

"Do you know Peter Smith?" He caught me unawares.

"Er... no I don't. Should I?"

"He is from New Zealand."

"New Zealand is a very small place, but it is possible I do not know him. I promised to tell him if I ever met him and walked out a free man. I noticed something else new in Japan. All the guards outside the police station were armed with jo.

As luck would have it, I met Peter Smith sometime later at a party; he was not someone you would miss in Japan, being six feet tall and blonde. I mentioned the inspector's concern, he was unrepentant.

"Yeah, I know they are looking for me, but I have used up all the extensions they give on visas, so I'll just stay as long as I can until they catch up with me. They can only deport me."

"Why don't you go and see them, and just say you forgot? They seem quite serious," I suggested.

"Nah."

I found out later that they caught him. He was in for a nasty shock. There is no 'habeas corpus' in Japan; they let him cool his heels in a detention centre for nine months. His girlfriend had to supply food to him. He was then deported, his passport stamped with something negative.

With no senior karate grades, training at Kyokushinkai I decided to travel south to the island of Shikoku, to meet up with an old friend, Ashihara Sensei, who had opened a new branch dojo in Yahatahama. He lived with his wife, also a black belt, above the dojo. It would be good to get away from Tokyo.

The journey seemed long, changing trains several times before taking the ferry across to Shikoku. Ashihara met me off the train. Like me, he had put on a little beef, but was unchanged otherwise. He was pleased to have someone overseas visit his dojo.

Ashihara's training hadn't changed; it was as hard as ever. During free sparring, one of the blows that landed started my nose bleeding; I carried on, letting the white belts mop up the blood.

After the training session ended, Ashihara Sensei gave his students a long training speech on training spirit and how I had come all the way from New Zealand to improve my standard and get a bloody nose in the bargain.

I had the entire long journey back to Tokyo to wonder about that.

Ashihara's students had their own style of fighting, and were begrudgingly respected at Honbu in Tokyo. They were to do well in future competitions.

I arrived back in Tokyo to a frosty reception. Oyama Sensei wasn't speaking to me, apparently annoyed that I had gone to train with Ashihara, a subtle indication that perhaps Honbu wasn't good enough.

Dismayed, the senior belts at Tokyo apologised for advising me incorrectly.

I was not the only person in the 'poo' at the dojo; later the phantom crapper was to strike.

Anyone who has ever used a Japanese toilet, hygienic as they are, will know that they can be initially confusing. Most people work out that you must face the cowling, some do not. The phantom crapper struck at Kyokushinkai, leaving a pile of faeces neatly on top of the cowling.

A junior in charge of cleaning toilets reported it to a senior who gathered all the foreigners, as prime suspects, into the changing room.

"Who has done this?" demanded the Sensei.

"It can only be a foreigner, one of you!" he insisted.

"Or some Japanese is trying to get us in trouble," mumbled someone.

"Silence!" screamed the Sensei; such a suggestion was unthinkable. He then proceeded to instruct all foreigners on the correct use the Japanese Benjo, following which, he stormed off muttering and clicking his tongue.

Several days later, the phantom crapper struck again, depositing an offending pile on top of the porcelain.

This was serious, Oyama Sensei himself took control of the investigation, haranguing all foreign students, and promising to get to the bottom of it.

Nobody sniggered.

Finally the phantom was caught by a ninja spying on the toilet, facing the wrong way. The luckless creature was dragged upstairs to the dojo, suitably punished by all senior belts during free fighting, and sentenced to endless toilet cleaning. I don't know what became of him.

My refresher course in Japan was over; I was to return to New Zealand to a newly born son and a karate system that had changed politically and permanently.

Chapter Eight

In New Zealand the karate organisation was polarising. There were those who had no problem with a transplanted Japanese system; others called it a dictatorship and formed their own organisations, some of them with impressive sounding names that did not make sense. Many local instructors realised they would not rate in an international and carved out their own fiefdoms, sometimes bonding together for strength. I don't recall any of them producing a student of international standing.

The organisation was given a boost by a visit to New Zealand by Sensei Oyama (Shigeru) and Nakamura. The two sensei had been invited by the Christchurch dojo and arrived from New York to teach a training seminar before travelling north to visit North Island dojo and to sightsee. They were to depart for home from Auckland.

A large contingent descended on Christchurch from all over New Zealand for the visit of Kyokushin senior ranks from overseas. There were some noticeable absences of New Zealand karateka.

The seminar was an outstanding success with Sensei Oyama and Nakamura working in tandem to up the tempo of training and attitude.

At the black belt grading my wife, Maureen, was graded provisional first dan.

"Fix the kata," ordered Oyama Shigeru, looking at me.

The seminar ended with a demonstration of budo at the new Christchurch Town Hall. A reasonable crowd ensured that expenses would be covered.

Backstage a small crowd gathered around the ice that had been ordered for a tameshiwari demonstration by Oyama and Nakamura. They were not happy; the ice had not been made properly and the sempei in charge had a long face: all chances of future promotion were in doubt. I never found out what exactly the problem was but, after muttered conversations in Japanese, some of the ice was brought out onto the stage and set up, dripping into the canvas covering. I have always doubted the wisdom of breaking large slabs of ice set up with two inch gaps between them. Most people can work out the domino effect where you break the top slab which falls onto the second, its weight breaking that and so on, but Christchurch spectators were enthusiastic with their applause.

The two Sensei stopped for a day in Wellington and visited Rembuden. I phoned ahead to Wanganui to arrange a Maori welcome for them at the Ratana Pa. While stopped for lunch at a small town on the way, I carefully explained the format.

"Sensei, a Maori warrior will approach you doing 'kata' with a long club. His job is to look both fierce and intimidating." They nodded, knowing all about that.

CHAPTER EIGHT | 197

"After a lot of formal posturing he will carefully and slowly lay a carved dart in front of you. You must carefully and slowly pick it up."

"What happens if I don't?" asked Nakamura

"Then it is three against the whole tribe."

"Bad odds." grunted Oyama.

I then went on to explain how in the company of elders we could then walk onto the Marae. I went over the complete procedure again just to make sure. They both nodded and smiled and said,

"Yes, Sensei."

As we turned off the main highway onto the road to Ratana we noticed a car stopped beside the road with several people standing around; one of them was the black belt instructor. We stopped. It was a group of elders concerned that our honoured guests were knowledgeable about procedure and protocol. They carefully explained the procedure all over again. I gave the two Sensei a quick look but they were masking their growing impatience well.

We arrived at the entrance to the Marae and there were drawn up over a hundred dancers and dignitaries. The dancers began one of several beautiful welcoming songs that made the occasion emotional as only Maori culture can make it. Oyama and Nakamura were spellbound; they had never experienced anything like it in their life.

As the songs died down the challenger appeared from behind the concert party expertly swinging the taiaha in menacing gestures, his facial expressions made even more fierce by temporary tattoos. He approached Nakamura, slowly taking the dart from behind his back and placing it on the ground. He then took up a straddle position, not unlike karate, holding the taiaha high above his head, similar to the kendo jodan, and stood there, thigh muscles bulging and sinews straining.

Nakamura was in full defence mode; never once had he taken his eyes off the challenger and there was no way was he going to break eye contact in that threatening situation.

The challenger was obviously had a great love for food and as a result his centre of gravity was similar to that of a sumo wrestler. He was finding it increasingly painful to hold his position and repeatedly flicked his eyes from Nakamura Sensei down to the dart and back again. A hint of panic was setting in.

Finally Nakamura snapped out of it and remembered his duty. He looked down to the ground for the dart. It wasn't there. Nobody had remembered to tell us that, because of the short notice, there wasn't time to carve a dart; they had used a twig instead which is a common practice. It wasn't common practice for Nakamura. He looked around in vain for the dart; the challenger's knees started to wobble and I wondered what it would be like to be a party to the first Maori challenge refused in New Zealand for over a hundred years. Finally, in desperation, Nakamura bent down and picked up a stone. This was too much for one of the elders who hurried forward, picked up the stick and gave it to Nakamura.

The rest of the program proceeded without incident with Sensei both straight-faced and formal.

As we drove away for the long drive to Auckland I decided to never mention the incident. I needn't have worried: as soon as we were clear of Ratana, Oyama punched Nakamura on the arm.

"You idiot, picking up a stone. We almost had a war on our hands." Both of them dissolved into laughter, tears running down their cheeks.

CHAPTER EIGHT | 199

The last letter I received from Nakamura Sensei, years later had a postscript:

"I still have the stone on my desk in New York."

My old friend, the challenger from Sydney Town Hall, reappeared, claiming he was the world champion. Sydney's karate instructors were not impressed as there was uncertainty about what the tournament was and who had fought there. Annoyed, the 'world champion' issued a challenge in the newspapers. None of the locals were keen and I was asked to accept.

I did accept and at first it seemed a 'just' crusade but it started to go wrong once the news media got hold of the story. The news media were, for some reason, anti the world champion and their coverage favoured me but I noticed the talk around town was that Sydneysiders did not like 'their' world champion being challenged by an 'outsider' who should pack up and go home. I did wait on neutral ground at the local boxing gym for a no rules contest. He failed to show but later, after I had returned to New Zealand, he issued a counter challenge. I initially agreed but with the situation becoming sour, I suspected a set-up and, on the advice of my old mentor Don Draeger, did not participate. This caused some justifiable ill feeling on behalf of some of the Sydney senior ranks. One later tracked me down in Canberra to demand an explanation, which made one wonder why they didn't handle the situation in the first place.

True to my promise I made several visits to Aubrey in Newcastle. For the first of many visits I took my wife and two sons, the younger being only six months old.

After a long train journey from Sydney we arrived at Newcastle and were met by Aubrey and all of his senior belts. On the drive to his home we passed along Hunter Street, made famous some months earlier in a song. A very large truck and trailer unit bedecked with horns and lights was coming in the opposite direction. Aubrey yelled something unintelligible out of his window as the rig thundered past. With a hiss of hydraulics and the smell of brake pads burning, the unit stopped. So did all the other traffic on Hunter Street. I should mention now that Aubrey's station wagon had 'Rembuden Karate Club' painted in large script on the sides and rear.

"How ya going mate?" Aubrey had eased out of the wagon and shouted up at the driver of the truck.

"Great mate, just got back from ... " the driver yelled back some unpronounceable Aborigine name.

"Come on down and meet Sensei," Aubrey invited the driver who started to make the long climb down to ground level. I looked around apprehensively. Some of the traffic had eased around Aubrey's vehicle but on the other side was a standstill. Surprisingly there was no sign of a riot.

"Peter, this is Sensei," Aubrey introduced the driver, a rugged looking individual with a bushy moustache.

"Great to see you in Newcastle, mate. Looking forward to your training sessions." A few desultory horns sounded, they were ignored.

"How's the wife, mate?" Aubrey decided he was talking to him.

"Great, mate, how's your missus?" Doors slammed as several irate motorists got out to see what the hold up was. Several saw Aubrey and got back into their cars again; others stood around in suppressed silence.

"OK, mate, see ya later."

"Drop in for a few stubbies." They both clambered back into their vehicles and we drove off. Neither seemed to be aware of the disruption they had caused.

CHAPTER EIGHT | 201

There was to be no rest: I was launched on a series of TV shows, demonstrations, radio shows, had lunch with the Mayor and I even found time to take the odd training session.

One evening Aubrey invited his entire dojo around for a barbie at his place. Aubrey was in his element: cars filled the cul de sac where he lived; his barbecue dominated the back section with meat and sausages spitting and sizzling. He presided over everything like a ringmaster.

One lad from New Zealand, a vegetarian, was looking in vain for something to eat. Aub grabbed his plate and filled it with half cooked flesh oozing blood.

"Er, actually I don't eat meat," ventured the lad.

"What," screamed Aubrey, "Is wrong with my meat?"

"Nothing, nothing," said the lad, more terrified of Aubrey than the meat and temporarily returned to being a carnivore.

"Come and look at this, mate." Aubrey proudly led me into his garage and opened the door of a large refrigerator. He knew I liked to drink wine on occasions and here, stacked four abreast across the top shelf, were four litre casks of white wine, with a backup row behind them. On the second shelf casks of rose wine were stacked in a similar fashion and yes, there on the lower shelf, were cold burgundies and Cabernet Merlot. He didn't intend for me to go thirsty.

The next day, while sitting in the sauna of the local Rugby League Club and trying to get rid of the toxins, the local wholesale butcher came in.

"Gidday, Aubrey, how ya going?"

"Great, mate, great."

"How did you get on with all that old second grade meat you paid me peanuts for?"

"For Christ's sake, shut up." It was impossible but Aub's sweating increased.

"This is my Sensei; you'll get me hung."

"I won't do that, Aub," I said in a friendly way. "I'll put up your affiliation fees instead." Aubrey headed for a cold shower.

One of Aubrey's students invited us all to a party. It was held in the social room at a fish wholesaler on Newcastle's seafront. I was not told at the time that there used to be several fish wholesalers in Newcastle but now there was only one. Nor did I find it peculiar that everyone introduced to me had a name ending in a vowel. I thought the two handsome young men that attended to me throughout the function, never letting me out of their sight nor my glass be empty was a nice touch. So did my wife.

Later Aubrey's brown belt asked us to go fishing with him on his private boat. My wife, a keen fishing person, was delighted. Feeling the social strain somewhat, I politely declined. Towards the end of the evening Aubrey huffed up to me.

"Listen, mate, you have to go fishing tomorrow."

"Sorry, Aub, I need a break, I have a class tomorrow evening."

"Look, mate, I've never asked you for a favour but I'm begging you to go fishing tomorrow." Aubrey did appear uncharacteristically distraught.

"Aub, I'm beat. Take Maureen by all means but I'll pass." In any event the weather turned nasty and the fishing trip was cancelled. Aubrey was a relieved man.

I was told discreetly afterwards by someone not involved in the karate club that Aubrey's brown belt was the local 'chief' or 'friend of friends'. Need he say more?

The social calendar continued with a trip to the vineyards in the Hunter Valley. Wisely we were put on a chartered bus and enjoyed the trip to one of Australia's premiere wine growing districts. We were not to be disappointed, visiting all the famous name vineyards plus a few of the not-so-well-known which were, nevertheless, equal to the high standards of the area. During a visit to one of the well known vineyards we were shown the old stone house with loopholes in the walls so that uncooperative locals could be kept at bay with musket fire. The Hunter River looped nearby, and I was surprised to see that the vineyard still used underground storage tanks.

"The Hunter River rose so high during the Maitland floods a few years ago that we got seepage into our tanks," explained our guide.

"Good grief, what did you do with the wine?" I asked.

"Sold it, mate. That year we won two gold medals."

The Hunter River must have something good in it, but let me hasten to tell wine buffs that that particular vineyard no longer uses underground storage tanks.

Training in Newcastle was completed, and we survived the long drive down to a new dojo in Canberra. Canberra is something of a 'toy' town, but does have several endearing features. The restricted advertising was a relief after Sydney, and the local bylaw that ensured that all property owners grew trees was a positive move towards a clean green environment.

Canberra dojo had a different atmosphere. The students were mainly state servants, and knew quite well how to fit into a structured system. They lacked the 'characters' of other dojo, but had a good all round standards. I was to return there later with a new style and a new head of Ryu.

The organisation was growing rapidly, assisted by the rising popularity of Bruce Lee. It is somewhat ironic that films depicting the ideals and symbolism that budo tries to avoid fill the dojo with people joining for all the wrong reasons. For the first, and only, time Rembuden had a waiting list. Honbu dojo expanded down another floor. This increased 'turnover' did provide the organisation with more students who remained training after those with a more casual attitude moved onto flower arrangement or the tea ceremony. It was time to look for a new dojo.

The building we were in seemed vulnerable. Built in the last century, it was an earthquake risk. During one training session an earthquake struck, rattling the old sash windows and their counterweights in their frames, and dislodging several bricks, long abandoned by mortar. I gave permission for a disciplined evacuation but thirty or so students thundering down the narrow stairs like a herd of stampeding pachyderms caused an aftershock.

Traditionally, Sensei does not go down with the dojo but, nevertheless, I felt it more dignified to emerge from the rubble unconcerned. I walked out the ground floor door to see that the students had sprinted out onto the road and onto 'Pigeon Park', still wearing their gi and startling the passers by.

"Wow, how big do you think that earthquake was?" asked one of the class.

"What earthquake?" said a pedestrian.

The earthquake had not even been felt at ground level.

With the 1970s building boom under way, our premises looked

a sure candidate for demolition. We began planning for a new dojo but we needn't have hurried: the original building is still standing and in use.

Planning was easy. An architect, with little input from me, produced the drawings for a modern dojo with accommodation on top. The ground floor had a hint of a fortress about it with adequate floor space, changing rooms, and sauna and plunge pool. The first floor featured two pagoda type structures containing the living areas and bedrooms joined together by the service rooms.

Putting the idea into practice was difficult and continually frustrating. The accounts estimate showed that the cost of my own home mortgage and the lease of the dojo would be approximately the same as a loan drawn to cover the new building. The accountant couldn't have known about the rampant inflation that was about to inflict itself on New Zealand.

Finding a site was a problem: those within our budget were too far out in the suburbs, while those centrally located and handy to transport were being absorbed by property developers at high prices.

The Wellington City Council was no help at all. Initially they did not know how to class the organisation. Were we a sports club, a business, a professional service, or even a religion?

In desperation I gained a meeting with the Mayor Sir Francis Kitts. He went on about supporting 'physical fitnessers' and 'keeping kids off streets' and even suggested the possible use of council land. The council administrator meanwhile had been giving me a baleful look and had the decency to take me aside after the meeting.

"Don't rely on the Council for help," he advised. "Do it all yourself."

We agreed then to make it a commercial venture; that decision was to cause far-reaching financial problems.

We made an offer on a small site in Tinakori Rd, diagonally opposite the ramp for the northern motorway. It was an ideal situation. The City Council then demanded more car-parks than the site could provide; permission denied. We found a large site at the bottom of the hill in the suburb of Kingston; local residents complained about access; permission denied. One half of the site was sold immediately at a small profit, the other half we ended raffling to get rid of it. Aubrey Brooks won. Who else?

Finally the ideal site was purchased at Newtown, handy to all bus routes with access to two roads. It was fifty metres from the building in which I was born. Being zoned commercial, no planning permission was required, but the Council staff insisted on more car parks than a drive-in movie (and they have still yet to build one in New Zealand).

A knowledgeable friend came to my assistance. A Council employee was taken to lunch, mellowed with wine and liqueurs, and then asked for his help in solving the problem. The next day I had a worthless piece of paper from an amused manager of a hire pool next door allowing the use of their car park in the evenings. Permission was granted; the local street kids saved on demolition fees for the old house on the site by burning it down after a party, and the foundations were laid for a new Rembuden.

The design of the building had been radically changed from the original. We were classed as being in a 'mid-city area' which meant that not only did the building have to be structurally stronger, therefore more expensive, but the upper stories would have to be built in permanent materials. I appealed to the architect, "Who wants to live in a cell block?" His solution was a mansard roof which wasn't classed as a second floor. It was also cheaper. While considering this, the Council approved the bottom floor which had not changed much from the original plan.

Most unwelcome surprises followed: a concrete floor (safety), heavier steel frames (strength), double thickness fire stop (fire), and a water reservoir (drought). The costs mounted, fuelled by 16% inflation.

The building inspector was not helpful. He insisted on the steel beams being covered by fireboard to prevent warping in a fire but waited until the beams had been covered in before telling us. He would not allow any work to be done on the second floor until the permit was approved. This meant temporary plastic covers, allowing the water to seep down, ruining completed work. Finally it was suggested to him by a large, less patient member of our dojo that upsetting the karate-ka could be dangerous to his health. From then on he refused to come on site during the day and would leave messages under blocks or in boxes after hours. They were ignored.

The Council took us close to financial ruin by demanding that the steel structure for the second floor be changed. Being part of the overall structure, it was already in place and changing it was not financially possible.

It was back to lunch again, this time with a well known local bender of the building laws. He suggested,

"Building by laws would be difficult to substantiate in court, they are subject to too much interpretation. Go ahead with it anyway." We did, overruling the builders' complaint.

"It's all right for you – this is a once in a life time event; I have to live and work in this town!"

We were past the point of no return. The building now had to be completed, regardless of cost. The extra borrowing was to be a millstone around the organisation's neck until inflation made it less overbearing, many years later.

The ambassador of Japan, His Excellency Tanaka San (no relation to the Prime Minister of Japan), himself a kendo ka who practised in our dojo, questioned the height of the ceiling, when laying the foundation stone. We assured him it was adequate. We were wrong. The particle board laid on top of the concrete was unsuitable. When coated with polyurethane it became dangerous, sweat causing the students to slip badly.

A new and more expensive third floor, of the native timber matai, was laid on top. After being coated with linseed oil, it was excellent both visually and to touch, but the increased height meant that any kendo Ka over six foot tall would clout the ceiling when striking from 'jodan'. My sons loved this; the resulting noise was a perfect excuse to stay up late and watch television two nights a week.

Finally, it was completed. Aubrey Brooks and students from Australia joined members from all over New Zealand at the opening ceremony. The local Member of Parliament, never one to give up the opportunity to speak, joined the Japanese ambassador and an Anglican Minister, who having survived the rigours of a Maori challenge from the Wanganui dojo, blessed the building (ignoring the Shinto shrine). Demonstrations of the four budo to be taught at the Rembuden changed the 'building' into a 'dojo'.

Moving from the old dojo that had served us well for eight years was a little sad, but this was more than offset by having our own dojo and the facilities it provided. My family shifted into the top floor accommodation, the car was sold as we prepared to weather the financial storm of increased overheads and the inevitable loss of membership a change from mid-city to near suburb incurs. For a while it looked like we wouldn't make it.

CHAPTER EIGHT | 209

After the formality of the dojo opening and the subsequent training sessions, Aubrey Brooks and his henchmen needed a break. They heard that Wellington boasted a mixed sauna; a form of socialising that had not yet reached Newcastle, possibly because it was too near Queensland's border. I explained that one could not guarantee that there would be ladies present at any particular time of the day. They were undeterred, and we descended on 'San Francisco' sauna en masse.

They all changed in record time and rushed into the first sauna. No ladies, only a few overweight businessmen doing penance for an extended lunch break. There was a mad scramble to the second, smaller and hotter sauna only an annoyed regular shouted,

"Shut the bloody door!"

They waited around in vain, like fans for a pop star, filling in the time by taking quick saunas and swims in the plunge pool. Disheartened, they began changing, and were ready to leave when two attractive young women with towels wrapped around them went to sit in the sauna. Within seconds, twenty fit, muscular and bronzed Australian maniacs burst into the sauna looking at them.

The two young women ignored the unwavering gazes, and made conversation between themselves. When it became too hot for them, in more ways than one, they went into the cold plunge pool, slipped out of their towels and under the water. When they surfaced, there were twenty Australians treading water in unison looking at them. Annoyed, the ladies went to the small sauna where it was the same story, with only half the Australians inside, the rest arguing outside as to who was going in next. The regular clients gave up and went home; the two young women had finally had enough and left early as well. The Australians, jubilant in surviving Wellington's sex spots left for a few days' recuperation in Rotorua's Thermal Wonderland.

Aubrey knew his troops well and arranged with the manager of the large hotel for the area around the swimming pool, well away from other guests. They could let their hair down without threatening the hotel's occupancy rate.

Service in New Zealand at the time could hardly be called world class, and it wasn't long before Aubrey and his merry men were out of beer. The waiter was fetched and told in no uncertain terms to keep up the supplies. He responded in the time honoured fashion of avoiding eye contact, and disappearing for long periods, Aubrey dispatched two of his heavies to bring the reluctant minion to his presence.

"Look, I told you, mate, we wanted beer and food service, what do you think you're playing at?" The waiter did not like it one bit being addressed by a rude Australian.

"I will not serve rude Australians who make comments about the way I walk and talk." The waiter made to stalk off.

"Men," ordered Aubrey. They grabbed the unfortunate employee by the arms and legs, swung him backwards and forwards three times and threw him fully clad into the swimming pool. He crawled out like a half drowned rat and squelched off to complain to the House Manager, who appeared within minutes.

"I will not have you treating my employees in this fashion. You will pack up; pay your account and leave!"

"Men," ordered Aubrey, and the House Manager followed the waiter into the pool, tuxedo and all. By now the path back to the hotel was spotted with pools of water. Aubrey then played his master stroke, and ordered all his men up into the trees surrounding the pool, and to keep out of sight.

The hotel manager, flanked by two assistants, had the common sense to check the pool area first. All he saw was Aubrey and his wife laying in deck chairs and enjoying their drinks. Emboldened, he advanced to the pool and began to assert his authority.

"We do not want your type here; you will leave before I call the police and lay a complaint of assault." He was willing to forgo any money owing.

"Men," ordered Aubrey. They all fell out of trees like trained baboons, grabbed the Hotel Manager and threw him into the pool. He still had his mouth open in surprise as he hit the water.

The hotel surrendered. Aubrey got his beer and food. I received a long letter of complaints.

Financially we had struck the bottom. With the car sold and Maureen going back to a hospital career I had to look for another source of income.

It was almost, but not quite, back into the army. The seventh battalion Wellington and Hawke's Bay Infantry Regiment were to form a reconnaissance platoon of the support company. Being a territorial unit they wanted us to use black belts as 'scouts'. The Minister of Defence, Mr. Faulkner, was in favour of the idea.

The original plan, to use us as a part of the First Ranger Squadron of the New Zealand Special Air Service, had proceeded as far as inviting me to take part in a S.A.S selection course. In a typical army way, I was given forty eight hours notice to attend the only selection course that year. Due to a full teaching load and no one available to cover for me, I had to decline. I wasn't too disappointed, being well aware of S.A.S selection procedures. Eventually the idea was canned; most of our black belts lived in Wellington, too far to travel to the Auckland based S.A.S unit. We did get as far as being issued with kit and waited for something to happen. Nothing did. The paperwork must have fluttered to death in some obscure office of the Ministry of Defence. The kit was returned and I looked for something else.

Something else came in the form of an invitation to teach physical education at Onslow College in Wellington. The college had not received a reply to all the advertisements they had placed for a P.E. teacher. With the reputation of the college at the time perhaps they should have advertised for a warden instead.

I found the new career challenging. Students had always come to me wanting to be taught; now I had to motivate young people, many of whom did not want to be taught. When I asked an old friend who was also a secondary teacher whether I should change my approach he gave me some good advice.

"Just be yourself."

I was to teach at Onslow for two years before moving on to teach at St Patrick's Colleges, Wellington and Silverstream.

With two assured incomes the financial crisis was over. We even bought another car.

Mas. Oyama's first open world championship was to take place in Tokyo in 1975. Kyokushinkaikan would cover the costs of a five man team from thirty five countries. A universal feature of the tournament was that all contestants would have had to demonstrate tameshiwari, breaking techniques, prior to contesting. This was to cause some selection problems for the New Zealand team. One member from the South Island was to break his hand during a pre-selection test, another during pre-tournament training. Several of New Zealand's top exponents did not make themselves available, following Rembuden's policy on tournament fighting. I had already made the decision that this was to be my last involvement in competitive karate; I did not realise it at the time but this would also be one of my last involvements in Kyokushinkai.

The team gathered for training in Wellington which included training in the water at the local swimming pool, a technique later to be used by Mohammed Ali and Olympic athletes. Training using water as a resistance has to be carefully monitored. One black belt training at a gasshuku had over trained in water, then attempted speed punching immediately afterwards. His first punch tore most of the forearm muscle away from the bone; he never regained complete use of his arm.

The team did not lack fitness; it was the lack of international competition since Sydney in 1971 that concerned me.

The air fares were sponsored by Japan Air Lines. This meant detouring through Sydney and Hong Kong to connect with J.A.L flights. We arrived in Haneda more than a little tired.

I had brought my sword back with me along with its licence. It had suffered surface damage over the years and needed minor repairs and repolishing. This could only be done in Japan. Despite my explanations, the team and I were delayed for over an hour while the Tokyo customs' officers treated me like a suspected terrorist. Dropping Kuroda Sensei's name in was of little use: he had retired several years ago. Finally, after long discussion, they decided to confiscate the weapon and gave me a receipt. I could apply to have it returned later.

We staggered out of the terminal to find that we were one of the first teams to arrive. A bus was waiting for us; in charge was my old friend from the restaurant confrontation that seemed so long ago. In a gesture of reconciliation I sat down beside him, intending to ask how he was, and what was the inside talk about the forthcoming tournament. Ignoring me, he looked around at the bus and said,

"All these seats and you have to choose one next to me?"

Some things in Japan never change.

With a few days to spare before the tournament commenced, I visited Kuroda Sensei, and explained how my katana had been confiscated. He insisted on driving me to the airport himself.

Being a passenger in Sensei's car was definitely a once only event. Kuroda Sensei is a 'Zen' driver, in as much as he expects the world (in the form of traffic) to revolve around him rather than the other way about. He blissfully drove anywhere he wished on the road, ignored all the road signs, and took traffic light changes personally. He seemed completely unaware of vehicles swerving to avoid him, screeching to a stop when they shouldn't have and he chattered all the way to Haneda. I arrived, more terrified than I had ever been in my life.

At first the airport police said no, the sword would not be returned. That was a good sign in Japan, a definite 'NO' means it's negotiable. A studied silence would have been the worst news. The police informed us that such confiscated weapons are taken out and run over by a bulldozer before being dumped at sea.

Kuroda Sensei pulled rank with one of the officers; a former student. A compromise was reached; the sword would be released to the custody of Kuroda Sensei who would arrange to have it repaired and re-exported. Later Sensei told me emphatically,

"Do not bring your sword back to Japan again; you can borrow one of mine."

The only positive feature of the car trip back from the airport was that if he had been attacked by any incensed motorists, we had the advantage of being armed.

On the day before the tournament, all the contestants gathered at the Dai Ichi Hotel for an introduction of teams, and explanation of tournament rules. Few were surprised at Japan gaining hometown advantage by entering two teams. The word 'team' was a misnomer: all the contestants were to fight as individuals the following day.

The rules were simple; no contact to the head with the hands or elbows which nullified the longer reach advantage of the

Europeans; no groin or knee kicks (the latter was be constantly abused during the tournament), and a knock down or knock out constituted a point. Three warnings were given for accidental or intentional fouls with disqualification on the third warning. Minus point would be given for continually stepping out of the contest area.

The 'draw' was simple, bordering on a farce. All the top Europeans and Americans faced each other in the first round, where half of them would be eliminated. Japanese contestants faced threats from Singapore, India and Easter Island.

The opening ceremony was a mixture of Japanese martial culture with an excellent display on the taiku (drums), and American hype with baton girls twirling everything they could. An orchestra finished with the playing of the Kyokushin 'Karate no Uta'.

In the opening round, contestants had to 'qualify' by breaking timber thicknessed according to their weight. Later, several draws were decided by the number of boards the contestant had broken.

Initially the Westerners provided all of the action, the Japanese all of the comedy. Royama, who was an old dojo 'mate', provided the first knockdown with an excellent middle thrust; his opponent the first of many to leave the mat on a stretcher. He was one of the few Japanese who could really punch. Many later in the competition would pound away at each other's mid sections with no success. Royama was to end up in the finals.

The team from Hong Kong might have been picked up off the streets, given free transport and accommodation plus the promise of glory. Dressed in black gi, some of them, after seeing the flow of stretchers did not want to fight. One unfortunate lightweight, when faced with a Japanese juggernaut, decided to disqualify himself by running out of the contest area. The announcer was relentless.

"Kung fu, where are you?" he asked. The Japanese audience loved it, but I suspected the Hong Kong Chinese would retaliate immediately by making scores of trampoline assisted kung fu movies, showing Japanese heavies being pounded into oblivion.

Two of the New Zealand team were eliminated on the first round, and the other two on the second. As expected, it was an all Japan final between Royama and the all Japan champion, Sato. The contestants had different fighting styles, neither able to gain a decisive victory. One extension after another could not produce a clear cut winner.

Finally Oyama Sensei called me and the three other judges over and told us we must make a decision after the final extension. Sato's weight and stamina told in the final minutes, and when the whistle went for a decision, three red flags went up for Sato, mine the sole white flag (very fitting) for Royama. I couldn't let an old dojo partner down by making it unanimous; several senior ranks of our age nodded in approval.

With some trepidation, I walked over to Sato to congratulate him before the ring was flooded with trophies and microphones. I was in for a surprise.

"You trained with my older brother; he always spoke highly of you, Sempei." The handshake was friendly and genuine.

Later I found out that Sato had been spending much of his spare time between bouts coaching junior belts in kata while others had been banging walls or gazing into space. He was a true world champion.

The fighting in the ring was over but political in-fighting was already under way. Kyokushinkai was in danger of breaking up. There was a half-hearted attempt to bring problems out into the open or to sweep them under the tatami, at the Branch Chiefs' meeting following the tournament.

CHAPTER EIGHT | 217

A Branch Chief from Holland said we were all in for it for the money, why didn't we just get on with it? This was far too direct for the Japanese. A branch chief from Malaysia responded by claiming that no one made money from karate in Malaysia, they were all strictly amateurs. Oyama Sensei defused the situation by presenting everyone with a new Seiko watch.

The real wheeling and dealing was going on behind the scenes. It was widely believed that Nakamura Sensei would go, he was not happy in the number two spot. When I asked him, he would not say directly that he would go, neither would he say directly that he would stay. In Japan speak that means, it's only a matter of time. The big question everyone was asking was who would go with him?

Steve Arneil told me privately that if Nakamura went, so would he, but he also would not say when. It would be over ten years later that Steve carried out his promise.

The problem I faced for both the organisation and myself, was, "What was right for the future?" I was concerned that Kyokushin had no central tree of knowledge to draw from now that Oyama was no longer training. In other classical budo, kata was always a reference for correct technique, but in Kyokushin kata was constantly being changed, either deliberately by head instructors who had their own ideas on how things should be done, or by accident. The problem was that nobody practised the applications of the kata; they were either not known or interpreted incorrectly. The result was a meaningless dance.

With all the large sums of money spent on the world tournament and all the talent that had gathered together, no one had benefitted technically. Those senior ranks who did join in the training at Honbu dojo had to content themselves with kihon, moving backwards and forwards across the dojo and being criticised by junior black belts who considered their authority threatened.

I returned to New Zealand to think about the future. Soon after my return, Nakamura left Kyokushinkai to form his own style, Seido. I put out feelers to join him, but he was adamant that he would initially keep his new organisation small. Not many teachers would have resisted the monetary lure of an organisation with over a thousand members and twenty dojo; my respect for the man increased further.

Feeling uneasy about 'shopping around', while still part of Kyokushinkai and, tired of the politicking, I resigned in October 1976. I was now in the same position as others I had criticised in the past, lacking links or responsibilities to a recognised authority.

Again I turned to Don Draeger for support and advice; the following are excerpts from two of his letters in reply.

2/Nov 1976

Kyokushinkai hinges on the dynamic Oyama. He is temperamental as you know, and creates as much ill wind as he does balmy air. He cares not who stays or goes against him, and with this policy, some day his central line will be dead. Splinter branches will continue, to be sure, but these are only what they are.

I have no ill will toward Oyama or Kyokushinkai, for those who know, know that I have defended both many times from violent and potent opposition here in Japan here and abroad. But your resignation comes as no surprise, though Nakamuru's startled me. You have hit the right circumstances in relation to Kyokushinkai, but these are common faults of all modern budo forms... with no exceptions. This is why I, long ago, got stuck into the classical arts where there is no commercialisation, small numbers, and headmaster-all-the-rest-are-students attitudes prevails and makes for enjoyable training. Maybe you too, now, can understand if not appreciate this.

But go on you must in karate-do. There is no better one for me than the Okinawa Goju Ryu under Higaonna Morio here in Tokyo. Here is a man who exemplifies the word do: humble, resilient, skilled, silent, friendly, strong, all at the right times. His technique is the best in Japan, and in a real fight I know nobody, including Oyama, who can best him. He is damn tough! He does not run around proselytising his art, nor is he keen on going abroad, but with the proper approach can be pried loose to set up a new group that would in your case be useful. Kyokushinkai and Goju are not so far apart as to create difficulties, and the man, John, the man Higaonna, is a gem... I have no words for this fine gentleman. Don't go it alone... tie in with somebody. My vote is for Higaonna. If you want me to talk for you I will be happy to do so. If you come up we can do it together. If you invite him down, I cannot come at this time, but you will get on well with him. Trust my judgment; you are his kind of man.

And 11/May 1977

Contacted Higaonna Sensei and enclosed a short blurb to give him. He will look out for you I am sure... but he is all business in the dojo and there are no pussies in his class... you'll have no trouble, but be in shape. He is the match of any karate man without the usual showmanship, bullshit and arrogance that usually accompanies this type. He is humble par excellence.

When you come out of Yoyogi station walk to your right-front corner and down a long street next to the tracks... ask and they can tell you where the dojo (old garage) is. It can be seen from the train as you pull in Yoyogi from Sendayaya.

I was to return to Tokyo, to start all over again.

Chapter Nine

Following Donn's directions, after arriving at Shinjuku station I had no trouble in finding Higaonna Sensei's dojo. Standing at the doorway, watching the students train, I remembered that I had been here before and wondered what my career would have been like had I changed styles ten years ago, rather than start all over again now.

My new career did not get off to a good start. A youngish looking black belt detached himself from training, approached me and politely asked,

"Can I be of help to you?"

"Is Higaonna Sensei here?" I asked in my best Japanese. I had been practising various phrases on the train.

"I am Higaonna Sensei." He smiled, anticipating that I had expected someone older.

After the shoe shedding, he took me to his office. It had to be so, because it was the size of a telephone box, and only one person could fit inside. No sets of secretaries here, or letterhead paper or a telephone to interrupt training, just a simple filing system for students.

Sensei read my letter of introduction from Donn Draeger but was obviously expecting me. He asked a few polite questions about my family, and then offered an application form for me to fill out. I was now one of his students.

I had considered putting on a white belt again, but the first thing I noticed in the dojo was that overseas black belts from many different styles, some of them senior, were training with Higaonna Sensei. He didn't seem to mind that these students would drop in, spend some time training under him, and then move on. One of them, a senior grade from England and a top tournament fighter told me that he always trained with Higaonna Sensei when he came to Tokyo, and not with his own teachers.

"I enjoy the traditional down to earth training methods; there are no 'posers' in this dojo."

I began again at the back of the dojo; the basics required very little adjusting; the kata almost had to be relearned again. Higaonna Sensei understood and, when I began to fall behind, he would allot me a senior belt to go over the movements for as long as it took, both of us being glad of the physical respite.

The applications were the key to the kata, and unlocked the door to understanding them. For the first time I felt the kata had meaning and continuity, not just a dance pattern that looked good. Any movement, however, could not be effective if it lacked the necessary strength, and it was here that Okinawa Goju Ryu supplementary training, (Hojo undo) provided the 'glue'. Putting it simply, the techniques won't work without it.

After being witness to the never ending mutation of karate styles, it was a breath of fresh air to return to the roots of Japanese karate. In the fourteenth century, there had been a period of rapid development in Okinawa. Formal contact with China, Korea, Japan and trade with Arabia and Southern Asia had made Okinawa a melting pot of weaponry and empty hand fighting methods. Chinese delegations included Masters of Kempo who began to teach the nobility on the islands. The interaction was two way, with Okinawans travelling to the Fukien provinces of China for further study. History records that their assistance at times against pirates was appreciated.

In the fifteenth century, Okinawa's King Sho Shin, in a fit of pacifism spurred no doubt by threats to his realm, ordered the confiscation of all weapons. These were locked up in his castle at Shuri. This edict, that was severe enough to limit villages to one knife chained to a post, stimulated two major schools.

One was Ryukyu Kobudo that developed very efficient weapons from agricultural tools. Knock the top off a pitchfork, and the pronged weapon developed into the truncheon 'sai'. The shaft, into the roku shaku bo, a near six foot staff used in similar fashion to the English quarter staff. The kama, or sickle, was later to be adopted and adapted by the Japanese into the kusarigama, still practised today by the Shindo Muso Ryu. The tun-fa was a device used primarily as a handle for a millstone and developed into an extension of 'te' movements, the spinning action a very effective defence. There are few masters of the tun-fa today, and the art is in danger of disappearing. This is not helped by worldwide misuse of it as a police baton. The 'nanchaku', a universal hinged wooden flail still used for beating out husks in Asia, was developed into a combat system subordinate to the 'te'.

All of these weapons are not indigenous to Okinawa and have their origins in Southeast Asia, but their means of employment took on distinctive Okinawa characteristics. I recall the first time a bank was robbed in the U.S.A. (where else?) by a villain armed with nanchaku. After being handed the money, the clown couldn't resist giving an impromptu demonstration before he left and subsequently knocked himself out. He awoke later beside a policeman interested in being helped with his enquiry.

'Te' or 'hand', later Okinawa Te, continued to develop even after the Japanese invasion of 1609. The Japanese, knowing a good thing when they saw it, carried on the banning of weapons and allowed the Okinawans the facade of remaining loyal to the Chinese emperor.

Early in the twentieth century, two major styles emerged. 'Shuri te' and 'Tomari te' merged and became known as Shorin Ryu. 'Naha te' later became known as Goju Ryu, a name given by the founder, Miyagi Chojun. The lineal strength of Goju Ryu is underlined by the fact that only two sub schools have formed from it in Japan: Gojukai and Kyokushinkai. 'Shuri te' has formed Shotokan, Wado Ryu, Shito Ryu and scores of splinter groups.

'Te' has always promoted the correct use of great physical strength, and developing maximum strength for each trainee. Hojo undo, supplementary training techniques, were far in advance of modern weight training, and are technique specific today, except perhaps for one. 'Kanshu', or penetration hand, an ancient Chinese training method uses a pot or jar filled with light powder. The student then practises thrusting his hand into the powder which is gradually changed to rice, sand beans and pebbles. There is some evidence that this can affect the nerve ends in the fingers and some suspicions, not backed by evidence, that eyesight can be adversely affected. It is certain that Kanshu is practised now only by a few devotees, probably wearing glasses.

Prior to 1940, combat or sparring was not permitted. Correct training in basics and constant attention to form was considered by the 'te' masters to be sufficient. Historically, competitions between dojo were settled by demonstrations of kata rather than free style fighting. This had the advantage of choosing the superior practitioner without anyone getting injured. It was only after Japanese influence in recent times that Okinawan karate permitted sparring and sport applications. Today many Okinawa masters acknowledge that competition karate has a small place in the development of a student who needs such an outlet. Traditional training has not changed to accommodate it.

The following Goju Ryu supplementary training techniques are reproduced from the Rembuden Institute of Martial Arts and Ways training manual.

The 'Kongoken' (iron ring): introduced by Master Chojun Miyagi this instrument is employed by Goju-ryu stylists. Weighing almost 100 lbs the ring is twisted and pressed in several ways; solo or two-man forms. It is intended to give the feeling of handling the weight of a man, so as to understand offensive balance.

The "Fukushiki" (double Makiwara): a post thicker than usual has a 2' vertical slot sawn down it. This provides a second resistance during the strike, giving feeling for penetration.

The useful moving Makiwara - "Temochishiki": this implement is invaluable for focus against a target moving in various directions. Thus, timing and distance are improved.

The pad, upon which the strikes are made, can be made of straw, leather, or rubber. A straw rope, wound around the post and flattened with a hammer, is the traditional striking surface. It is still regarded as ideal for conditioning the skin on one's hands. A leather pad (often designed to slip over the permanent straw, or rubber pad) tempers the bones of the knuckles. A thin layer of dense rubber is probably the most common surface now. The Okinawans say that it approximates the feel of tensed flesh!

In the past any cuts caused by Makiwara practice were treated with slices of 'Rugai' which is a cactus-like plant. Nowadays, it is usual to supply mercurochrome.

The 'To' (bamboo bundle): before kick-bags were introduced into Okinawa the 'To' fulfilled many of the requirements of this implement. A sturdy central post was sunk into the ground, then bamboo evenly distributed around it, forming a thick bundle. A leather sheet was fastened around the central portion to act as a striking area, and to distribute the force into the bamboos. Full power hand and foot attacks were unleashed upon the 'To' from static or mobile postures. The apparatus was particularly utilised for the training of 'furi-geri' a swing-kick which was the forerunner of the modern 'Mawashi-geri' (roundhouse kick).

The "Makiwara" (striking post): this is, without doubt, the central tool of karate conditioning. It is a common misconception to regard the 'Makiwara' as a device for producing hardened and enlarged knuckles. These characteristic callouses are merely the external indication that such training has taken place; the real value is to the wrist and elbow joints and the muscles of the armpit, chest and back. The 'Makiwara' is essential, too, for the 'feel' of a technique, to absorb the recoil and to vary the depth of 'Kime' (focus).

Several types of 'Makiwara' exist. The "Tanshiki" or 'simple' model which is the kind found in dojos the world over. Lunge and reverse punches, elbow strikes, back fists and knife hands should all be practised on this post, from a variety of stances. The post should be firmly embedded in the ground, so that the top is at chest height. In Okinawa dojo it is usually the job of the new student to dig holes for the 'Makiwara', as the powerful thrusts eventually break even the best posts! A native wood 'shi-ja' is the best, having terrific resilience.

The 'Tan' (barbell): this is similar to a modern barbell, but has either metal or stone weights, with a wooden stock. This stock is quite thick, which enables the 'Tan' to be rolled along the arms to condition the blocking edges. The 'Tan' is also used for conventional weight-training exercises, e.g. squats (especially in straddle stance), curls and vertical presses.

The 'Udekitae' (arm tempering post): this device is a thick round post (usually a length of young tree trunk) firmly embedded into the ground, with two longitudinal slots which cut the post into quarters. Blocks are performed on it in order to condition the forearms and wrists. Such attacks as 'Empi' (elbow), 'Shotei' (palm-heel) and 'Shuto' (knife hand) can be very effectively used on the 'Udekitae' as the round section is similar to a human skull.

The "Chi'ishi" (strength-stone): the 'Chi'ishi' strengthens the arms, shoulders, abdomen and stance for a variety of techniques. Known also as 'Chikara-ishi' the 'strength stone' is based on the principle of leverage. Grasping the wooden shaft at one end the user rotates lifts and presses the device in various ways. The leverage of the stone weight at the other end of the shaft concentrates the force upon the wrists, and isolates the muscles, tendons and joints used in specific exercise. Set routines are highly related to the demands of karate, especially blocking techniques. Breathing and tensing methods are incorporated into 'Chi'ishi' work for added efficiency. Most 'Chi'ishi' exercises involve finishing in a strong straddle stance, which further benefits the exponent.

The "Sashi" (thrusting stone): used in pairs the 'Sashi' assists the user in achieving a powerful punch. Particularly utilised by those styles having 'Sanchin' kata, the two 'Sashi' are held in a Kamae, then alternate left/right Sanchin thrusts and withdrawals are performed. The device can also be hooked through the foot to practice slow-motion stamping kicks to the front, rear and sides.

The most characteristic factor distinguishing Okinawan karate is its emphasis on physical power. Much of Okinawa Goju Ryu was adapted from Chinese "Chu'an-fa" from Fukien Province which itself has a heavy reliance on applied force and conditioning methods. The rigours of the feudal times, particularly following the Satsuma Invasion of 1609, necessitated karate's employment as a strictly combat art with the central principle - "one punch to kill".

To condition the body and achieve powerful technique Goju Ryu uses a variety of methods, including solo exercises, two-man routines and the use of supplementary equipment. Traditionally, wood and stone provide the materials for karate equipment, as the old masters liked to test themselves against natural objects. A wide range of devices exist for the practitioner to choose from which fit his particular needs. Such implements as the 'Makiwara' (striking -post), 'Chi'ishi' (strength-stone), 'kame' (jars), 'Kan-shu' (sand/gravel pail), 'Kongoken' (iron ring), 'To' (bamboo bundle) and 'Sashi' (thrusting-stone) have specialised uses applicable to different aspects of technique.

Specialised equipment for a strong grip: a powerful grip is considered an undoubted asset by the Okinawans. Whether used defensively, to catch an opponent's arm, or leg, after blocking his punches, or kicks; or offensively, to attack throat or groin, several methods exist to increase the potential of this stratagem.

Weighted jars, known as 'kame' are a vital requisite for an effective grip. These are lifted, either empty, or with sand or metal-inserts to give increased weight, and the wrists turned from side to side. Often, a special grip excluding the thumb is used to isolate the fingers, thus subjecting them to added stress. Stepping forward and back in stances is practised with the 'kame' with emphasis on the shoulders being properly down and back.

A simple stone of suitable size, as can be found on Okinawa beaches, is used to hold and grip. Known as 'Nigiri-ishi' (grip stone) emphasis is based on a uniform clenching action involving all the fingers. The stone can also be thrown from hand to hand and caught.

Identical to a modern wrist-roller, the 'Makiage-gu' develops grip, wrist area and forearms. A wooden shaft about forty-five centimetres long, is held between outstretched arms at shoulder height. A cord is attached to the wood, with an iron or stone weight on the end. Rotating the shaft raises then lowers the stone. Some types are fixed to a wall-rack.

A particularly practical training method involves suspending a small canvas bag of pebbles at about face height. The bag is thrust away with a Nukite (spear hand) thrust, and then intercepted on the return swing with a grasping technique.

Some trainees may feel encouraged to add some conditioning routines to their workouts. If so, certain points should be noted. Always start within your capabilities. If using 'Chi'ishi', for example, select a size which enables you to do at least ten continuous repetitions of each exercise. Regarding the 'Makiwara', don't overdo it on the first day and be unable to strike it on the next day. Train so that daily 'Makiwara' striking is possible. Concentrate fully with all equipment; in this way you will get more out of your workout. With all practice involving weights or resistance training, beware of pulled ligaments, etc. Make steady progress from a modest beginning.

Most of the above equipment can be quite easily fabricated with time, imagination and effort. Moulds for Chi'ishi', for example, can be found by using large cake-tins or plant pots. Filled with concrete around a suitable wooden shaft they make ideal examples. 'Makiwara' are no real problem to build, providing a suitable space is available. A rubber sandal makes a good pad.

To assist those considering making equipment and trying out the Okinawa conditioning methods the approximate weights of the various implements are as follows: Chi'ishi: ten pounds minimum and twenty-two pounds maximum; kame: seven pounds empty; Kongoken: ninety-five pounds; Sashi: ten pounds; Tan: fifty pounds.

The most significant aspect of Conditioning Training is that it extends the limits of ones ability. Some devices, like the 'Chi'ishi',

'Sashi' and the 'kame' provide a sort of series of slow, relentless barriers to progress, each overcome only by gritting ones teeth and enduring. Other aids, such as various 'Makiwara', 'To', 'Udekitae' and the two-man 'Kotekitae' exercise enable the practitioner to go all out in the practice of his techniques. Nothing must be held back on these training aids. Total power must be released, for it is only by continual maximum output that one can push back the parameters of power and prowess.

My retraining time in Japan was over. There had been little time to train in iaido or jodo. I had been staying with Phil Relnick and his family and Phil, being a seventh dan, ensured I did some jo training in the morning, but most of my energies had to be channelled into Goju Ryu. Sensei Higaonna rewarded my efforts somewhat by regrading me third dan and I returned to New Zealand with the challenge of 'converting' the organisation to Goju Ryu.

The strain of the extra work proved too much for my family life. Maureen and I separated and I was left with two sons – aged four and six – to raise, to prepare the organisation for Sensei Higaonna's first visit the following year and to complete a diploma in Physical Education. Perhaps, fortunately, this left no time to worry.

The two full time students who studied at Honbu dojo over the next two years made it all possible. Disciplining my two boys wasn't a problem. I returned home one day to see one of them being held off the 1st floor balcony by his ankle, until he agreed to behave.

Sensei Higaonna's visit to New Zealand was a complete success. Those harbouring any doubts about changing to Goju Ryu had them dispelled by Sensei both as a wonderful person, and as a top exponent of his art. Several branch dojo which had decided to stay Kyokushinkai asked to be reinstated after meeting Higaonna Sensei.

CHAPTER NINE | 231

It was Australia's turn next. Aubrey had been terrifying his troops for months prior to the visit. They were prepared for a thousand kick basic warm-up; they got two thousand. Afterwards in a sauna Aub said it all,

"I wonder if you can be so sore that you die?"

Sensei indicated that he would like me to sit another grading test. The place he selected was unusual. Beacon Hill overlooked Newcastle's wonderful beaches that improved as they stretched southwards. There were only four people there when we assembled in the early morning: Sensei, Aubrey, Peter Oberecker and I. An inshore sea breeze kept the air cool before the sun rose to drain everything of energy.

Uneven ground is a great leveller; I recalled seeing an accomplished tennis player defeated on an uneven court. He had been anticipating where the ball should be while the novice waited until the ball bounced before he looked and hit it.

The steps in kata had to be adjusted to allow for the changing terrain, but in free fighting it can be used to advantage. The free fighting test was simple: I was to fight Aubrey and Peter at the same time. Knowing Sensei, this could go on for over an hour.

The grass area of Beacon Hill ended with a steep drop of over thirty metres down to the access road. Aubrey, true to his domineering spirit, charged in to attack, head down, the only thing missing being horns. Peter hovered vulture-like, to take advantage of any favourable outcome. Moving back to the edge, I grabbed Aub sumo style and pivoted. Aubrey, being built like a battle cruiser and taking about as long to stop, dropped over the edge with a bellow. Peter looked decidedly uncomfortable at having me all to himself while Aubrey began the long drag back up the hillside. By the time he arrived, mostly out of breath, the grading was over. I suspect Sensei had tired of keeping a straight face.

There was no let up in training when we arrived in Canberra. Sensei was obviously out to make a point. After one long and grueling session, Sensei had everyone relaxed and sitting cross-legged while he gave advice on training. Sensei managed quite well in English, but needed some help from me now and then with some phrases. For some strange reason, Peter Oberecker thought it necessary to translate from Kiwi to Australian. The students got the message three ways.

Sensei: "You must not forget to do daily stretching exercises to avoid damaging your ... ?"

Me: "Tendons and ligaments."

Peter: "Avoid damaging tendons and ligaments."

Sensei: "Practice with the chi'ishi will ensure your wrists become strong along with these muscles?"

Me: "Latisimus dorsi and deltoids."

Peter: "Strengthen your lats and deltoids."

Sensei: "If your muscles are sore after training, after a hot bath give them a ... ?"

Me: "Massage."

Peter: "Sensei will give everyone a massage after training." There was a stunned silence; there were over sixty students present.

"Erm, I think Sensei meant that you should do it yourself," I put in quietly. Peter decided to go out of the translation business.

For recreation, Sensei and I were taken for a picnic beside the lake. The thought of lazing around for a few hours was quite foreign to Sensei, who decided we should rent some paddle boats. These were two small two-seater fiberglass affairs propelled by side paddles. The motive power was provided by two sets of rotating pedals.

Aubrey, always at the forefront of everything, decided to go with Sensei to protect him from unknown natural hazards. Now, Aubrey's weight does not quite match that of Sensei's, so as a result that craft took a dangerous list Aubside. Unperturbed, they both paddled away happily.

The Queen had graciously gifted a fountain for the capital's lake. Ungrateful Australians grumbled about its running costs, but that day it turned on its majestic splendour. Jets of water spurted hundreds of feet into the air and the base was shrouded peacock-like by smaller sprays. Because of their list, Aubrey and Sensei were headed straight for it. Fearing the worst, I and crew mate tried to intercept, but a strange feature of the rubber paddles was that if too much power was provided, they curled, and the craft slowed down. Dismayed, we could only watch while Aubrey and Sensei curved in towards the fountain, and disappeared under what seemed to be tons of water. I could already see the headlines: "World's Top Karate Master Disappears in Boating Mishap."

It seemed to take an eternity to paddle to the fountain. As we approached it, there appeared from the opposite side a sodden craft and two laughing occupants who had the gall to challenge us to a race back to shore. We, suffering from a severe loss of adrenalin, came second.

The first Goju Ryu International Gasshuku held in Okinawa brought together, for the first time, exponents from all over the world. Most members had never met each other, so it was an important social occasion. At the time I had an unsympathetic bank manager so I stayed at home to watch another great martial event, the 1981 Springbok Rugby tour.

The New Zealand team was impressed by the depth of the international organisation, and the level of skill of the senior ranks, both Japanese and foreigners. Elderly masters who were senior students of Miyagi Chojun inspired everyone. The displays of traditional Okinawa Te and Kobudo gave the visitors some insight as to how martial traditions are a way of life for Okinawans. Unlike in Japan where only devotees practise, in Okinawa almost everybody practises karate. It is as commonplace as rugby is in New Zealand.

One student arrived at a well known dojo and waited around for a training session to begin. None did. Senior and junior students alike wandered in to train for whatever length of time they had available, then wandered out again. Disappointed, about to lose patience and leave, he noticed an old man with a hacking smoker's cough slowly make his way towards the Hojo Undo equipment. Fascinated, he decided to stay and watch.

The old man lit up a cigarette (not allowed in the dojo area proper), gave a raucous cough that would give a thoracic surgeon nightmares and wandered over to the kame jars. He put his cigarette on a the charred edges of bench, which suggested that this wasn't the first time, bent down and grasped the tops of the jars. Standing upright, his back rigid and keeping his arms locked straight, he raised first one jar almost to the horizontal position at right angle to his body then the other. He took time out to nod and smile at his one man audience, take a drag on his foul smelling cigarette (followed by another hacking cough) and then resume working on the kame jars. After twenty minutes and two more cigarettes he gave a departing rasp, slapped his chest vigorously, smiled again at the young man and departed. The young student walked over to the jars; he couldn't lift them. They were three quarters filled with sand. It was almost enough to make one take up smoking.

Somewhat surprisingly, the gasshuku ended with a tournament. Politics became part of Goju Ryu when the Japanese Government prevented the strong South African contingent from participating.

CHAPTER NINE | 235

Back in New Zealand, Rembuden's rear entrance opened onto a road that was a pedestrian access to rugby's Athletic Park. Anti Springbok Tour supporters lined the route determined to give rugby supporters a hard time. Police, many of them ousted from behind office desks, watched the Anti-Tour supporters, determined to uphold law and order, and we watched all of them in case any melee spilled onto our property. Some of the anti's sat on our fence for a better view.

"Could you please get off the fence and go somewhere else."

"Why?"

"Because we have longer batons than the police." It was taken in good humour, and they moved on.

Observing our small corner of the nationwide disturbance, it seemed that for many of the demonstrators (genuine ones excepted) this was perhaps the one chance in their life to do something dangerous. They could dress up protectively, defy authority, and occasionally run the risk of being hit. I had seen the same look in the eyes of soccer fans in London. They made a poor comparison with the Zenkaguren in Tokyo.

The New Zealand team came home with a wealth of experiences. Rembuden now felt a valued part of the International Goju Ryu organisation. We began planning for the next Gasshuku in Washington State, U.S.A.

Our small branch in Suva, Fiji had been requesting a visit for some time. I decided to combine teaching with a holiday and take my two sons. Fiji agreed to pay half the cheap airfares, teaching fees were waived.

We landed at the Suva airport, walked out of the plane and into an oven; it was the wrong time of the year to visit, hence the airfares. Despite the late hour, everyone had wonderful smiles, but no-one seemed to be doing anything. After a delay we cleared customs, were met by a pleasant young man, and driven by taxi to our hotel. Our hotel in Suva had seen better times when plantation managers and remittance men had used it as a far flung outpost of the Empire. Today all the good hotels are down on the waterfront, with swimming pools plus hot and cold running waitresses.

The room we were ushered into had no windows; only an opaque skylight. The solid concrete walls had yellowed with age; brown water stains left by ancient hurricanes patterned their surface. A nineteenth century ceiling fan converted to electricity dominated the ceiling. My two lads complained that they couldn't breathe; I took the chance and switched it on. A spark spat at me, there was a few seconds delay, and then slowly the blades began to rotate. Unfortunately the apparatus was unbalanced and as it worked itself up into frenzy, bits of plaster began to flake off the ceiling. We gave up, and tried to sleep in the humid still air.

Some time later, when I was about to drift off, I was awoken by a muffled sound. The sound was vaguely familiar, but there was something about it that was not quite right. It came to me as I became wide awake. The sound was that of flesh being hit. What was wrong was that it carried on repeatedly with no respite. Loud voices shouting in Fijian but muffled by the walls provided no answer; the muted sounds of rock music did; we were next to the back entrance of a night club. The sound of a body falling, thrown down the stairs was followed by a brief period of silence, then it started all over again. The bouncer was obviously earning his money that night. Next morning we insisted on, and got, a room with a window and safe air conditioning at the other end of the hotel.

For the next few days we led a Jekyll and Hyde existence: eating wonderful salads and fruits at the Travel Lodge down by the seaside, and only going to the Hotel to sleep.

Rounding up students to attend training reminded me of the film 'The Magnificent Seven' based on Kurosaura's 'Seven Samurai'. I would be collected at the hotel by a senior rank from where we would begin our walk down the streets of Suva. As we passed the tailor's shop a member would stop his work, pick up his gi and join us. At the next street as we passed the window of an appliance store, another member grabbed his bag and hurried out to join us. And so it went on, all that was missing was the theme song, so I hummed it to myself as we collected our karate club.

The local dojo was too small for all the members to train at once, so we trained on a field, which was fine, as long as you didn't step on the frogs.

Being isolated for so long the general standard was not so good; a lot of hard work had to be put into the basics.

At the end of the training, a farewell party was held at the house of one of the black belts. I was presented with the traditional gifts of kava bowl and tapa. During the 'thank-you' speech I was informed with regret that the club could not honour its commitment to pay their share of the air fare: they were broke. It must have been true, because months later I received irate letters then phone calls informing me that the hotel bill had not been settled.

Feeling somewhat embarrassed, two of the members offered to obtain for me a mini stereo set that were all the rage then, at the best possible price. True to their word, I was taken to a shop owned by their friend, who sold me a set at close to wholesale. It was a 'Sencor', made in Switzerland under a Japanese license, which just goes to show how far Japan was advanced. I was to pay more for the set later in New Zealand.

Auckland customs had a flap on; there must have been a drugs tip-off, because everybody was being checked, down to prodding tins of tobacco. A jumbo landed behind us and crowds backed up through the terminal. Tempers were becoming frayed. When it came to our turn, the Customs' Officer looked at the stereo, still in unopened cartons.

"Have you got a receipt for this, sir?" he asked, checking my declaration form. "Are you sure this is the correct receipt, sir?" He looked unconvinced.

"Yes, it says so there, Sencor mini system." He checked his list of stereo sets and prices; Sencor wasn't listed, so he grew more suspicious.

"I'm afraid you can't buy a Swiss stereo set at that price."

"Well, I did get a very special deal."

"I'm sure you did, sir. Would you please come this way?" We zipped up the bags and followed him to an office, where a senior customs officer quizzed me all over again. It came down to the fact they would not accept the receipt I offered.

"We will have to hold the set in bond until you can prove to us that was the purchase price," the senior of the two told me.

"That's an imposition," I objected, "We are travelling on to Wellington." The officer sighed and tried a new line of arguing.

"How did you buy it so cheaply?"

"I was teaching karate there on a tourist visa which, as you know, prohibits working for remuneration."

"Can you prove that?" I was saved, and produced several newspaper cuttings. The officers became conciliatory, and explained that many people these days were obtaining two receipts, one specifically for the customs.

CHAPTER NINE | 239

They did have the last laugh, however, and charged me 100% duty. They didn't accept credit cards then, so I had to make a special trip into Auckland to arrange the cash. It turned out to be an expensive holiday.

The Government was keen to bring together all the different factions of martial arts under one umbrella organisation. A Martial Arts' Forum was set up by the Council for Recreation and Sport to bring the diverse groups together, Government funding for a united organisation was the carrot. Human nature being what it is, people whose philosophy differed and hadn't spoken to each other in years found themselves in the same room competing for a financial share.

The Rembuden organisation had two strong reservations. One was the 'grandfather' clause, which allowed anyone presently operating, whether they had genuine qualifications or not, to join with standards set and agreed to for future admissions. The other was that if the Government paid the money, they could quite rightly dictate how the funds should be used. The concern was to know the extent of this and how much interference could we expect within our martial arts/sports. The question was:

"Would the price be too high?" We decided to find out.

We had a long standing invitation to visit South Africa and, although we had no plans at that stage to tour the republic, it would be strategic to know what would happen if we did. Find out we did. Details were leaked to a local newspaper reporter, and the headlines shouted,

"Karate Kiwis to Chop Gleneagles in South Africa."

At first the results were as expected, the Minister of Foreign Affairs wrote to us in accordance with the Gleneagles agreement, explaining the implications of sporting contacts with South Africa. The chairman of Halt all Racist Tours condemned the tour and said,

"But there are words to describe people who are paid for their favours." (One of our members had to be restrained from visiting a few favours gratis on him.)

The T.V. front man seemed immune to it all when he arrived at the dojo.

"Here we go again, same old questions and answers, hope you don't mind?" I didn't mind.

A university professor with some Maori blood launched a campaign to have a tapu (ban) on South African money; he had earlier asked Maori rugby players to impose a rahui (a ban on themselves).

A parent of one of the pupils at St Patrick's College questioned my right to teach at the school, and talk back hosts kept the telephone busy.

The news media were generally fair in their coverage and published some of the points I felt should be made. Karate in South Africa had always been non racial. It's difficult to discriminate against your Japanese master, even if you do make him an 'honorary white'; he would not accept segregation of students. Many of the senior members in dojo in South Africa were coloured or black. Would we be discriminating against people in South Africa who had always fought against apartheid by not sending a team? Was New Zealand being targeted because we are small enough to pick on? A French rugby team had recently completed a tour of the Republic and France did not have to withdraw any ambassadors for consultation, and there was the question of African countries trading with South Africa. Apparently it is all right to make a buck out of them, but not to play with them.

Finally the chairman of the Martial Arts Council condemned the tour and recommended it be stopped. Big Brother had spoken.

The problem for them was that Rembuden was not a member of the council and now would not be. Other larger organisations got the word and also declined to join. The council was not to be a success.

A tour to South Africa would not take place until 1985. Before then we were to attend the third international Gasshuku in Spokane, Washington.

"Why Spokane?" someone asked; its only claim to fame being the birthplace of Bing Crosby. The reason was Chinen Teruo, an Okinawan, who had arrived to conduct a three month karate class, and had stayed on for ten years to become the western hemisphere director and number two Goju Ryu Sensei out of Japan. He was later suspended from the International Federation for trying too hard to become number one.

We had arrived from New Zealand by a roundabout route to take advantage of the U.S. internal airfare price wars via San Francisco, Los Angeles and Salt Lake City. Spokane was a good place in the U.S.A. to be in; the people were laid back and friendly and always went out of their way to be hospitable. All visitors were instantly recognised; we were the only ones walking.

Training was held in the gymnasium of Grant Elementary School; it could only just hold 150 people from ten countries. The world class gathering was kept low key by intentionally maintaining a distance from the public in an area that barely provide room for the participants. The training was as intense as I have ever experienced, leaving little time for socialising.

When there was a little time, the New Zealand and South African teams seemed inextricably drawn together. South Africa suggested a 'friendly' game of rugby; I found excuses partly because of Gleneagles, and for the most part their scrum would have twice our size and weight.

One of the highlights for the New Zealand team was the grading of John Marrable from Shodan to Nidan. The exceptional part about the training was that John couldn't walk. A paraplegic since a fall down a hillside when he was eleven, John had never been given (or expected) any favours and had joined in all training sessions only substituting punches for kicking training. He used his wheelchair as a weapon whenever possible, and on more than one occasion somebody had threatened to let his tyres down after nursing a bruised shin. Some students at the grading were overly cautious when throwing jabs and kicks at him, but Higaonna Sensei ordered,

"No sympathy."

Sensei was impressed that John had substantially developed muscles in his upper body since attending the last Gasshuku in Okinawa. His success was an example to all people in wheelchairs who refuse to be thought as of second class citizens.

In the few days we had for sightseeing we were overwhelmed by American hospitality. I have always found an American on his or her home ground to be a most hospitable and generous person; the few who do not export well are mostly responsible for their poor reputation overseas.

A visit to the "Veterans of Foreign Wars Club" proved so embarrassing we avoided our promised return the next night. We had not been allowed to pay for any food or drink all night.

I had to stop at a gun shop while I was there, and I was not disappointed. A sign over the door read "Register communists, not guns". Inside was an array of ordnance from .22 Saturday night specials up to war surplus rocket launchers, presided over by two ventricose characters who believed citizens should protect themselves by shooting attackers dead.

"They didn't re-offend."

They gladly showed me around the displays, informing me,

"We can't sell to non residents; it's against federal law." Wink wink.

The gun laws in Washington State were strict. They included a waiting period between ordering and uplifting while the purchaser was checked out by police, a law not introduced federally until the Bradt Law ten years later.

Driving over the border into Idaho, a little later, guns could be found scattered around on display tables at fairs and could be purchased with no questions asked. One young lad who was with us poked a vicious looking .357 magnum with his finger, as if it might go off on its own.

"Pick 'er up," invited the vendor, amused at the reticence.

That weapons were a part of life for many American citizens, was reflected when one of our team shared a lift at our hotel with two well-dressed businessmen.

"Got your piece?" asked one, as if it was an everyday article like a wallet or a key ring.

"Yep," replied the other, patting his shoulder holster. They were going out for an evening on the town.

A stop at Honolulu did wonders for some bodies, although several other holiday makers looked suspiciously at the bruises many of us were carrying.

"Football team?" asked the bartender.

"Bouncers convention," I replied. He nodded sympathetically.

The South African problem would not go away. When I returned home I received a call from the Department of Education.

"There were South Africans attending the event in Washington," he accused. Did we have a mole in our organisation?

"They did not compete in the competition," I replied, quite truthfully.

"Well, I suppose that's all right then."

Chapter Ten

Donn Draeger had organised an international jodo Gasshuku in Taiping, Malaysia. Members would be attending from as far away as Europe and the United States and as my technique was sorely in need of improvement, I was glad to be able to take up the invitation.

Travel was via Auckland to Singapore by Singapore Airlines and the flight was one of the best I have been on. To be fair the aircraft was only half full but the service was excellent. They seemed to have more cabin staff than other airlines and French wine and cognac is not usually available on economy class. For some strange reason my travel agent had booked me into the Mandarin Hotel for the one night. It was an unnecessary extravagance but at least it was kept clear of predatorial pimps and sales agents.

I was leaving for Taiping early the next morning so I presented myself at the Emperor's Room Restaurant at 6:30pm. The place was empty, and didn't really, "Come alive until very late,"

I was told by a waitress who must have been short-listed for Miss Singapore. I dined in imperial solitary splendour like an emperor; you would have needed to be an emperor to buy imported wine.

"Try some dry Chinese white wine," she suggested then, noticing my reluctance.

"If you don't like it there will be no charge." It was most acceptable and complemented the fine Cantonese dishes that I chose.

I didn't have time to appreciate the expensive room, falling asleep as soon as I flopped into bed.

The train journey to Taiping was interesting but too long, a sort of once only event made bearable by air-conditioning and the wonderful array of cheap chilled exotic fruit juices.

Taiping station was small and I had called ahead advising of my arrival time but as I waited around watching all the taxis being fought over I realised there must have been a mix up. There is nothing lonelier than being by yourself on a foreign railway station. I looked about and saw that, perhaps, I wasn't.

One Pedi cab driver, rejected by the departed crowds, stood hopefully by his machine like a dog wanting a kind word from his master. His age could have been anywhere from sixty years to a Guinness Book record; his stooped body looked frail apart from his legs with calf muscles knotted out of proportion. He would have weighed seventy pounds wringing wet. His Pedi cab must have been passed down through his family: a fixed wheel, no gears and a canvas awning made from material left behind from the invasion (the Portuguese one). The only modern piece of equipment was a parasol folded and tucked into a cavalry holster.

He knew he had me; I was too tired even to negotiate the fare.

"Where to, misir?"

"The hotel."

"Which hotel, misir?"

"The best one in Taiping."

"Okay, okay," he laughed and helped me into his machine and then stacked my suitcases, one on my feet, the other on my lap. Because of the canopy I had to hold the joo in its cover out on an angle like Don Quixote looking for a windmill. I feared we would never reach take off speed. I was wrong. He pushed the contraption until it started rolling then leaped onto the pedals and, standing up, leaned first to the left then to the right for maximum pedal weight. The grass started to pass by. He was lucky Taiping is flat; he would have starved in Hong Kong. We arrived at the hotel entrance which was choked with Mercedes and Morris Oxford taxis that don't exist in any other country apart from in museums. He found a gap and delivered me, smiling through the rivulets of sweat. To add to the embarrassment everyone stopped to look as I tried, with what little dignity that was left, to untangle myself and pay the outrageous fare. A porter finally took pity on me and, trying to keep a straight face, helped me inside with my bags. I stayed in my room until hopefully a new shift came on.

When I arrived at the King Edward School, Donn was all apologetic; they had met the wrong train. Training started immediately. I found myself the subject of some attention; students who had exclusively studied under Shimizu Sensei were becoming rare.

One of the formalities of many of the classical budo is that senior ranks never line up facing the students, the one spot in the middle of the dojo is reserved for the head of the Ryu. Instead, senior ranks line up at right angles to the right hand side of the front line. The turning point, rank wise, depends on the number and how high the ranks are. There may be a third and a fourth dan, in Taiping it was an eighth and a sixth dan. To make matters a little more complicated seniority can take precedence over rank, therefore a third dan who is senior both in age and in years of training will be invited to stand out at the end of the line ahead of younger fourth of fifth dan. This is now carefully explained to all students after a foreigner caused a major upset at Rembukan in Tokyo by refusing to stand to the left of a junior ranked but senior member of the dojo. I was made to feel quite ancient by being bustled in a light hearted manner towards the end of the line.

In training my timing was out but came right very quickly. Donn had done an excellent job of training the Malaysian students, many of whom were of Chinese and Indian descent. Later he took one of his senior students back to Japan where he completely dominated the Japanese, whose technique had become weaker after the death of Shimizu Sensei. This did not endear Donn to the new hierarchy in Shin do Muso Ryu.

My jo, the one which had given me all the trouble going through Customs, the same one they suspected of being a new kind of hijack weapon, was of great interest to the locals. They all wanted to look at the maker's mark on the end. This type of jo is no longer available.

I had no sooner settled in to enjoy the training and the restaurants of Taiping than I was given a rude awakening: an invitation to take a Nidan grading on completion of the Gasshuku. I began to try too hard, and my technique suffered. Donn's only encouragement was to smile and shake his head. Somehow I got it together on the day and passed. My partner for the grading, a Swiss who had spent many years in Japan, made an interesting comment afterwards.

"Your style reminds me vaguely of what used to be in Japan but is now suppressed." Perhaps being isolated in New Zealand has its advantages.

CHAPTER TEN | 249

We had a good send off at the completion of the camp. Being Muslim, there was no alcohol allowed at the school so we adjourned to the ubiquitous Chinese restaurant.

It was the last time I was to see Donn. Sadly he died a few years later. His contribution to Westerners' understanding of Japanese martial arts can never be overestimated; thankfully much of it is published.

On leaving Malaysia at Penang airport I noted that the authorities left none in doubt about their drug laws. "The maximum penalty for dealing in drugs is death," painted in large letters above the entrance hall.

Donn's interest in studying the weapons' systems of South East Asia caused me to become involved in a bizarre series of events that could do justice to a full length novel.

He had already made several tours of Malaysia, Indonesia and the Philippines but still needed some more information on some of the lesser known systems in the Philippines. He had given me several contacts there, should I visit the country before he did. I had previously sent him information on Maori and Fijian weapons for his thesis on hoplology.

Two well known Wellington businessmen had been involved in promoting the successful tour to New Zealand of Mohammed Ali. An Auckland accountant also associated with the tour, put before them a proposition to invest in a mining venture in the Philippines. Subsequently, they began to raise funds locally, and I made a modest investment, despite my solicitor advising me,

"You will be throwing money into the ground and not pulling it out!" The great idea of the time was that the investment would give me an excuse to visit the country and claim a tax write off as well.

I was interested to make comparisons between the Japanese 'Tanjo' (stick) and the Philippine 'Baston' used in the arnis system. There had been several migrations of Malays to the Philippines but it was the third migration from the start of the fourteenth century until the middle of the fifteenth that introduced stick weapons. Pigaletta mentions in his records that on the island of Mactan where Magellan was killed, natives carried a short hardwood stick hardened by fire and used in combat. It was called a 'Takak'.

There are many similarities between the fighting systems of the Philippines being suppressed by Spanish colonisation and the Okinawa systems under the Japanese during a similar time in history.

The best known fighting system in the Philippines today is 'arnis de mano' or 'hardness of hand'. It is thought the term came from the Spanish word arnis which described the fittings or 'harness' used by 'Moro-Moro' actors and 'De Mano' meaning hands. What the conquistadors did not realise as they sat about in their finery, completely unsuitable for the tropics, and sipped wine, which hadn't travelled well, was that the intricate hand movements were martial art skills. The word was corrupted to arnis and is believed incorrectly, even amongst some Philippinos, to be a Spanish system introduced by the invaders. In other regions it is known by other Spanish names 'Estocada' and 'Astoque'.

The systems Donn was interested in were the single stick (solo Baston) used by the Pangasinense, Batangas and the Viajevos from Macabebe and the two stick system, 'Sinawali'. The movements of the two Mutan is said to resemble the bamboo-rush weave patterns used as matting by the natives. The mats and walled coverings were called 'Sinwali'. The sticks are slightly longer than the Japanese Tanjo, about thirty one inches in length and one inch in diameter. The Illecanos use the longest 'Muton'.

CHAPTER TEN | 251

Arnis uses hand and arm actions including feints. Trainees practise offensive and defensive swinging movements, striking and thrusting in set forms similar to Japanese kata and free practice where pairs attempt to outdo one another without the use of protective armour. Main targets are the wrist or hand if the attacker is armed; any of the body's weak points if not.

Training similar to Japanese Zanchin is given where trainees have to practise staring at an opponent's head for long periods without blinking. Like 'Zanchin', an expert can mentally reach out and grab his opponent's mind and dominate it. I had to agree with an old boxer, who once told me,

"Never watch his eyes; he can't hit you with his eyes."

I was told to expect some resistance from experts. Although 'arnis' today is regarded as a self defence discipline, traditionally the best styles were secret and training practised in out of the way places. I was looking forward to discovering if experts today still retained and practised traditional methods, or whether, as in other countries, arnis was becoming sport and contest oriented.

The two Wellington businessmen had arrived in Manila with their lawyer to meet with principals and to discuss the investment. A new company, 'Philzeal', had been formed and registered in Hong Kong. There wasn't much they didn't know about business in English speaking countries but they had a lot to learn about doing business Philippine style. All the business people they had dealt with had President Marcos as their ideal and faithfully copied his business practices; everyone had to be paid.

The mine site was in the province of Zambales known as the 'House of Chromite', about 350 kilometres north of Manila, the nearest town being Santa Cruz. Encouraged by good assay reports of fifty percent Cro23, they decided to check out the market for Chromite. South Africa and Russia were the big players internationally. Having their own geologist, they made an appointment with a 'professor' not averse to private consultancy fees.

The previous night had been a heavy one. It had started pleasantly enough in the bar of the Hyatt Hotel but had gone sour with the arrival of a flashily dressed young man, complete with bodyguards. The bodyguards' gaudy shirts did not conceal the bumps on the back of their trouser belts that indicated firearms. The spoiled young man was obviously used to being the centre of attention; dominating the waiters time and attentions, and insisting the band play the songs he requested. It all got too much for the New Zealanders.

"We want a little service around here too, you know," said one.

"And we didn't pay that band to play someone else's requests," added the other. The bar manager looked alarmed and whispered into a telephone. The bodyguards took up a position where they could either dispense a beating or have a clear line of fire. The hotel manager arrived, took in the situation and hurried across to their table.

"You must leave the hotel now, please," he turned and smiled at the scouting bodyguards and indifferent young man who was picking his teeth with a gold toothpick. They decided to leave, ignoring the smirks from the bodyguards.

"Who is that little prick anyway?" one asked the concierge, who looked apprehensive.

"That is Bong Bong, sir."

"Who?"

"President Marcos' son, sir." He accepted the ten peso note and bundled them into a taxi of unknown manufacture.

CHAPTER TEN | 253

The next morning, feeling somewhat the effects of San Miguel beer, cigarette smoke and cognac, they grabbed one of several sample rocks and headed off to see the professor. The professor was a shrewd, dry little man with a face that resembled the material he studied. He listened patiently while they expounded the proposals and when they had finished, politely asked for a sample. They proudly presented the rock.

"This isn't chromite, it's zinc." They had grabbed the wrong rock!

Trying to tie something up legally in the Philippines is an exercise in patience and frustration. Lawyers had to be paid along with judges, government officials, agents and the 'New People's Army'. At the end of ten days, hundreds of thousands of dollars had disappeared into claims that didn't exist; 'rights' that were wrong and contracts that were useless. The final financial crunch came with the bill for the ten days at the Philippines Plaza: U.S $23,800. At least one of the pair were still philosophical about the country,

"What can you expect after three hundred years in a Spanish monastery and fifty years of Hollywood?"

They returned to New Zealand, resolved to try again. The Reserve Bank didn't consider the mining venture to be New Zealand's answer to its rising overseas debt. The request for overseas funds was denied so 'other' methods were used. The unofficial exchange rate for New Zealand dollars overseas carried a heavy discount rate.

The timing of all this dealing in cash was unfortunate. This was the time of the 'Mr Asia' drug trials and scandals. Two well to do New Zealand businessmen travelling between New Zealand, Australia and Asia with large amounts of cash and a lifestyle that would attract the attention of any revenue agent, soon became an entry in the computer of Interpol. They could not at first understand why they were always singled out for individual attention, including body searches every time they passed through customs. The wife of one of them, not known as a placid person, finally had enough at one airport, whipped off her high heeled shoe and threatened to skull any of the stunned officers who came near her.

This brought things to a head in more ways than one. Lawyers, Police and Customs Officers were consulted and, with the threat of legal action, the computer entry was 'erased'. The two remained under close visual scrutiny.

Finally, an option on a mine site was taken up with the assistance of a multi millionaire dealer in machinery from Quezon City. For supplying the machinery to get the mine up and running, he charged a twenty percent share in the company. Labour was not a problem; US $1.00 a day was above award rates.

It was a fifteen hour journey to the mine site. Later, when Japanese contractors sealed the road, the trip would be cut to eight hours of easier driving. The road to the mine site proper was cut through the red soil of the area. All the original hardwood trees had been cut and milled at the turn of the century; only secondary scrub remained, dotted with rocky outcrops.

The mine was 1700 feet above sea level at the top of a small mountain range; access was by way of a valley and across a swift running river. It was here that several members of the N.P.A. arrived to check on the new activity in 'their' area. They were easily recognisable. Apart from their M16s, they wore imitation designer jeans with false labels and had shoes. It was a tense moment but they were happy that 'their' people were receiving above award rates of pay and, like good unionists anywhere, accepted their fees, fortunately in rice rather than in pesos.

Success does not always breed success; it can cause apprehension amongst competitors. No sooner had the mine begun to produce ore for shipment than a large multinational moved into the claim area and dared tiny Philzeal to contest through the courts. Paying your dues in the big league was going to be costly.

Some judges in the Philippines are aptly named: they can judge to the peso which litigant to back and for how long. Philzeal's 'legal problems' were to drag on for eight years until the demise of Marcos and by this time there was no money left to pay all the new 'administrators'.

To save money, Philzeal's directors moved out of the luxurious Lagespy Towers and into more modest quarters where they augmented their income by flying bangus up from Mindanao and selling it on the Manila market. This involved dealing in a lot of cash; most of it (no disrespect for the peso) was in U.S. dollars. Their faithful Philippino retainer suggested,

"Why don't you buy a safe to keep all this money in – very dangerous to leave lying around?"

"What a jolly good idea," replied one of the New Zealanders. A safe was purchased, installed in the apartment and U.S. $60,000 locked securely inside. Satisfied, one of the Kiwis went to feel better by drinking endless bottles (never cans) of Heineken beer. When he returned late that night (or was it early in the morning), the faithful retainer was gone, along with the U.S. $60,000. The police were called and looked sympathetic until a 'reward' was paid in advance, they then moved into action. The culprit was finally caught and shot dead. The police maintained they could find no trace of the missing money.

Using the 'when in Rome' principle, the New Zealanders hired a local taxi driver to enforce company rules. He was immediately effective; problems disappeared at the mine site along with those who were causing them, presumably transferred to an undersea site. Philzeal was finally being taken seriously.

My visit to the Philippines was by a roundabout way after attending a court case in Sydney. One of the Philzeal's director's sons had been walking out of the garden bar at the Golden Sheat Hotel in Double Bay with his girlfriend. The young man was previously a karate student of mine and had a good strong physique. Two car loads of hoons pulled up, disgorged and advanced on them, loud-mouthing threats and obscenities. Understandably, he felt that he and his girlfriend were in danger. The leader of the pack came too close and was hit once only. It was enough; he dropped to the ground unconscious. The rest of the mob flagged round, two picked up their mate, got back into their cars and drove away, still mouthing obscenities from the safety of locked doors.

The father of the hoon who had been hit was a professional man and well off financially. He laid a complaint of assault with the police. They agreed to investigate. The one blow had broken the jaw and cheekbone; rebuilding the jaw and teeth had cost $5,000. The police in their own time and in their own way tracked the young man down and interviewed him. After hearing his side of the story they decided they had far more important crimes to deal with and decided not to prosecute. They also gave him some advice.

"Go back to New Zealand and that should put an end to the matter." It didn't. They underestimated the father's need for revenge and his considerable wealth. The father paid for the prosecution and a detective sergeant to fly to Wellington to investigate extradition proceedings.

I was called to give evidence of a technical nature regarding the blow and the damage it caused. The defence counsel began by making my status clear to the court.

"Mr. Jarvis, what is your rank in karate?" I mumbled something about having a black belt. He wasn't satisfied.

CHAPTER TEN | 257

"Mr. Jarvis, modesty aside, are you not the most qualified martial arts' instructor in Australasia?"

"Yes."

"Can you explain to the court what happens when a blow strong enough to cause the damage shown in the photos marked exhibit A makes contact?" I took a deep breath, I had been well rehearsed.

"When a blow of that power lands, the opponent must be knocked backwards."

"I refer to the witnesses' statements that the complainant dropped at the feet of the accused." Counsel turned back to me.

"How could that happen?"

"It could only happen if the person who was hit was advancing more than probably quite quickly onto the person who struck the blow."

"Thank you Mr. Jarvis."

The detective sergeant had no questions; the Judge did.

"You can't be sure that this was the only way such damage could occur, could it happen in other ways?"

"It could, Sir." I thought of demonstrating to him what happens when somebody moving hits a stationary person but by the stuffy look of him I didn't think he would appreciate American style theatrics in his court, besides defence counsel was giving me the crooked eye. I stood down.

The talk amongst the legal profession was that it would have been thrown out. The reserved decision therefore stunned everybody;

the young man was ordered to be extradited to stand trial in Sydney, Australia.

The young man's father was also a person of some wealth and appealed the decision in the High Court. This was now becoming a very expensive exercise for both families. The High Court ordered the young man to be extradited.

I travelled to Sydney with the entourage to attend the trial. To show there was no ill feeling, the Australian detective sergeant accepted an invitation to lunch with the father prior to escorting the son back to Sydney. The lunch included copious quantities of wine and liqueur. By the time the sergeant was delivered to the airport he wasn't feeling any pain.

"This is a dangerous criminal!" he told the terrified air hostess. "Make sure he gets plenty of drink to keep him happy." All the drinks, of course, were immediately confiscated by the Sergeant who was getting happier by the minute.

By the time the Qantas Boeing landed at Kingsford Smith Airport the Sergeant was paralytic and had to be escorted off the aircraft by the extraditee. The son propped him up in a corner of the airport and rang the Rose Bay Police Station, asking them to come and pick them up. The Sydney police, who have a reputation for looking after their own, arrived swiftly and accepted the fact the son had 'given himself up'. The sergeant was hustled away.

The father was less well behaved on the flight over. He had a system that worked of trying to upgrade his ticket to business class, knowing it had been booked out for weeks. While helpful young ladies at the counter unsuccessfully attempted to upgrade him, he sat in the first class lounge enjoying complimentary champagne and club sandwiches. We joined him as his 'guests'.

CHAPTER TEN | 259

One of the privileges of being in the lounge is that you are called last. He ignored that call and the repeat call. I and the others began to get apprehensive.

"Don't worry," said the father with a slight slur, the bubbles in the champagne causing the alcohol to be absorbed more quickly into the bloodstream.

"Once your luggage has been checked onboard, they will never take off without you, security, bombs and all that stuff." He helped himself to another free drink.

Finally a hostess came for us and insisted that we board. The aircraft was full of impatient passengers who glared at us as we came through business class to look for our seats in economy. Fortunately my seat was away from the others in another aisle. I scuttled into it and hid behind a copy of emergency instructions. One of the passengers must have said something to the father.

"Who the f'ing are you to tell me what to do? I've paid my f'ing fare and don't need your shit." A hostess rushed in to attempt damage control and asked him to sit down and buckle his seat belt.

"And don't you f'ing start, I have to fly economy because you can't do your f'ing job." The hostess went for reinforcements; they arrived in the form of the purser and co-pilot. The co-pilot was explicit.

"You will sit down and be quiet otherwise the aircraft will taxi back to the terminal where you will be arrested." The father gave in immediately and, for those that knew him, far too easily. The passengers let out a collective sigh of relief as the aircraft lifted off and began a slow turn towards the sunset. At twenty-thousand feet the seat belt sign went 'ping' and turned off. The father unbuckled his seatbelt and 'pinged' the hostess who reluctantly answered the call.

"Now you can't f... turn around, now it will cost you too much f... money so we are going to sort out our f... problem." Sort it out they did by silencing him with a half a bottle of cognac from first class.

We arrived in Sydney and were driven to the Commercial Travellers' Club off Pitt Street. The rooms must have been designed by a Tokyo architect but were sufficient for a few nights' stay. The location was central and the room rate reasonable. The trial was to start the next day.

From the beginning there were some ominous signs that the trial verdict might not be in our favour. Defence counsel failed to nail down important facts; prosecution witnesses had obviously been very well briefed (some by the police we found out later) and the judge seemed to be only interested in the prosecution statements.

Luncheon recess was at Doyle's Restaurant. Perhaps it was the mood everybody was in but I was unimpressed with the place and rated it as a glorified fish and chip establishment.

The trial finished the next day.

"Guilty," said the judge and accused the young man of 'king hitting' the complainant. Later the sentence for the first offender was nine months jail with hard Labour.

We were to fly on to the Philippines but the saga was to go on to the Australian Court of Appeal. The judge and the complainant's father turned out to be friends and were often seen together at the same club. The Court of Appeal reduced the sentence to a fine. The overall costs of the legal battle were above $100,000 which for one punch put the lad in the top earning bracket for professional boxers.

The gap between leaving the air-conditioned Manila International Airport and the doors of the Philippine Plaza's Mercedes courtesy cars was filled by hundreds of people living in hope. The drivers ignored them as if they were part of the discomforts of life, like the heat or the falling peso now that Imelda and Ferdinand had vacated the Malacanang Palace.

At the traffic lights young children with practised looks of helplessness put out their hands towards the stationary cars and cried.

"No money, no money." Having not changed currency, a few of us new to Manila felt somewhat embarrassed until the driver muttered something to them in Tagalog. They fled.

"They would only get a little of what you give," he said over his shoulder. "The cop in charge of this area gets most of it."

The Philippine Plaza is a world class hotel with a world class tariff based on the U.S dollar. Fortunately it was off season with half rates and a further ten percent discount for the Philzeal Mining Co. It was an ideal place to sally forth on business or pleasure ventures then return, hot, discontented and financially fleeced, to recuperate.

We were introduced to the night life of Amita. Piling into a taxi, its suspension gave up the uneven fight and collapsed; the party had to be split in two for the journey.

The bar looked great at night with an endless supply of attractive young women dancing in shifts, watched by mainly unattractive old men, who one suspected, would be very much alone at home.

Our two N.Z. executives were well known and popular. Once on a previous visit they could not agree on which girls to take back to the hotel so they ordered up the Philippine Plaza bus and almost emptied the bar. Business expenses can be hell.

At a lower pulse rate level, shopping was interesting. Every known and famous brand name of clothing was manufactured locally (not under license) and sold at a fraction of the genuine article's cost. One of our party bought a bottle of a well known aftershave only to come out in an allergy reaction to whatever unknown ingredient was used (probably the Pasig River).

I was amazed at the number of antique bronze cannon recovered from sunken Spanish galleons and selling for around U.S. $5,000 until closer inspection revealed they had never been fired. One of the dealers laughingly offered to tell me how they were made if I bought a small one at a 'special' price.

It was not possible to visit the mine site; the roads were washed out. Our party decided to take a weekend's 'rest' in Hong Kong while I visited the Islands of Negros and Cebu in search of information on 'arnis de mano'.

A young man, who came from Negros, offered to be my guide and interpreter for a salary of next to nothing. He took his duties seriously.

"To save money we should fly to Bacolod in Negros then take the buses and ferry to Cebu," he suggested.

"How long is the bus trip?" I enquired. The island of Negros is about fifty kilometres across, but I had no idea what the terrain was like or what condition the roads were in.

"Only about three hours," he assured me.

It was settled; we flew to Bacolod, a pleasant seaside town on the west coast of Negros, where I faced my first disappointment. The contact person Donn Draeger had recommended was away in Manila. We would have passed each other in the air. After a day's sightseeing we boarded the air-conditioned bus for the trip across the Island. The natives were kept quiet and happy

CHAPTER TEN | 263

watching in-bus C grade videos. The bus trip took four hours and I was reminded of the saying, "Seen one jungle seen them all."

We arrived at the ferry terminals which consisted of a ramp way, a shop and a scattering of huts.

"Where's the ferry, Miguel?" I asked my guide.

"Don't worry, sometimes it is late." He went back to sleep. Two hours later a smudge of smoke on the horizon excited everybody.

"It's our ferry," said Miguel needlessly.

It was another two hours before the smudge of smoke turned into the ancient ferry that would have made the 'African Queen' look state of the art. As it churned its way towards us it gave an asthmatic wheeze rather than a hoot and circled about to berth stern first.

"They are not going to put our bus on that are they?" I asked, not wanting to hear the answer.

"Oh no, they will put two on to keep an even keel." I looked around to see another bus had arrived from somewhere.

Somehow they got the buses on board along with a horde of passengers, pigs and chickens. The land slowly receded as the single propeller churned up the local sewage system.

The voyage across the Tannon Strait was pleasant, the sea breeze a welcome change from the humidity of the jungle. Several hours later the western coast of Cebu focused into buildings, trees and, finally, people. We didn't make it all the way. Being so far behind schedule the tide had turned and run out; leaving us stranded fifty metres from shore. A crew member dived overboard and swam to shore with a line to secure us to the tantalizingly close wharf. Many passengers were clambering down ladders and into outrigger canoes to be paddled ashore to a waiting bus. I assumed they were locals. One obese lady succeeded in shoehorning herself and her shopping into a canoe. With the freeboard almost non-existent she signaled the paddler, who was also overweight, to commence. Unfortunately, as the paddler leaned to port for his first stroke, so did the lady. I didn't think outrigger canoes could capsize, but this one did, spilling its occupants and contents into the tepid sea.

It was like a scene straight out of a Hollywood movie: young boys dived off the wharf to help, everyone on land welcomed the diversion and all work stopped on the ferry as captain, crew and passengers alike rushed portside to see what was going on. The resulting list gave everybody a better view.

Surprisingly the fat lady and the canoe owner were laughing along with everyone else as they salvaged her shopping and tried to lift her back into the canoe. This was not an easy task. Every time they managed to heave a fat leg and buttock over the gunwale, the canoe tilted dangerously and began to sink. Finally, through the combined efforts of tilting and levering they got the (by now exhausted) lady back into the canoe and the boys towed it ashore while others looked for the lost paddle.

The bus started up and drove away.

"Where is the bus going?" I asked my guide.

"To Cebu City," he smiled. It took a while for this to sink in.

"Why didn't we go ashore and catch the bus?"

"I didn't think you'd want to travel in a unairconditioned bus," he said importantly.

We waited for three hours in thirty-two degrees temperature for the tide to change.

The bus finally arrived and we departed for Cebu but the drama had not quite finished. There had been rumours of yet another coup and the military were jumpy. They stopped the bus for a search out side of the city and I groaned expecting an East German style delay. I need not have worried. A young man, who looked all of fifteen, M16 slung over his back, wandered down the coach smiling and shining his torch into the luggage rack gave us a sloppy salute and left. In five minutes we were on our way again. We arrived at a Spanish style hotel at two in the morning. A pair of tatty, tired eagle-hawks were chained to perches on either side of the entrance foyer; I commiserated with them.

My stay in Cebu was frustrating. Even armed with Donn Dreager's introduction I lacked the go-between to smooth the way for in-depth research. I was met politely by several local masters but I could not escape the feeling that what I was being shown was the same as the usual tourist fare.

I decided to enjoy the city which has the reputation of having the most beautiful woman in the Philippines. The flight back to Manilla took just over an hour.

"Are you not happy that we saved twenty-five pesos on the trip down?" enquired my guide.

Chapter Eleven

My flight back to New Zealand was routed through Melbourne. The visit was not only for a training seminar but also to buy several good quality jo that were becoming increasingly difficult to obtain. Jo are too long to send through the post and too expensive to air freight, the easiest way was to bring them back personally.

With the seminar completed I was taken to one of the excellent bring-your-own restaurants for which Melbourne is famous. The food was Mediterranean, the host garrulous and the patrons friendly and noisy.

My hosts were unconcerned as the check-in time for my flight grew near, they assured me I would make it to the airport on time. There was, after all, plenty of wine left on my table. Finally, continued glances at my watch had an effect: the bill was settled; we piled into a car and headed off for the airport. Fortunately breath testing was way in the future.

Most airlines prefer you to be at the airport one and a half hours before an international departure, an hour is calling it a bit fine, but we arrived only twenty minutes before departure time. The departure hall was empty; we were the last flight out that night. The man behind the check-in counter looked annoyed as we bustled in, my companion obviously the worse for wear.

"Left it a little late, haven't you, mate?" He gave my ticket a hard look.

"Blame them," I said, jerking a thumb at the three grinning idiots. As he weighed my luggage I prayed I was not over the limit and he began to throw the cases none too gently onto the conveyer belt. The carton of jo broke open, spilling the contents all over the floor.

"Christ, this is all I need," said the Qantas man.

"Let us help," said my friends who stamped across the scales and tried unsuccessfully to put back the jo.

"Bugger off," screamed the Qantas man and did the job himself. I was busy filling out a departure card and pretended not to notice.

He finished using up the last of his sticky tape and punched viciously on the keys of his computer.

"Economy is full, your seat has been allocated to someone on standby," he said triumphantly.

"There are a few seats available in first class," said a sweet young hostess who had come to help sort out the disturbance.

"Argh," was all the man could manage as he handed me a boarding card and stomped off.

Sitting on board in a large comfortable seat with my legs stretched out I accepted a glass of champagne.

"Champers is the only drink after 11:00 pm," said my companion.

"It's the only way to travel," I agreed.

Sometimes the years slide past faster than a waiting taxi meter; the fourth international karate camp was upon us with extra attendant problems. The Gasshuku was in South Africa.

The event proved to be low-key. Many of us who were in government employment were refused leave to attend although some circumvented this by taking annual holidays. A small team did attend from New Zealand; other countries were in a similar position. Rembuden's loss was one black belt who felt our organisation should have set an example by not attending.

I attended a course of a very different nature but one that confirmed many of the traditional teachings of the martial ways and introduced modern psychological procedures. The course was run by Canadian Dr Brent Rushell, a man suspected of being influential behind Canada's snatching of a gold medal off New Zealand in the prestigious rowing eights at the Olympics (an event very dear to the hearts of New Zealanders).

I had always been concerned that much of the training both in the martial arts and in some modern sports concentrates too much on external motivation. Trainees are subjected to the direct instructions, tactics and will of the teacher/coach, with fear often the force behind performance. There are nu-merous examples of when the external motivation is removed in the form of an instructor leaving the dojo or a coach moving on, and then students are left high and dry, often collapsing back into shallow standards and achievement.

No two trainees are the same but the difference is often not physical. Trainees not suited physically to their chosen martial art or sports are either culled out at an early stage or remain in the lower ranks of achievers. A famous photo of the start of the Olympic men's one hundred metres shows all eight starters are physically similar and their technique almost identical. The main difference is in their psychology. It is here that the trainee in a martial art and a participant in a sport differ, even though some psychological procedures are transferable. A sportsperson has an event to focus on: he or she can psychologically arouse him or herself to a peak prior to performing. The focus can be solely on the competition at hand and so avoid all distractions. A famous lady golfer playing a well known course next to a railway was about to make a crucial winning putt when a train passed by. After sinking the putt an impressed official asked her,

"How could you concentrate on that putt with the noise of the train going past?"

"What train? "She asked.

Good coaches will know how to arouse their teams or charges. They will also be able to spot anxiety symptoms and deal with them by having their trainees engage in continuous physical activity, focussing on the task rather than on themselves. This can include physical interaction to shock the trainee back to reality by pushing or shoving them. The Japanese slap on the face was not, as seen by some, egocentrism but an effective method of eliminating anxiety.

Sportspeople can be protected against factors that will adversely affect their performances (a sudden change of goals, home town pressures, parents, press and other intrusions on their preparatory procedures). To become an elite performer the sportsperson faces the same barriers as a trainee in the martial arts. All sportspeople need more and more input into their own training but in the end each must, psychologically, be able to stand alone. A good coach or martial arts' teacher should slowly fade into the background, leaving their charges unaware of their lessening attachments.

Trainees in the martial arts face an entirely different type of psychology. They must not only focus on the task in hand (their performance) but on the individual facing them and also be able to ascertain if any distractions are relevant to the situation. When facing more than one opponent their task becomes an exponential problem.

A practitioner in the martial arts may have to 'go into action' immediately without the luxury of physical and mental warm-ups. It is possible to physically warm-up 'on the job' by using evasion, defensive tactics and even temporarily running away. Battle, whether individually or en masse, is ninety percent movement and ten percent fighting.

For a trainee in the martial arts the spark that ignites a cold start is kiai. The juice that keeps them running is adrenalin. This is nothing new; almost all martial cultures have used a war-cry and/or dance to psychologically prepare their warriors. In the west, the Romans countered that with group and individual discipline working hand in hand with superior weapons and tactics.

Even today those armies that have not consigned their bayonets to ceremonial, use a war cry when practising bayonet drill. The reason is simple, a non-commissioned officer cannot calmly tell an educated young man to run down 'there' and stick another young man in the stomach with his bayonet and expect him to do it. He has to be psychologically aroused through fear (and sometimes animal blood in training) so that his 'animal' instincts will override any civilised thoughts; he doesn't think, he reacts.

The ancient Chinese were aware of this and had a maxim, 'Civilise your mind but keep your body savage.' This 'fear factor' is the body's internal self-defence system. Adrenalin can override thought and allow a mother to lift a car to free her child, a police officer to notice details on the labels of cans behind someone who is shooting out at him and a famous baseball star who insisted when asked that he could determine the seams on a pitched ball even though eye specialists declared that this was physically impossible.

In some modern budo the practice of kiai is given the same status as bayonet practice in modern armies. Yet modern sportspeople practise it unknowingly: as the song goes - weightlifters do it, throwers who are short do it, even tennis players on the court do it. They shout, scream and grunt to get the spark going.

In a simple, physical test, thirteen year old boys at St Patrick's College were divided into two equal groups of seventy. One group practised throwing a shot from a standing position, the other group were kept well away and had to shout as they threw (press-ups if they forgot). No explanations were given. At the end of the six weeks the group that had to 'shout' averaged sixty-five centimetres further than the group that did not. A significant improvement for that age group.

Kiai to Japanese masters has a very wide application and could be described as the potential power which governs the course of human life. The word kiai is a compound of ki meaning 'will', 'spirit' or 'mind' and ai from the verb awasu signifying 'to unite'. In a psychological sense it means the ability to concentrate the whole of one's mental energy on a single object with the determination to achieve or subdue it.

Kiai is the active use of the mind, the force that becomes the spark to gain the initiative (sen). A combatant or competitor who secures this will win. Sword master, the late Yamoaka Tesshu, advised his students not to 'fix' their minds on their rival's attitude or their own but to cast aside any specific designs and rush into the attack. There simply isn't time to think, only to react as you have been trained to.

In a physical sense kiai is about breathing. Expelling the air with the use of lower abdominal muscles adds power to a technique (try lifting a heavy weight and breathing in at the same time). In combat, therefore, timing is crucial. Attacking an opponent at the instant he has expelled his breath will give an advantage - a reason why masters develop sound counter attacks.

An old method for practising breathing was to wrap a sash tightly around the stomach below the lower rib then attempt to inhale air deep down into the 'stomach' (meaning using the lower abdominal muscles). The instructors advise holding the shoulders down, back bent forward and, when walking, 'Project your abdomen beyond your feet.' (Some unkind people might say that this has never been a problem for me).

This concurs with the theory of 'hitting your opponent with your hips'. By shifting his centre of gravity forward a swordsman can 'cock' back his weapon over his head and drop his hips behind, the descending blow adding body weight to the technique.

A lunge punch is initiated from the hips as are all turning movements. Judo and Sumo exponents are never ones for subtleties and get right down to it and can either throw you or smash you with their hips.

The projection of the abdomen is a natural way of moving, not a concocted one. Observe how young children walk along the beach abdomen first until the boys' hormones start firing in all directions and they adopt the 'macho' style of shoulders back and chest out.

Correct posture is essential for the practice of breathing. When the mouth is shut and the chin is drawn back the principal muscles of the throat are kept taut and the spinal column straight. Physically correct posture stimulates blood circulation which in turn invigorates the muscles and other organs. Mentally, the mind is also refreshed for the application of kiai. The old Bushi maxim, 'First eyes, second alacrity, third courage and fourth bodily force,' gives an indication about their emphasis on mental preparation.

The psychological aspect of kiai was explained by a famous philosopher of the Ming dynasty, who advised,

"If the mind is kept one and undivided it will accommodate itself to ten thousand varied circumstances. That is the reason why a superior man can keep his mind empty and undisturbed."

Kiai can be kept in readiness to meet an emergency that arises and to deprive opponents of initiative by distracting them to your own advantage. In the West we say, "A strong mind in a strong body." Kiai implies making a strong body by means of a strong mind.

Training in the martial arts and in some sports (whether individual or team) advances in stages. An individual's character is also developed in stages similar to the process of forging a sword. In the initial stage fire is generated by youthful enthusiasm, positive attitudes and strenuous physical activities.

The second stage douses it all with cold water. The martial arts trainee, realising it was all basic stuff, sees the enormity of what lies ahead and doubts his ability. The sports person will suffer an injury or reach a plateau where there seems to be no hope of improvement.

The third stage is the resulting steam which clouds progress and direction, the groping around in the dark, on your own without a teacher or a coach to lean on. It is the trying, the discarding, and the attempt to move in different directions not knowing what the end result might be and finally emerging all the stronger for it.

Like the making of a sword the process is repeated many times only now it is the individual who becomes the 'forger' and has to seek out what will 'reheat' him or herslf. The process doesn't end with a polished person or performance but with the words, "My career is over."

'Winning' is a relevant term, something the kendo instructor at Rembuden was attempting to convey to his students.

The facilities at St Patrick's College, Wellington had always been made available for visits by the Japanese Self-Defence Force Navy and Youth Goodwill courses. A wider range of sports and activities could be catered for at one central location, in return I always received tickets for on-board functions that included Japanese food.

One year, a naval visit included a very strong kendo team of more than twenty kendoka, many of them third dan or higher. In desperation, urgent invitations were sent to other kendo dojo around New Zealand and in Wellington a senior rank was plucked out of retirement to make up the numbers.

It began badly and deteriorated. The retiree had no time to work into his timing. His Japanese opponent flew at him as if he had been catapulted and, with a shriek, landed a mighty mean blow on top of his protective helmet. A cloud of dust rose up off the previously mothballed helmet, but not enough to obscure the four judges' flags that stabbed into the air signifying a point. His knees buckled under the force of the blow and although I couldn't see his eyes through the grate of his helmet I knew they must be spinning.

"First round to Japan," came the smug voice of the Japanese interpreter.

"Japan wins again," he said a few minutes later, his satisfaction obvious.

"Another victory for Japan," later again and, "Japan wins again," as his team dispatched more reluctant Kiwis.

"Well, we won the bloody war," someone muttered from the butchered New Zealand team.

The instructor plotted revenge. A huge totara post that navigator Kupe had probably tied to his canoe to, was sunk deep in the ground outside the dojo and a rubber pad tacked over the top, resembling a kendo helmet. All kendo students had to practise striking this at first with 'bokken' (wooden swords), but this proved too expensive for as they grew stronger they broke the blades. Special heavy bludgeons were designed – the instructor wanted to use iron bars but had to be restrained.

This monstrosity proved to be embarrassing later when Higaonna Sensei stayed at the dojo and began to shift it in the ground.

"Your makiwara is too hard!" he admonished. No-one had the nerve to tell him it was for kendo.

Chiishi training weights, described earlier, were also pressed into service. Trainees at first could hardly manage to lift them over their heads, let alone practise a cut. Crushed toes were often the result of failure but they persevered and their wrists grew stronger. By the time the 'Nippon Maru' arrived in Wellington for another youth 'goodwill' visit they were ready.

The kendo instructor, being a man of strategy as well as tactics, asked for a friendly training session at the dojo the day before the demonstrations and competitions at St Pat's. The Japanese students, expecting easy beats, did not know what hit them. Three shinai were broken over them in as many minutes. Being their host, it did not seem appropriate to stand in the dojo and watch their demolition. I went and sat in the sauna and listened to the sounds of smashing bamboo and screams with Japanese accents.

After about twenty minutes the door of the dojo leading to the sauna and weight training area crashed open. I could hear laboured breathing. Minutes later someone else came out, obviously a Japanese 'Sempai'. The Japanese dialogue was rapid but I got the gist of it.

"I am not going back in there!"

"You will! Remember your duty." The door closed again, muting the sounds of conflict.

After the training session drinks and finger food were provided for our guests who made a brave face of it. Several took a long time to pack up their gear; others had to be helped onto their bus. The instructor stood there beaming surrounded by his 'team' dressed in faded hakama, patched up armour and bamboo splinters.

"We won the training!" he announced. The next day Japan won the competition narrowly but that didn't seem to matter.

Japanese arms and armour had long been underrated in the west, especially items other than swords. Many collectors consider them unattractive or just plain ugly.

Martial art instructors who had trained and studied in Japan realised this and began, wherever possible, securing items as they came on to the market. These investments were not always appreciated by wives who preferred mundane items like washing machines to an aesthetic piece of chain mail cluttering up the display cabinet.

Jon Blumming had made an early killing by seeking out an Amsterdam antique dealer who had two sets of Japanese armour for sale. One of the sets was fairly recent and was in very good condition, the other older and in fair order.

"I will pay you full price for that set." Blumming indicated the better of the two. "And you throw that one in for free." The dealer looked up at Blumming and decided to make a smaller profit rather than a fuss and agreed. As you have already probably guessed, the older tatty set was by a famous maker, had a history and was worth a small fortune. Word of his success spurred many others to keep an eye open and try to emulate it.

I began with some success. An antique shop in Pitt St, Sydney had a part suit of armour that looked impressive with gold coloured lacquer and fine embroidery, but it was made for wearing socially rather than in combat. It was not worth the high asking price. A drab looking helmet was much more interesting. Made in the last century it was in good condition with original chin strap and inner fabric lining. We haggled a little and agreed on fifty dollars (several days wages in those days). As the dealer was about to place the helmet in a cardboard box, he remembered,

"Wait a minute, something came with it, it's out the back, I think, and I'll get it!" The 'something' turned out to be a maedate (forecrest), an addition designed to take the focus out of a sword blow similar to the Graeco-roman crest or Viking horns. These are one of the first items to be lost off helmets over the years. The maedate was bronze and circular with a badly cracked red lacquer covering. With the intention of replacing it, I chipped this away with a bronze chisel and revealed underneath, carved into the bronze, was a wonderful pattern of trees with the Japanese kanji (character) of a nightingale. It is signed by 'Fujiwara', an ancient family, and, if authentic, it would outdate the helmet by several centuries. It is also possible that the maedate is in fact an old mirror but this has not been substantiated.

A full set of armour became available later in Sydney and the price was good but it was beyond the budget of most individuals of modest means.

Japanese armour earlier than the sixteenth century is rare. In Japan only sixty full suits of the earlier periods exist although some suits made up at a later date include earlier parts. The earliest forms of armour recovered from the dolmen burial mounds appear to have been first a type of leather harness upon which metal plates were laced and secondly a plated and riveted cuirass of metal fitted to the upper half of the body. Helmets were well formed and fitted with earpieces and neck protectors.

With the introduction of horses into Japan in the fifth century, fighting on horseback became popular, with bows and arrows used extensively. At the same time armour made of small plates laced together and overlapping was introduced. Suits of armour were modified and adapted with the period of the rise of the great military families in the tenth to twelfth centuries.

During this era two basic forms of armour were developed. The 'great harness' (oyoroi) was worn by warriors of high rank; it was complete with helmet and large shoulder protectors, the latter taking the place of a shield which was never carried (the hands had to be free to use the bow.) The second type was called 'haramaki' (wrapping the belly). It consisted mainly of cuirass and tassets and was worn by common soldiers who dispensed with helmets and shoulder pieces. It was less elaborate and protective than the 'great harness' but was lighter and more flexible becoming more popular as fighting on foot became the norm.

The Kamakura period of the thirteenth and fourteenth centuries was perhaps the golden era of Japanese armour as it was for the sword. The military class was increasing in numbers and powers and the defeat of the Mongol invasion in 1281 extended their privileges. Fighting on horseback was now in decline and the gap between 'oyoroi' and 'haramaki' was closed by the wearing of helmets and shoulder pieces with the 'haramaki'. Greaves were introduced and an apron to protect the thighs. Protection for the face and neck in the form of iron masks and gorget were added and chain mail used to protect the forearms.

During the fifteenth and sixteenth centuries the use of family crests (Mon) became general and were used in the decoration of armour. The sixteenth century was a time of almost continuous civil war. It was also the time when the Portuguese introduced firearms. Foreign influence on Japanese armour was not extensive but a number of examples of strong plated cuirasses, inspired by European models, and helmets with a brim resembling a casset have survived. Warriors of high rank often wore helmets of freakish design but the long suffering common soldiers had to be content with the lacquered leather war hat or jingasa.

During the peaceful isolation of the Tokugawa shogunate (1600-1868) armour became progressively less practical and more ornamental. At first armourers concentrated on making it bullet-proof but once peace was fully established they occupied themselves in luxurious adornments and imitations of ancient armour.

The last occasion when Japanese armour was worn was during the battles for the restoration of Meiji. Suits made at this time were often largely of cowhide – tough, light and practical.

One of the more unusual and lesser known martial arts is the practice of crossing rivers and smaller lakes in full armour. Bushi had to jump into the water, sink down to the bottom (presumably this had already been established), trudge along a few paces and then rise to the surface like prehistoric reptiles for air, and then repeat the process. It could only have instilled fear into anyone watching. If they had no route for escape and a sense of humour they would have died laughing.

A syndicate was formed by four members of the Rembuden Institute to purchase that suit of armour and future items. Our combined buying power would give us some bidding 'clout' at arms and armour auctions.

We soon became favourites with the auctioneers by advising and valuing items for them. Sometimes we were given the 'the quick knock' where the auctioneer would quickly accept our bid without giving another bidder time to reflect. On one occasion this was disputed, carrying some ill-feeling and a higher final bid from our syndicate.

One auction listed a fine example of Naginata, the Japanese equivalent of a halberd, complete with original wooden sheath (family crest) and extensive marking of pearl inlay. The blade was slightly pitted but in good overall condition. It retained a very sharp edge. The auction house had that suppressed air of excitement and smelt of old wood, oil and musty fabric. Most of the excitement had been centered on a set of German boxed flintlock pistols which sold for three thousand dollars - an incredible price in New Zealand for those days but not for the overseas buyer.

There was little interest in our lot when its turn came. Most dealers would not bid on an item that may take a long time to shift unless it went very cheaply. The auctioneer described the Naginata and added a few embellishments (they can't help themselves) and opened the bidding. Our syndicate took it in turns to bid at auctions; I was in the seat on this occasion.

"Fifty dollars," a token bid from a dealer.

"Seventy-five dollars," from a gentleman on the other side of the room.

"I am not taking five dollars at this stage, sir, will you bid eighty?" asked the auctioneer. The gentleman nodded.

"A hundred?" questioned the auctioneer. I indicated with the catalogue.

"Against you, sir," the auctioneer addressed the gentleman on the other side of the room. There were only two of us left in, he nodded at a hundred and twenty dollars. The auctioneer's gaze returned to me; I decided to go for the big hit.

"Two hundred dollars!" I called and started to talk casually to my fellow members as if that was a mere bagatelle. In fact my pulse rate was racing, this was our limit.

"Against you, sir." The gentleman looked somewhat taken aback, not expecting such a change in tempo.

"At hundred dollars then?" A pause.

"Sold to the syndicate," he announced and tapped his pen on the lectern. Heads swivelled round to look at us, expecting dark glasses and white ties. Our opposition looked furious.

In the euphoria of our success we missed the next item in the catalogue. It was listed as a Chinese armour 'puncturer' and did not interest us. I looked up as it was knocked down to a dealer for thirty dollars. It was a very old Japanese Jute, both a symbol of authority and a defensive weapon against a sword. The colour of the metal suggested it was very old. I button-holed the dealer later and casually offered to 'take it off his hands' but he smiled, suspecting a 'steal', and said he would get back to me. He never did; I heard later that it was sold overseas.

Our reputation grew and I was 'requested' by the Dominion Museum in Buckle St to identify and catalogue Japanese polearms that had been in storage since the turn of the century. None of the staff I talked to knew how the museum had come by them.

A trip to the basement in the Dominion Museum is both fascinating and depressing. Stepping out of the lift underneath the Dominion Museum could be likened to entering Aladdin's cave. The air is kept dry and at a steady temperature, there is no sound, only the lagged pipes of the heating system give the impression of a basement. Nothing sparkles here, only thousands of items unable to compete for space in the galleries above, stacked row after row, shelf upon shelf, waiting.

"We can't sell items we don't want," explained the assistant curator, a pleasant, intelligent young lady, and intent on bringing some order to a small part of the underground surpluses.

"Almost all the items have been bequeathed to the museum; our by-laws do not allow it."

We came to an area with a chalk mark on a concrete column informing 'Eastern'. There, stacked on a shelf, were over a dozen Japanese polearms.

"I'll leave you to it then and come back in an hour." She switched on a single light bulb and disappeared back the way we had come.

Historically polearms are among the oldest of Japanese weapons. Along with the sword, they were important weapons used by early settlers in driving back the barbarous aboriginal Yemishi, who were finally expelled to the northernmost islands. Even today it is considered inappropriate to sleep with your head facing north, a direction from where, in the past, the barbarians would attack. The sword was the main weapon of the Bushi and developed into a perfect hand to hand weapon both in use and in beauty. Polearms ran a close second. Different applications of polearms ensured that they developed for specific tasks.

The nagimaki was usually a sword mounted in a shaft complete with tsuba (guard) but was considered too ungainly and gave way to the more graceful naginata (halberd) which rivaled the sword in popularity in the Heian period. It later became a weapon favoured by women and today is practised as a sport similar to kendo (but with much needed knee protectors). Both the nagimaki and the naginata were favoured weapons of the warrior monks.

During the centuries of civil war the long bladed su-yari displaced the naginata, with many high-ranked warriors recorded as using them. Later in the Tokugawa period the magariyari, a trident type three-bladed spear, became a ceremonial lance carried symbolically at the front of a noble's retinue.

The museum's selection consisted of several different types of yari (spear), some of them with their original wooden scabbards. Given the conditions, they were all in a reasonable order although many of them couldn't be stripped down for a more complete inspection. Age had glued them together and they would have to be dismantled professionally. I did what I could, taking rubbings from inscriptions of the blades or tang, listed them in possible order of value and left precise instructions on how to clean and care for them.

"I don't think we will be able to manage that," said the young lady sadly, as we returned to daylight. "We just don't have the staff available."

A doctor from a well-known Wellington professional family died and was taken by ambulance to hospital to be examined by the duty doctor. On opening his dressing-gown nurses were shocked to see two Colt .45 pistols in holsters strapped along with ammunition to his waist. The police were called and removed the offending ordnance and drove to the late doctor's residence.

He had lived alone in a house full of antique weapons, over three-hundred items lined the walls and it took three police van loads to secure the arms in the basement of the central police station. The collection included cased Wogden flintlock dueling pistols, Rigby percussion pistols and another fourteen original cased weapons. Many collectors aspire to owning a German broom-handled Mauser; there were five in this collection which included an eighteenth century Japanese matchlock.

Firearms were introduced into Japan by the Portuguese in 1543. The Lord of Tanegashima purchased two matchlocks for a small fortune and turned the guns over to his swordsmith to copy. The sword smith failed to overcome small technical details like how to close the end of the barrel which caused the 'volunteers' who were firing them no end of embarrassment.

When a second Portuguese vessel sailed in several months later the Lord, great family man that he was, exchanged his daughter for lessons in gun making. His workshop was soon turning out homemade products as good as the originals. The form of the weapon adopted continued almost unchanged until the middle of the nineteenth century when the American Admiral Perry sailed into Yokohama, his ships armed with rifled cannon.

The Japanese never used the wheellock, snaphaunce or flintlock and passed straight from the matchlock to percussion and pinfire. With their usual skill at adapting and improving their models, however, they brought the primitive matchlock to as near mechanical perfection as was possible. Their gun barrels, although generally of a heavy type, are of a quality compared to the best produced by Persian gunsmiths. They are often adorned and inlaid with precious metals and many bear the signature of the maker.

The Japanese never accepted the use of firearms in warfare as being consistent with the Bushi code: what the British might call 'unsporting'. They are rarely mentioned in the recorded history of battles yet they played an important and often crucial part in the outcome.

The fifteen thousand men in the military service of Shimazu-dono in the late sixteenth century included:

- three hundred banners, hand spears (te yari)

- three hundred long spears (naga yari)

- six hundred small banners (sashimono)

- one thousand five hundred teppo (matchlocks)

Firearms played an important part in the Kawanatajima campaigns (1553 to 1563) between the naval war lords Takeda Shingen and Uyesugi Kenshin.

It is possible that the peaceful Tokugawa shogunate in the following centuries made development along the lines followed in Europe less urgent. The Japanese must have known of the newer types of mechanism from the Dutch trading at Nagasaki and an accurate drawing of a flintlock pistol is to be found among the works of Hokusai.

Firearms continued to be popular in hunting.

One of the questions I often ask my students at seminars is that given a musket (depending on type) can fire a round a minute, accurate to a hundred metres, compared to a Japanese or English long bow capable of six arrows a minute with a range of three hundred metres and in some cases better penetration, "Why did an inferior weapon supersede a superior one in both the west and the east?" Few get it right. It is all a matter of supply and demand. It takes up to five years to train an expert archer; a musketeer from the more numerous lower classes, with no previous experience, can be efficient in a few months, and easier to replace.

The bow and arrow maintained their position in Japan until the middle of the nineteenth century. When the forty-seven Ronin entered the palace of their enemy Kodzuke no Suke, their leader posted men on the roof to pick off anybody attempting to obtain help from the outside. These men were armed not with guns but with bows and arrows with which they carried out their instructions with deadly accuracy.

The auction of the collection of antiques was attracting buyers from as far away as Australia and the United States, several of them arriving to bid in person. I voiced my apprehension at bidding for the matchlock against such heavyweights to the auctioneer. He replied that I shouldn't be too concerned because Japanese firearms were not popular with collectors. He was right, there was no serious opposition. It was knocked down to us for four hundred and seventy-five dollars.

I received a telephone call from a gentleman in Wanganui. He sounded mature and his voice had a soft distinct Scottish burr to it. He wasted no time in coming to the point.

"I hear you buy Japanese swords!" It was a statement not a question.

"We do sometimes; yes," I replied. The 'we' referred to the Institute Iai Do students who were always on the lookout for suitable katana.

"Would you be interested in a naval sword with a history?"

"Yes, sir, can you give me some more details?" He did, and an hour later I was on the two and a half hours drive to the city of Wanganui. Crossing the river and turning north I followed the directions to a large gabled double-storied residence set back from the banks of the river.

The owner of the sword was six foot three, his large frame topped by a mane of white hair, he was in his eighties. He was also going through the throes of a divorce, deciding after a good slice of the century that they were not suited. He needed money for the settlement and had to sacrifice part of his precious collection to meet the costs.

His collection was impressive, not large by most standards but very selective. A revolver once owned by Von Tempsky, a soldier of fortune during the Maori wars, and a Spanish pistol from the time of Cortez was two examples. Every item had a history.

The sword was a kaigunto, much as he had described it, in naval mountings with a hilt that extended over the handle, western fashion. Faded red tassels proclaimed the past owner had been of general (admiral) rank. Its history was interesting. A Japanese admiral had been present at the signing of Japan's surrender after the Second World War on the deck of the battleship 'Missouri'. The admiral had a duty to face the surrender of his country but could not surrender his personal sword and attempted to throw it into Yokohama harbour. It bounced off a rail and fell into the scuppers where an enterprising British commander draped his cloak over it. Many owners later it ended up in New Zealand.

It was the blade that attracted my attention. If it was a naval issue blade of pressed steel it would be next to worthless but this could be unlikely going by the rank of the owner. Many officers of high rank substituted the issue blade with a family heirloom making the weapon very valuable. It was a true Japanese sword blade in very good condition but unsigned (not unusual). This made valuing it a bit of a punt. I offered $250.00, a price a little under what it would fetch at an auction, but I suggested he 'shop around'.

He rang back in four days. "I'll play!"

A school teacher friend of mine was returning to London. I asked him if he would deliver the sword to Sotheby's, it was time to see if the punt would pay off. He also transported several teppo (matchlocks) that were to be sold at the auction. Sotheby's entrance is not particularly imposing, being neither particularly old nor modern in appearance. The receptionist made quite an impression on my friend, though. She was a blonde-haired girl who had obviously had a very expensive education, and they had performed wonders on her self-confidence, while apparently abandoning, at a very early stage, any development of her mind. It was to become apparent that they had good reason, because she seemed to be straight out of the pages of P.G. Wodehouse. She may not have been the dumbest blonde in

CHAPTER ELEVEN | 289

the Home Counties, but she would definitely make the short list. Even Bertie Wooster would have found her vacuous.

My friend explained that he was calling on my behalf and was expected, so she smiled and said she would get someone. It was to be a long wait, because as she picked up the phone, another girl came in, and she called her over.

"Could you possibly cover me for half an hour after lunch, it's really desperately important, and I can't be quite sure of getting back on time?" She said this in that tone of great concern with which English public schools seem to endow their pupils. The other girl, however, was of the same milieu, and knew how to parry this approach. In a similar tone, suggesting she was just as desperate to help if she possibly could, she made her opening.

" I'd love to help, but are you absolutely sure you'll be back within half an hour - you were awfully late yesterday, and it did get a little embarrassing, I'm afraid, and today, I have an appointment, that I've simply got to be on time for..." This went back and forth for a while, both competing in their voices to sound more solicitous than the other. Finally, a deal was struck, and the first girl seemed to get what she wanted, but the definite impression was that the second would make her pay dearly in the end. All this done, the receptionist, as if coming out of a trance, realised that she was holding a phone, and she clearly suspected that the call was something to do with my friend.

"I'm so sorry, what was it that you wanted?"

My friend went over the facts of my case as briefly as possible, and she seemed to remember why she'd picked up the phone. A representative of the Armaments Department was asked to come down and see if they could possibly fathom why this person had come in with some antique guns and swords. He appeared a few minutes later. Neither particularly formal nor casual in appearance, he looked at the muskets as my friend explained the situation. He seemed impressed, though not overly so, rather as one pleasantly surprised to see that someone had not intended to show him some junk. My friend never did speak to anyone who knew of the correspondence between me and Sotheby's, let alone who'd seen the photographs of the muskets. Everyone seemed to think he was just another person who'd found something interesting in his attic and wanted a free appraisal. When he mentioned that the muskets were Japanese, the expert stopped and said in that case the Japanese Department would have first call on them, and asked the receptionist to call someone else down to the foyer, which she managed to do with suitable guidance. My friend never did get past the foyer, which shows just how impressed they were with him, but at least he wasn't cast back into the freezing cold outside.

The Japanese expert came down, rather more formally dressed, and as soon as he looked at the muskets and began to speak, it was clear that he knew his stuff. He also seemed pleasantly surprised that my friend hadn't come twelve thousand miles to show him junk. He also had a surprise for him. Picking up one of the three muskets, he said,

"Those two are very nice, but I'm afraid this one isn't Japanese, it's Indian." My friend pointed out that he had been assured they were Japanese, but the expert obviously knew what he was talking about, so the Indian musket was taken by the Armaments Department, and the other two by the Japanese department, whose representative left with his booty, giving the receptionist instructions to write out a receipt. She looked up at them, rather puzzled, as if we were slightly deprived in the matter of education.

"Did you say 'muskets'?"

"Yes," my friend said, still amazed that her skull hadn't imploded long ago. "These things here, like rifles." The armaments man tried to help: "As in musket, fife and drum". My friend thought of mentioning The Three Musketeers, but decided not to push his luck. Between them, they managed to half-convince her that such a word existed, but only just enough to persuade her to humour them, and as a result, my friend left with the receipt for "Three musquets and one sword," which he passed on to me when he got back to Wellington.

It was listed in a subsequent auction along with an impressive array of eastern art works one would expect from Sotheby's and sold for six hundred pounds less commission. The 'punt' had paid off.

Chapter Twelve

The lady at the Japan Cultural and Information Centre in Wellington had been a long supporter of the Rembuden Institute of Martial Arts. In turn, we had always been willing to assist with arrangements for any Japanese naval or youth goodwill visit. In recognition of this support, I was offered a position on an educational tour of Japan. All expenses would be covered by the Japanese Government.

The offer came at a bad time school-wise. Earlier that year I had taken the St Patrick's College Athletics' team for a tour of Western Germany; to request further leave with pay would be straining the system. I mentioned this fact to the lady at the cultural centre who told me politely, but finally, to apply for it anyway. A week later the Rector came to see me, shaking his head.

"I have just had a phone call from the Department of Education. The person in charge of granting leave told me that normally he would never have done so, but he had been 'told' from higher up to grant permission. He sounded quite miffed." The lady at the cultural centre pretended surprise when I telephoned to accept the offer.

Few details were given to me about the tour other than that I would be accompanied by someone from the brand new Ministry of Education. We would be joined in Sydney by two Australians and we had to supply a speech in writing so that it could be translated prior to our arrival. With only a few days remaining before our departure, I desperately tore out a section of the newly published 'Tomorrow's Schools' and posted it away.

The fact that we travelled business class to Kyoto via Tokyo should have given me an indication that this was a visit of some status. The black Ministry of Education limos complete with gold 'mons' and white gloved drivers reinforced this feeling. A meeting with the Director of Education completed our unease, and when two Australians began exchanging gifts at ministerial level I felt my that briefcase full of St Pat's badges and rulers displaying different woods of New Zealand was somewhat inadequate. My New Zealand partner, however, was quick off the mark and descended on the N.Z. Embassy, forcing them to give up several expensive bilingual books, 'New Zealand in Colour'.

Our host was a retired principal of a prestigious private girl's school in Tokyo and I had noticed with interest that the D.G. of Education had deferred to him; a very unusual situation in the strict Japanese seniority system. We found out later that he was from a very old and respected family, a famous scholar and a multi millionaire.

We travelled to Kyoto and enjoyed the temples and high schools. An average class of forty-five did not seem to bother the teachers, who professionally presented their lesson to the class, who in turn took copious notes. There were no questions and answers between teacher and students.

We took lunch at a beautiful lakeside resort, and dined on trout caught that morning. I passed on the sake and beer, so French white wine was provided. I shuddered to think of the cost of it all.

Returning to Tokyo, we were formally introduced to a meeting of principals from all over Japan. These would be the people we would be presenting our speeches to. There was a mix-up in my introduction. I had put in my C.V. that I had attended a course at Rikyo University. It was translated as if I was a graduate of this prestigious university, and I watched with dismay as several elderly scholars, possibly Rikyo graduates themselves, nodded in satisfaction. What would happen if they questioned me later? I mentioned the mistake to our interpreter. When he sat down, he pondered intently for a few minutes, then replied,

"Better leave things as they are, less embarrassing." Less embarrassing for whom?

Our hotel was near the Imperial Palace, a place for politicians; we were told we were the only foreigners. One strange aspect of the tour's organisation was that we had to pay for 'personal expenses' which included items such as laundry. These were checked meticulously by our financial minder, who seemed more worried about our Y fronts than the hundred dollar French wines we included in the food total.

We were invited to attend the Kabuki Theatre. Mindful of the lengths of such productions, my two Australian friends chose the play with the shortest synopsis.

"How long can it take to present a four sentence summary?" they asked. They found the answer four hours later.

I was more fortunate. At another theatre they were performing Chushingura Kanadehon, The Forty Seven Ronin. The story is one of the few well known outside of Japan, and illustrates the differences in morals that exist between Japanese and Western cultures. It is probably unnecessary to relate it in detail, especially since the historical setting has been altered beyond recognition in the stage version. Only the basic facts remain true to the actual events.

"In the early eighteenth century, Lord Asano made the compulsory visit to Edo (Tokyo) to attend the Shogun. Being young and somewhat provincial, he was unaware of the court politics and procedures. Master of Ceremonies, Kira, introduced the young lord but was dissatisfied with the gift offered in payment, and neglected to complete his education. The result was that Lord Asano was made to look foolish in court and smarting under the sense of injury, drew his sword to remove Kira's smile along with his head. He was thwarted by the guards. The penalty for unsheathing a sword in the Shogun's palace was death. Asano requested permission to end his own life. Given his rank, this was granted. The first Seppuku in the long saga took place.

Asano's family and supporters knew that their lord had been wronged, his enemy remained at large and Asano unavenged. In addition, the now masterless Samurai or Ronin should have also committed Seppuku for failing to protect their master. This would awaken the authorities to their duty to punish the man who had insulted their lord, they decided collectively to avenge their lord by killing Kira. This could be considered an extension of the Confucian principle that a man may not live in the same world as his father's slayer. Killings of this type were permitted, but due notice had to be given, which would alert the well protected Kira.

The Forty Seven Ronin decided to serve their revenge on a cold plate. Their leader, Oishi Kuranosuke, sent his children away, divorced his wife and took to a life of wine, geisha and song. Others acted similarly, even to the point of letting their sword blades rust, an unforgivable act. They were ostracised by society, and conveniently forgotten. Much later, rearming themselves from

CHAPTER TWELVE | 297

a fearless and probably expensive merchant, they made a surprise attack on Kira's residence. During the free-for-all which followed, where the impression of Shoji screens, lacquer bowls and heads fly in all directions, Kira hid in an outside toilet. A passing Ronin thrust his yari through the wall to check if it was occupied, with a bad case of constipation, but Kira wiped his own blood off with the sleeve of his kimono. His deception was short-lived; he was dragged from the outhouse and generously offered the chance to commit Seppuku. Coward that he was, he refused, and as a result had a sudden rush of blood from his head. The grisly token was laid on the grave of dead Asano. The Forty Seven Ronin then complete their duty and committed Seppuku one by one. They have remained heroes to the Japanese ever since."

A few months after their death in 1703, a play was performed and later the famous Chikamatsu wrote a puppet play, but changed the time frame to three hundred years earlier and drew his characters from appropriate historical personages of the Ashikaga period. This avoided antagonising the somewhat touchy authorities.

As I was leaving the theatre, I could read the smiles and expressions of the Japanese audience. How could I understand the true spirit of Japan?

The morning came for us to address the party of principals on aspects of education in our countries. The principals had selected the address they would like to hear, but each of us had about the same number to speak to. I began reading from Tomorrow's Schools, allowing suitable pauses for the translator. Soon several of the audience started to nod off, I could not blame them, and I wanted to do the same myself.

After about half an hour I decided to put us all out of our misery, and began to speed up the presentation, missing out some of the details. This caused consternation among the interpreters, who were reading from their script, not from my speech. I looked worried, pointed to my watch (we all had time allowance); the interpreter smiled, nodded and began to translate verbatim.

On completion, I bowed to the polite applause and sat down, not expecting any questions. I was wrong; several of the septuagenarians came awake and started asking searching questions about New Zealand's new education system. They were especially critical of decentralisation (an anathema in Japan). I found myself defending a system with which I did not entirely agree. Not a pleasant experience.

On a final night, we were taken to one of Tokyo's top traditional restaurants. Set in a park that once belonged to a prince, it shares the sculptured grounds with a hotel and reproduction church. Here an endless procession of couples, formally dressed, pass from service, to reception and on into married bliss. The restaurant was tastefully secluded from all of this. Space is money in Tokyo. The restaurant's reception area indicated its status with over five hundred square metres of secluded alcoves and seating.

Our private room was on the ground floor overlooking its own private garden. There seemed to be more hostesses dressed in expensive kimono than guests. They fussed around like pretty birds until we had all settled in. The tatami mats smelled new, and I remembered the Japanese saying that the two best things to have new were wives and tatami (not necessarily in that order).

Sake, wine and beer were served. I noticed on a side table a bottle of XO Cognac, Polish vodka, single malt whiskey I had never seen before and various liqueurs. On Tokyo's prices, that alone was a month's salary.

Soup was served in antique iron teapots. One poured the soup into exquisite porcelain bowls, and then removed the lid to reveal sculptured vegetables, twisted into beautiful patterns.

Endless courses followed, each outdoing the previous one in presentation, texture and taste. The Australian next to me nudged me in the ribs and said,

"I'd give my right testicle to know what this costs."

"And I would be delighted to cook it and serve it to you," I replied (they had just beaten us again in cricket).

When we left, we were escorted to our cars by a hostess, complete with parasol, "Tradition!" we were told.

On the drive to the airport, I discussed with one of our teacher guides some of the shortcomings of Japanese education. He sighed,

"From the day we are born until the day we join our ancestors we have to compete, there can be no escape for us." I looked forward to an 'escape' back home.

It was New Zealand's turn to host the International Goju Ryu camp. It was also time for me to announce my retirement. Like most decisions, it was made after considering several factors. It is a pity that we are not born with a, "best before" date stamped on us somewhere. An old boxer once sighed, when he recalled staying on too long,

"First your timing goes. Then your legs go. And finally your friends go."

I had been training against a few health problems that were restricting me to aerobic supplementary training such as jogging and swimming. Anaerobic training, which included sparring, was not advisable and this could be likened to training all week for a game, then not being allowed to play.

Family was important to me. Being a solo parent involved a time commitment not always honoured. I remembered seeing one of my sons play in a junior college rugby game and score a try. I passed on my satisfaction to the coach, who replied,

"Yes, he is really quite good." I didn't know that.

Being a head of an organisation, I was the one to deal with periodic bushfires, but after stamping them out there was always a bitter taste left in the mouth.

Finally, the organisation was changing nationally and internationally. The big budo systems, born out of smaller identities, were moving back into regional groups who were demanding, and getting, more authority. I was a product of a simple system where Sensei gave an instruction and it was carried out down the line with no questions or deviation. I am not suggesting that this is the best way, but I was uncomfortable with any other, and was beginning to feel quite Jurassic.

Making the decision was easy, informing Higaonna Sensei was not. He suggested at first that I might stay on in an administrative role, but I pointed out that a good cut should be clean and decisive. In the end he was worried about my health foremost; he is that sort of person.

The international Gasshuku was not a great success. The financial strain of attending every two years was beginning to show, and New Zealand was a long way from the numerically strong centre of Europe and America. The South Africans declined, not wanting to risk being demonstrated against, which was a shame, because I had a 'ring in' rugby team, stacked and ready for them. Japan provided the largest group, the rising yen diluting all their expenses.

At my farewell speech in the assembly hall at St Patrick's College in Wellington, I was asked to relate two of my favourite stories about the martial arts.

I will leave the reader to decide which two I chose.

Postscript

In the time that has elapsed between my retirement and the date of publishing there have been many changes.

In Japan there has been an exodus of senior teachers overseas caused in part by changes in Japanese society. Young Japanese (and this is not confined only to Japan) are reluctant to undertake the rigorous methods of traditional training. They bring water bottles to the dojo and expect breaks in training to use them. Young people now have a wide range of choice in sport and leisure activities and face less parental but more peer pressure in making these choices. The Kurodas and Shimizus who were police officers in name only and free to train full time in their Martial Ways have gone. There can never be a 'new' Donn Draeger and very few if any can today achieve their standards. Fortunately in some traditional schools teaching licences remain separate from dan ranks acknowledging the difference between personal techniques and teaching skills. A small number of traditional Ryu have resisted change and demand that students rise to the standards set, not the other way around.

Internationally many school teachers no longer teach sports or martial ways because of teaching pressures and this is a shame. Children can benefit from karate for example by learning balance, timing and coordination. These skills are transferable to any sport and this is born out by the success of many sports men and women who trained in karate as children.

Eastern Europeans now dominate because they still place their athletes into the police or armed services allowing them to train full time.

My father once told me that the best boxers were produced in the depression era and this is still true today.

Western athletes by contrast are usually forced to seek sponsorship.

Many dojo can no longer financially support a group of highly trained and ranked practitioners and are forced to import 'Stars for Seminars' in much the same way as mercenaries were once used to bolster local under-skilled soldiers.

Karate will continue and it will adapt and change because this is the nature of human endeavor. I have been privileged to have been part of it.

Finally, one should be wary of 'legends.'

Years ago I was asked by a student if I had ever killed anyone and I said I hadn't but I did know of a karate master who had, and told him that story on more than one occasion.

Some time later another young student said to me in class,

"You have killed someone, haven't you, sir?"

"No!" I said; and he replied,

"That's what they said you would say!"

The story teller had become the story.

John Jarvis Silverstream 2006.

Acknowledgements

The proofreading efforts of Heather Pigou and Barbara Stedman in their quest for correctness in a sometimes challenging raw script, are acknowledged. For the many hours you spent on this task, ladies, thank you.

John

www.ingramcontent.com/pod-product-compliance
Lightning Source LLC
Chambersburg PA
CBHW060943230426
43665CB00015B/2050